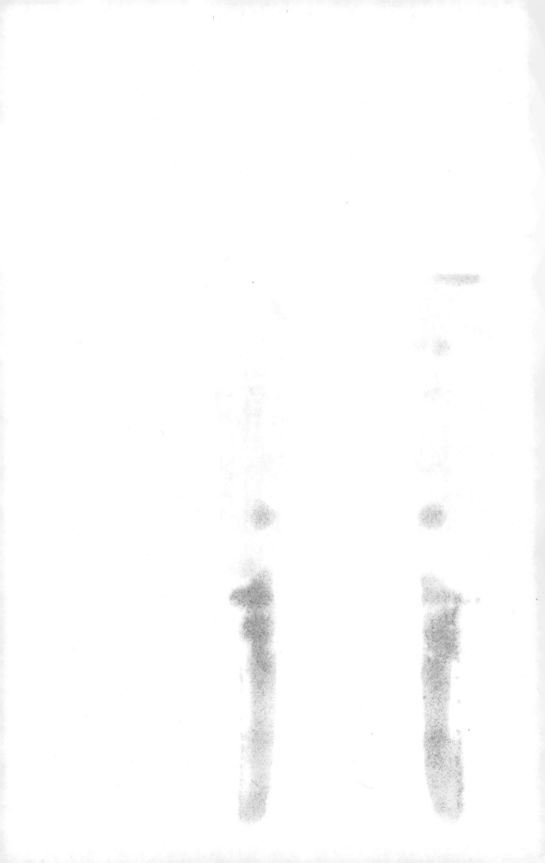

The Human Resources Revolution: Communicate or Litigate

ARNOLD DEUTSCH
Chairman, Deutsch, Shea & Evans, Inc.

McGRAW-HILL BOOK COMPANY
New York   St. Louis   San Francisco   Auckland   Bogotá   Düsseldorf
Johannesburg   London   Madrid   Mexico   Montreal   New Delhi   Panama
Paris   São Paulo   Singapore   Sydney   Tokyo   Toronto

Library of Congress Cataloging in Publication Data

Deutsch, Arnold, 1913–
  The Human Resources Revolution.

  Includes index.
  1. Personal Management—United States.

  2. Labor
and laboring classes—United States—1970–
I. Title.
HF5549.2.U5D48   658.3'00973   78–23256
ISBN 0-07-016593-9

1234567890   DODO   7654321098

The editors for this book were W. Hodson Mogan and
Virginia Fechtmann Blair, the designer was Naomi
Auerbach, and the production supervisor was Thomas G.
Kowalczyk. It was set in Palatino by University Graphics

Printed and bound by R. R. Donnelly & Sons, Incorporated.

To Frank Coss, Executive Vice President and Director of Research of Deutsch, Shea & Evans, Inc., whose ideas and effort made this book possible.

790652

Contents

Acknowledgments

The author would like to thank the many people who have had a hand, through discussions, interviews, letters and other contributions, in the creation of this book. Some of these contributors are identified in the text; to all, cited or not, my deep appreciation.

A number of publications and publishers have also permitted the use of their copyrighted material in the book, for which permission the author is duly grateful. These include:

Studs Terkel, *Working: People Talk About What They Do All Day And How They Feel About What They Do,* copyright © 1974 by Pantheon Books, a Division of Random House, Inc., New York.

Arthur Bryant, *The Age of Chivalry: The Atlantic Saga,* copyright © 1963 by Sir Arthur Bryant, reprinted by permission of Doubleday and Company, Inc.

Theodore Levitt, "Marketing When Things Change," *Harvard Business Review,* November–December 1977, copyright © 1977 by the President and Fellows of Harvard College. All rights reserved.

Fred K. Foulkes, "The Expanding Role of the Personnel Function," *Harvard Business Review,* March–April 1975, copyright © 1975 by the President and Fellows of Harvard College. All rights reserved.

"Caterpillar Film Credits Employees for Cat Quality," Reprinted from *Industrial Marketing,* March 1977, copyright © 1977 by Crain Communications, Inc., Chicago, Ill.

Excerpt from an article by Gene Lyons, *Harper's Magazine,* September 1976, copyright © 1976 by Harper's Magazine. All rights reserved.

CHAPTER ONE

The Human Resources Revolution

It was a harsh winter in Chicago, one of the worst the sixties had seen. Outside a local store, one of a national chain of supermarkets, a small group of black pickets marched in the bitter winds. "Boycott this store," their handprinted placards read. "This company does not hire black people."

A shot of the pickets appeared in *Time* magazine, then the story disappeared. The civil rights movement was making daily and more dramatic headlines. That the food chain's local sales had dropped by 30 percent as a result of the boycott apparently didn't merit editorial comment.

At that moment no one could foresee that this early and almost unnoticed demonstration of how a company's human resources policies could affect its bottom line would foreshadow a new revolution, one that would expand even beyond the civil rights movement itself and shake today's business world.

But now, like a great tidal wave, a revolution is sweeping through the work place, wiping out traditional attitudes toward work, flooding companies with litigation, battering the walls of the educational establishment, altering the nature of our working lives, and forcing a massive restructuring of the goals, characteristics, and operations of American business.

Neither violent nor political, this is a new kind of revolution—a human resources revolution—based on the changing views of people about their work, their employers, and their rights and aspirations in and out of the work place.

People are in revolt against traditional, mechanistic work practices, flaunting banners inscribed with slogans like "Human being: do not fold, spindle or mutilate." They are concerned at every working level about the right to have a job, to hold one, or to reject it. They want to help determine the conditions under which they work, and to reconcile the traditional business emphasis on profits with the individual needs of each worker on the job. The traditional work ethic and the mystique of career and company are being de-emphasized, if not discarded, in favor of an ethic in which work and the employer have diminishing importance. It is a revolution, moreover, that extends beyond the work force itself.

EVERYONE A LITIGANT

This is the age of the activist, in which everyone is a litigant, not least an organization's own employees. People today readily take court action against policies and practices they feel impinge upon their human rights or upon the rights of others for whom they feel a responsibility. Today's company operates within a sophisticated web of social advocacy organizations with experience in the weapons of boycotts, class-action suits, publicity, and lobbying.

Uniquely, this is a revolution with substantial government support. Congress has created sweeping new kinds of social legislation. Courts have responded with financially staggering penalties on organizations found to have transgressed against these new laws, and an extensive group of regulatory agencies polices their implementation.

This human resources revolution affects not only an organization's work force but other audiences important to the corporation as well. Consumers (who are also workers) have begun to use their leverage in the marketplace to support social goals; many of their efforts, such as the boycott of the Farah Company, a clothing manufacturer, relate to human resources. Stockholders peer anxiously over the shoulders of management to see how companies handle human resources problems. They are concerned that a slip may result in a multimillion-dollar penalty that will cut into company profits, and they are anxious not to alienate some of the major consumer blocs. There is also the threat, meagerly enforced but still there, of withdrawing lucrative government contracts from companies which do not comply with the extensive (and often conflicting) volumes of guidelines, regulations, and requirements governing such matters as employment, working conditions, and workers' compensation.

In the space of a single decade, the human resources revolution has become a dominant element in the operation of business and industry. Yet much of management is unaware that a revolution is occurring that will forever change the way in which organizations are run. Understandably, perhaps, they have yet to recognize the new revolutionaries who are creating this change.

THE NEW REVOLUTIONARIES

Barney C. and the Leisure Ethic

In a time when armed-to-the-teeth terrorists are a staple of the television screen, Barney C. does not fit the popular image of a revolutionary. He works as a maintenance mechanic on a Detroit assembly line, a well-paid, skilled expert who helps keep the highly automated operation running and troubleshoots breakdowns when they occur. No bomb builder, Barney's passion is fishing. His $6,000 bass boat attests to that and so does a basement full of tackle. So do his fishing vacations to Florida every winter.

How does Barney qualify as a revolutionary? Because he is making a long cast from his boat into the edge of a lily-pad bed in the back reaches of a Michigan lake this weekend when he could be making time and a half for overtime back at the plant. Barney is one of a growing percentage of the work force which prefers more leisure time to more money.

"Look," he told his foreman, "what's the use of coming in this weekend? A few more bucks? You know and I know that a big chunk of whatever I get is going right back in the government's pocket. I make enough to get by on. My wife's working, too. I've got a camper and a new bass boat and we're going to be up at the lake this weekend with the kids. I'd rather be there than on this damn line. And, don't expect me on Monday, eh?"

Barney is also part of that substantial group of workers which has been creating its own "four-day week" when its members happen to feel like it. In turn, they have created a massive absenteeism problem in many areas of industry and given rise to such consumer wisdom as, "Don't buy a car that was built on a Monday."

Edith B.: Employee Activist

Edith B. doesn't fit the traditional mold for a revolutionary either. At work she's a conservatively dressed, mature woman, a first-line supervisor of a major New York City bank who has a reputation in her department for being hardworking and conscientious.

Watching her at home tonight, a visitor would get the same impression. Piled on her diningroom table is a large batch of printed material issued by her bank: customer booklets, employee manuals and guidebooks, mimeographed copies of speeches by the bank's top executives, copies of the company house organ—even ads that have appeared in the local papers.

Edith is working her way carefully through this pile. Now and then she pauses to mark a page with a paper clip, underline a passage, or make a note on a yellow pad. Her manager might think she was doing company take-home work as she has done so often in the past. Not so. This is a project undertaken for a very different purpose.

Tomorrow morning the marked documents go to the woman lawyer who is representing Edith and a group of other female employees of the bank. The documents are part of the evidence being accumulated for a suit against the company charging discrimination against older women in pay and promotions. "It's long overdue," Edith says quietly. "For years I've had the bright new young men assigned to my department. I train them, teach them the basics here. Then they're moved on, and up. Now the bank has a so-called affirmative action program and I'm doing the same thing with bright young women right out of college. Same story. I stay here at the same job and they move up into management positions. It's not fair, and we're going to do something about it."

Edith is a member of the older generation in business which is in revolt against policies that discriminate—unfairly, they feel—against experienced older workers in favor of the young, and she is also one of the working women who seek equal pay and upward mobility. She is revolutionary in the sense that she is part of the current trend among employees at all levels to turn to litigation to redress grievances they see against themselves in the work place. These employees include women, minorities, older workers, the handicapped, and other groups who are "protected classes" under current government equal employment opportunity regulations.

Charlie S.: the "Noncompany" Man

Charlie S., striding down the hall of his company's office building, doesn't appear to be either "protected" or revolutionary. His contemporaries or his manager would spot him as a comer. He is young, alert, confident, with an air of aggressive intelligence; in the language of business clichés he would be called "a young tiger." At the moment Charlie is on his way to the division manager of his company, who has been impressed with Charlie's work and thinks he has a pleasant surprise for him. But it is the division manager who is in for a surprise.

"The company has been keeping an eye on you," the manager tells Charlie. "In your last merit review, we told you that you were in line for something good as soon as the opportunity came." He pauses for effect. "Well, it's come."

He watches the smile begin to develop on Charlie's face. "Starting in September, you'll be getting $2,000 more a year." By now Charlie is beaming. "You'll have a new title," the division manager goes on, enjoying Charlie's reaction, "assistant general manager of the Philadelphia plant."

Traditionally, Charlie should now be thanking the manager for the opportunity and showing his enthusiasm for the promotion. But he is one of the new human resources revolutionaries—although he isn't aware of it—a noncompany man with values he places above his working role.

The smile is gone abruptly from his face. He hesitates a moment, and says, "Thank you. I really appreciate the offer, but I'm afraid I can't take the job." While the division manager listens in astonishment, Charlie hurries on. "You see," he explains, "my wife has just been appointed marketing director for her company here. Making a move now would mean she'd have to start all over again with another organization. Besides, we like it here—much more than we would in a big city environment like Philadelphia. The girls are doing well in school, and well, you know we've been moved around a lot by the company and we've just decided that we don't want to move any more."

Charlie and his wife are representative of several aspects of the human resources revolution. One is the emergence of the two-career family, which has to consider changes on the basis of how they would affect each member. Secondly, they are part of a growing minority of families in revolt against the business practice of moving people around the country to fill corporate openings. The corporate gypsies of the fifties and sixties, with their endless moves in quest of promotions and pay, are giving way to employees who want stability. Charlie does not feel obligated to the company, although he likes his work. He is aware there are other organizations, other opportunities that will not conflict with his personal goals.

Sidney F.: Displaced Person

Taking a taxi in San Francisco, a visitor finds another revolutionary. Sidney F. feels that he has been shortchanged by the system and is willing to talk about it. "This is where I've gotten after five years of college," he says. "It cost my family and me about $20,000 to finance school and grad school. I graduated cum laude with a master's in history, and no job. I wanted to teach, but there weren't any teaching positions open. The universities are cutting back. They've got money problems and the birth rate is dropping. But nobody warned me when I was taking all those classes. The year I graduated there were only 200,000 teaching positions open in the whole country, and 400,000 of us were graduating with teaching credentials. That's a lot of talent just thrown away. It seems to me a country that wastes trained people like this is heading for trouble."

Sidney is one of hundreds of thousands of young people who have, at considerable expense, passed through an educational system which prepared them for careers that don't exist, or for fields that are so overcrowded with earlier graduates that the chances of these young people ever being able to use their training are almost nonexistent. This waste of time, money, and talent is one of the prime causes of the human resources revolution.

Laura M. Meets the Job Mismatch

In a suburb of the same city where Sidney F. drives his taxi and broods about his future, Laura M. is concerned about the immediate present. A drainpipe has backed up, her bathroom is flooded, the situation is getting worse—and she can't get a plumber. "I've called every number in the book," she cries. "All I get are answering services or someone who tells me the plumber is out on another job and will call back. The man who used to take care of our plumbing retired a few months ago and moved to Florida. Nobody's replaced him. The place is being flooded and I just don't know what to do. You can't seem to find a plumber when you need one—or an electrician, or even somebody who can tune our car properly."

Laura's predicament accents another aspect of the human resources revolution—the mismatch between the needs of the economy for skilled or specially trained people and the failure of the country's multiple systems of education to produce enough plumbers, carpenters, mechanics, nurses, and physicians, not to mention dozens of other vital specialists. We have millions of unemployed people, including hundreds of thousands who hold college degrees in fields like teaching and sociology, while at the same time millions of jobs go begging in this country for the lack of people with the appropriate skills to fill them.

Yourself: A Revolutionary Unaware

There are many other human resources revolutionaries, some of whom you will meet in the course of this book. But there is one more, who may best illustrate the extent of the change now going on within the American work force: you.

Whatever your own working role in the economy, changes have been happening to you and to your attitudes toward your work, changes that mirror the causes and effects of the new working revolution. How important, for example, do you rate your work and your employer? A decade or so ago you might have answered that next to your family your work was the most important factor in your life. You might have felt a fierce loyalty to the company that gave you your chance and held your future. Today opinion studies suggest that if you are typical, it is still your family and its well being that ranks above everything else with you. But then come your own concerns and personal interests, and only then your work.

As for company loyalty, your attitude today is more likely to be that of a baseball player toward the team he's currently playing with—a considerable modification of the "company man" syndrome. You are likely to rank working conditions and the nature of your job higher than the salary it pays. Your satisfaction with your job is likely to be qualified, whatever you do, and you well may be contemplating switching not only your job but the kind of work you do. A recent study suggests that about a third of the working population changed occupations within one recent five-year period.

If any of these points apply to you—if you are a member of a minority group or a working woman, if you have been displaced from a job by technology or economic conditions, if you value your leisure time above your working time—welcome to the revolution!

THE IMPACT OF THE HUMAN RESOURCES REVOLUTION

Defining Human Resources

The illustrations in the preceding paragraphs are familiar to most people in management today, but the context of "human resources" may not be so well known.

If a corporate executive were asked if his or her company is concerned with human resources, the answer might be, "Oh, yes. In fact, we have a director of human resources." Further inquiry, however, discloses that this director is usually a person solely concerned with implementing the company's program for recruiting and developing the upward mobility of women and minorities as required by the Equal Employment Opportunities Commission. In short, human resources is regarded by many companies as a synonym for affirmative action. Such action, although a key factor in the revolution, represents only one aspect of the term as it is used here.

To equate human resources with the total personnel function is still to limit its true dimensions. As this book will demonstrate, human resources affect *every* aspect of the organization, from hiring to marketing to investor attitudes, and extends beyond business and industry to involve government, education, unions, the economy, the consumer, and the general public in extensive, complex, and vital inter-relationships.

Unfortunately, business remains myopic on this subject. Executives may deplore the loss of company loyalty, managers may be dismayed by the caliber of graduates coming into the work force, and supervisors may curse the plague of employee absenteeism. Top executives may writhe under the attacks of stockholding activists at annual meetings, complain about the shortages of trained people to staff vital company operations, deplore the erosion of the work ethic, and blast the impact and costs in time and money of government policies from equal employment opportunity (EEO) to welfare. Yet business does not recognize that all these problems are aspects of the single, larger problem of human resources. Nor is business alone in its failure to perceive and deal with human resources as a whole rather than in isolated bits and pieces.

Government Fragmentation

Government is fragmented in its approach, particularly at the federal level. The Department of Labor is isolated from the Department of Commerce, as if there were no relationship between business and work. Education is incongruously mated with Health and Welfare. Literally scores of other agencies affecting human resources from the Department of Defense to the Bureau of Mine Safety are scattered through the sprawling federal structure.

There is no single voice that speaks within government for effectively creating, developing, and utilizing the human resources that are as important to us as our natural resources. There is not even a coordinating agency to bring some order out of the present chaos, nor a voice at cabinet level to speak for or against government policies and actions that will affect our own working lives and the single most important ingredient in our economy.

The End of the Buffalo

Some of us believe that part of the myopia of management and the failure of government to recognize and deal with the human resources revolution is due to a long-existing, conditioned response relating to the work force. This is sometimes known as the Buffalo Theory, applied disastrously to the bison herds of the West a hundred years ago: there will always be more. It was a comfortable conviction, but we know what happened to the buffalo.

It can be argued that in American economic history the labor supply has until now been one of the easier problems for business to solve. When there weren't enough bodies to take on the jobs that needed to be done—clearing the wilderness, building railroads, manning the machines for war production—we brought new ones into the labor force. Indians and Africans were captured and enslaved, and indentured servants were brought to clear and work the land. When slavery became illegal we imported the people we needed—Chinese and Irish work gangs who joined the rails of the continent; foreign engineers recruited to meet the needs of the space and armaments race of the 1960s; the Mexican *braceros* who come to harvest our crops. We geared up vast training programs to turn out "Rosie the Riveter" and her production-line kin, or we invented machines that would substitute for people.

Historically, the more difficult problems in American business and industry have centered on obtaining and managing capital or finding markets for the products that our manufacturing-oriented economy produced in such abundance. This has been reflected in the sources from which business chooses its top executives. For many years they came from the financial field. Then growing complexities introduced by government regulations affecting business pushed legal talent into top executive positions. After that marketing people had the inside track to the top positions as company success involved obtaining multimillion-dollar contracts for complex systems like computers and aircraft, or selling to consumer audiences comprising hundreds of millions of people here and abroad. The work force was taken for granted.

Now it is the people, the human element in business, that is changing. The Buffalo Theory no longer holds, in part because in the new post-industrial economy mere hands are no longer enough, as today's millions of unemployed can testify. The need is for trained hands and specialized minds, and there are not enough of them to meet the demands of the economy.

The worker as mechanical cog in the business machine is disappearing, and so, therefore, is the homogeneous, readily manipulated work force. Tried and true incentives no longer apply, and corporations are not the favored employers. The character, attitudes, and goals of people who work are suddenly becoming something new, more demanding and aggressive.

Other new voices are being heard as well, and broader views are being expressed about what business organizations owe to their own people, to the community, and to the social scheme of things. Other groups are looking over the shoulders of executives and taking action, sometimes with financially painful results, when the demands of business appear to infringe on the perceived rights of individuals or groups.

As a consequence business no longer deals solely with workers or even with the unions on matters related to human resources. Government has come into the work place. Activist groups launch class-action suits against companies. Communities reject company plans to relocate facilities. Even stockholders may sue corporate executives.

Organizations have suddenly found themselves scrambling, improvising, and changing to accommodate one aspect after another of this new and—for much of management—astonishing development. It has become a hostile, heterogeneous, and human working world.

HUMAN RESOURCES COMMUNICATIONS: THE NEW IMPERATIVE

Emerging: A New Kind of Corporate Communications

Not the least of these corporate responses, and the one with which this book is most closely concerned, is the burgeoning of new kinds of communications programs, each directed to critical audiences inside and outside the organization and each an attempt to establish an equilibrium, like that of a trained bear balancing on a ball, amid the fast-moving changes now occurring.

But only a painfully few companies perceive the total picture we call the human resources revolution, or have drawn the obvious moral from these developments. The moral is that corporate survival in a period of massive change requires a new outlook, not only in corporate policies and practices and in philosophies relating to human resources, but in their corporate communications structure as well.

Significantly, corporate marketing people in companies manufacturing consumer goods have already recognized the heterogeneity of American consumers. It is rare today to find a national advertising campaign for consumer products or services that does not include minority people in nonstereotyped roles. We are even beginning to see recognition in consumer advertising that almost half of today's work force is female, and that women work for a living and perform a variety of work roles beyond those of waitress and eccentric plumber. There are solid dollars-and-cents reasons for this, but most of management has yet to make the mental leap that relates human resources to the bottom line.

The human resources revolution has not made itself felt in corporate communications in an identifiable and organized way, even though workers at every level are demanding more information and more kinds of information than ever before. There are many varieties of communications relating to human resources, from recruiting to stockholder relations, but responsibility for transmitting this information is fragmented among a number of corporate operations. What happens is that as new communications needs are perceived, they are assigned in fragmented fashion to whatever company function seems most appropriate. In 99 percent of America's major corporations there is no single high-level executive directly responsible for this expanding mass of human resources communications. No one has yet identified it for what it is.

Danger Ahead

Danger lies ahead for corporations that fail to restructure their corporate practices and policies to meet this new challenge. The pages that follow will examine in detail the communications changes that the revolution is creating, and will offer a comprehensive program to deal with it.

Clearly, the first problem is a company's own work force in this new Age of the Activist. Recruiting people at all levels to staff company positions has generated a sophisticated and specialized new form of corporate communications. Then, too, a firm may have something it calls an "employee communications program," but the question today is whether such programs are sufficiently broad and diverse to meet the information demands of contemporary activist workers.

That leads us to the second problem. Unless a company wants to lose customers, it must extend its communications program to consumers as well. This is the practical way to forestall sales losses stemming from negative perceptions of what the company is or is not doing in the human resources field.

The third problem is how to let stockholders know what the company is doing about human resources. High litigation awards, chopped out of profits, are involved, and the stockholders know it. They want to hear what the company is doing to make sure that it won't wind up on the front pages in a costly class-action suit that may also alienate customers. An annual report that omits such information is not only antediluvian in today's climate but downright dangerous, because it implies that management doesn't understand the situation.

Another key audience to be reached is the potential investor and the financial community at large. But keep in mind that it isn't enough to take action on human resources. The company must be *seen* to be taking action, and that means communicating broadly and effectively about the human resources aspects of company operation.

Colleges and universities must be added to the list of audiences for human resources communication, not only because the campus is a major supplier of many kinds of workers but because it is also a major center for image building, generating long-lasting attitudes toward individual companies and toward business in general.

Companies are already communicating with government on aspects of human resources through the mountain of expensive paperwork they are compelled to do, but that is hardly enough. Government is a key audience because its view of a company can not only determine whether or not a firm becomes a primary target for punitive action, but also whether it receives government contracts. A controversial human resources situation can affect a company's opportunities in this respect. For all these reasons, what a business organization does about its human resources communications program affects the bottom line.

The aim of this book is to examine why the need for human resources communications as a new element in the corporate communications spectrum has come about. Particular attention will be paid to the new work force with which companies must now communicate, and the broad new range of audiences that the revolution has created outside company walls. It will outline in detail a new human resources communications strategy to replace the old-fashioned "employee communications" programs, or whatever names they have been called in different organizations. Finally, it will describe how to build a human resources communications capability into the corporate communications structure. Thus equipped, any business can face the complex, uncertain future with a good deal more confidence.

CHAPTER TWO

The Social Roots of the Human Resources Revolution

To say that we live in an age of change is a massive understatement. Even the familiar French aphorism, "the more things change, the more they remain the same," is no longer credible. "Somewhere around the mid-sixties," says Ian Wilson of General Electric in his 1976 monograph *Corporate Environments of the Future: Planning for Change,* "there occurred a radical change in the change process. Previously discrete elements of change started to interact and coalesce, and the process itself 'went critical,' much as a nuclear reactor does, starting an accelerating chain reaction in our societal 'feedback loops.' As a result, change is now more rapid, more complex and more pervasive than ever."

For Americans of the seventies and eighties future shock has become present shock, and the pace of social change is a key element in the human resources revolution.

THE MAGIC MACHINES

Part of the reason for the acceleration of change is that technology, itself a major creator of change, is recreating the social landscapes in which we live.

McLuhan has defined the impact of telecommunications as creating a "global village"; jet airliners have become the flying transit systems that put any neighborhood in that village within our reach. Television brings distant disasters and classic dramas into our livingrooms with equal ease. Nuclear technology offers both a ubiquitous threat and a slightly tattered promise of ending our energy problems, in the meantime stimulating social confrontations between the antinuclear and pronuclear groups at proposed reactor sites.

The automobile dictates the shape of our cities and the timing of our lives—where we live and where we work. The computer is having almost as pervasive an effect. Business is drastically reshaping its methods of operation to take advantage of the computer's capabilities in areas ranging from accounting to electronic "war rooms" for top management. Government is our largest user of computers. Campuses have installed computer terminals for ready student access, and the home computer, no longer just around the corner, is becoming a fact. Many people have made a hobby of building their own.

It is hardly necessary to expand on how the quality of our lives and our personal interests are affected by these "magic machines" with which we deal regularly. Their effects range from the "revolution of rising expectations" to the rise of tennis as a national sport, from urban sprawl to environmental pollution.

The social impact of technology is unchartable. It has played a role in promoting the growth of international corporations, and in enhancing antitechnological social attitudes often expressed by the environmental movements—objections to technology's impact on the natural environment and, in the case of the picketing of proposed nuclear power sites, potentially on the human environment. But nowhere has the impact of technology fallen harder than on the work place. Here it is revising the nature and content of many jobs, eliminating and creating many others with bewildering rapidity, and in the process fueling the new concern with human resources.

Technology in the Work Place

"In a world of cybernetics, of an almost runaway technology," Studs Terkel writes in *Working* (Random House, 1974), "things are increasingly making things . . . what with the computer and all manner of automation, new heroes and anti-heroes have been added to Walt Whitman's old work anthem. The sound is no longer melodious. The desperation is unquiet."

In a modern hospital, one nurse today can maintain remote watch over a dozen patients via a central console on which television screens provide readouts of their vital signs, just as utility workers monitor the fluctuation in power generating systems via banks of computer displays. On main streets across the country ingenious machines turn out hamburgers, cooked to order and untouched by human hands and set pins in bowling alleys from which the pin boy is exiled forever.

"It's kind of frightening," a supervisor in a modern manufacturing plant reflects. "When I went to work just after the war, I was what they called a 'semi-skilled worker.' I'd come in every morning and go to my machine and set it up and start it going, and it would punch out metal parts and they'd end up in this hopper and a guy with one of those electric carts would come along and move them to the next machine that would deburr them, or whatever. Then these numerically controlled (NC) machines came along. They operated off a punched computer tape, just like the old player pianos worked off the piano rolls with the little holes in them. I was a foreman by then and the main work was getting the right tapes in the right machines and maintaining them. Now I'm a supervisor, but I don't know for how long. They've started installing minicomputers on the floor that run a whole battery of machines. How long are they going to need me now?"

A steelworker in Studs Terkel's *Working* takes another view of technology in the work place:

> "Automation? Depends on how it's applied. It frightens me if it puts me out on the street. It doesn't frighten me if it shortens my work week. You read that little thing: what are you going to do when this computer replaces you? Blow up computers? (Laughs) Really. Blow up computers. I'll be goddamned if a computer is going to eat before I do! I want milk for my kids and beer for me. Machines can either liberate man or enslave 'im, because they're pretty neutral. It's man who has the bias to put the thing in one place or another."

Automation is no longer limited to the factory floor. "My daughter took a secretarial course when she finished college," a friend remarked recently. "She figured it would help her get into the kind of company she wanted, even though being a secretary is going out of style for young people these days. Know what they told her, the first place she applied? 'Sorry. We put in a word processing system last year and since then we haven't had any secretarial openings.' What the devil is word processing?"

Word processing is the newest of the technologies that have been transforming the office. Using a sophisticated computer-based typing machine, a skilled word processing operator can handle the work of a dozen or more stenos or secretaries. The photocopying machines are substituting for whole pools of typists. The computer has taken over the accounting department in processing bills and paychecks and dozens of other routine paperwork jobs, as the morning mail will confirm.

One clear-cut measure of the impact of technology on working humanity is a study of fourteen major paper companies by the United Paperworkers International Union. This study finds that in 1971 it took 1,000 workers to generate net earnings of $1 million per year for the average paper company. But by 1975, as new technologies were introduced, as few as 235 workers could generate the same income.

A perceptive view of how these new generations of technology are reshaping the world of work is provided by Dr. Seymour L. Wolfbein, Dean of Temple University's School of Business Administration. "Technology is a determining force in the kinds of jobs an economy provides," says Dr. Wolfbein. "Perhaps nowhere is this better illustrated than in agriculture. Productivity has now significantly advanced to the point where only 3.5 million farm workers produce all of the food, fiber and feed for more than 210 million Americans, plus many people abroad."

Manufacturing, as we shall see, is going the way of agriculture.

THE GOVERNMENT-SUPPORTED REVOLUTION

Much of the massive social change affecting us is underwritten by our taxes. There are now seventeen federal regulatory agencies concerned with social areas alone, *Business Week* pointed out in a recent special report on "Interventionary Government." These share among themselves a formidable $4 billion budget. The social legislation passed by Congress to establish the agencies provides the legal basis for much of the human resources revolution we are experiencing.

A Part-Time Leisure Class

Unemployment insurance and welfare, along with food stamps and similar forms of payment, have changed working from an economic necessity to an alternative life-style for some people. Intended as a cushion to enable people to survive the pressures of personal or national economic crises, these programs do provide the intended emergency support. Losing a job today does not mean an instant end to income as a worker. But the programs have also become something else—a means of choosing among available jobs, maintaining oneself (for example), as an actor or artist, or under some conditions, opting out of the working life entirely.

Take this young New York filmmaker, for example, who says, "I really wanted to get out on my own. I guess I'll never like working for other people. So when a film I made won an award, I decided it was time to quit and try and make it on my own. I talked my boss into laying me off by promising to do some work for him, because I needed the unemployment payments. It was my stake, you see. It gave me a year of bread, beans and beer while I tried to make it as an independent filmmaker."

"Unemployment insurance reduces—sometimes even eliminates— incentives to work," *The New York Times* notes in an editorial. The newspaper worked out the hypothetical situation of a family of four with two breadwinners, each earning $190 a week. If one is laid off, the *Times* concluded, untaxable unemployment benefits plus reduced taxes on the income of the working partner would cut the family's spendable income by just $30.

Nor is it simply the low-income groups whose life-styles are changed by government largesse. "Incentives created by unemployment insurance," the *Times* points out editorially, "go a long way toward explaining idleness among middle income workers, particularly in cyclical industries like automobiles, clothing and construction." Such workers—about one-third of all workers receiving state unemployment benefits—expect frequent layoffs, and expect to be hired back after six or eight months. Most are well-paid when they are working, thus greatly affected by tax incentives. With unemployment checks as a back-up, they have little reason to look for a new job.

Thus, government programs are subsidizing a part-time leisure class.

The Rights Brigades

The long and sometimes bloody struggle by black people for their full rights as citizens is one of the major social movements of our time. Many of its immediate goals were realized with the passage of the Civil Rights Act in the 1960s and the establishment of government apparatus to implement the new law. Other groups seeking to achieve their own social ends, including their human rights within society, have adopted the tactics and assumptions of the civil rights movement.

Most visible among these is the women's liberation movement, with social aims ranging from legalized abortion to upward mobility in business. The Hispanic community, American Indians, older people, the physically impaired, and homosexual groups are among the other segments of society that have organized, picketed, publicized, boycotted, and taken court action to achieve their goals, often under the aegis of a relevant federal agency.

Increasing government involvement in business has come from this flood of social, political, and legal activity. One example is the growing web of acronymic legislation affecting the work force. Government is involved in hiring (EEOC), on-the-job safety (OSHA), health insurance (HMO), the handling of pension funds (ERISA), and other, lesser known programs in specific industries.

These new laws and the agencies created to enforce them have served to proliferate litigation. People are going to court in large numbers to seek or defend their rights in the work place as they see them. The number of civil rights employment cases litigated, for instance, has mushroomed from some 300 in 1970 to 5,300 in 1976. Class-action suits have doubled in the past five years. The situation recalls a different period in history, when Edward I was successfully launching another new age in thirteenth-century England—the substitution of national law for baronial force. Sir Arthur Bryant, in *The Age of Chivalry: The Atlantic Saga* (Doubleday and Company, Inc., 1963), describes it in terms familiar to the modern ear:

> From the industrious, frugal peasant to the extravagant, indebted baron, everyone seemed to be trying to enlarge his rights at someone else's expense and to take advantage of the complexities of the law to do so. If, thanks to England's strong line of kings, law and its subtle complex processes had taken the place of the sword, it was employed with the ruthlessness of the battlefield . . . something approaching legal civil war existed.

If, 700 years later, we are fighting paper wars and legal battles as a means of reaching social goals, however, it is in a completely different context. In medieval England the clerical orders contained almost all the literate people, while in our own society one of the contributing factors to social change has been the increasing level of education that characterizes America.

Education: The Paradoxes of Plenty

A few years ago French author Servan-Schreiber was predicting an American takeover of the European economy, a judgment based in part on the huge cadre of highly educated people America was producing. In

1975, however, in the depths of a deep economic recession with more than 7 million people unemployed, there were a million or more jobs within the American economy that were open but could not be filled.

The paradox of American education is that although we are achieving new levels in the *quantity* of education as measured in high school graduates and college diplomas, the *quality* of that education has dropped steeply in the view of many observers, and the trained people our educational system is producing are *not* trained for the kinds of jobs being created by a rapidly changing economy.

The Job Mismatch

Immediately relevant to the human resources revolution is the problem of job mismatch, a subject which requires a more extended treatment than can be provided here. In essence, the problem is that despite United States expenditures on education, we have not developed a means of relating education and training closely enough to the economy's requirements to avoid a continuing series of shortages of some kinds of trained people and overloads of others. Recently we have seen hundreds of thousands of young people leave college with four-year degrees in such fields as teaching, sociology, and psychology only to find that there was a glut of graduates in these fields in a dwindling job market. The same phenomenon appears to be occurring in law, as well as in such popular fields as filmmaking and photography.

As a result we are building up what Europeans are calling an "educated proletariat"—masses of young people who have no opportunities to put their minds and skills to productive use.

At the same time there are ongoing, unsatisfied demands within the economy for many kinds of skilled people—nurses, welders, computer technicians, plumbers, and dozens of other specialists. As this is written, the market for computer-related positions—computer scientists and engineers, programmers and analysts—has gone wild, another instance of a high level of demand within the economy and too few trained people to meet it.

An inability to anticipate and react to these economic requirements is characteristic not only of our educational system but of our society itself. In an article headlined "A Million Jobs Go Begging," published in 1975, *Business Week* observed:

> Although unemployment heightens the drama of job shortages, manpower experts emphasize that the underlying problem is related to neither recession nor prosperity, but involves a basic malfunctioning of the U.S. labor

market. Workers seek jobs, hear about jobs, and even make their original job choices in a haphazard fashion that is increasingly impractical in today's complex economy, the experts say . . . Job shortages—and surpluses—are inevitable in a labor market that does not even possess a device for telling job hunters where the jobs are.

Education and Literacy: Down the Up Staircase

"Even those of us who would prefer to disregard the coming of a plague of semi-literacy must find the evidence persuasive," writes a college English teacher, Gene Lyons, an article entitled "The Higher Illiteracy" in *Harper's* (September 1976). "Consider, for example, the steady drop in the average national score on the verbal section of the Scholastic Aptitude Test; the fact that nearly half of the entering class at the University of California at Berkeley . . . failed placement exams and had to be enrolled in remedial composition courses; the news that applicants to journalism programs at Wisconsin, Minnesota, Texas and North Carolina flunk basic spelling, punctuation and usage tests at rates that vary between 30 and 50 per cent; a survey by the Association of American Publishers showing that college freshmen *really do* read on what used to be considered a high-school freshman level."

This paradox of the degreed illiterate is a common complaint. Executives say the ability to spell and write clear sentences is so deficient in many college graduates that some companies have had to set up remedial seminars for those who have other abilities the company wishes to utilize.

In terms of their usefulness to the work force, the products of schools and universities are suffering from a disease which has multiple causes. This disease does not rise from lack of money alone, even though the effects of the economic squeeze are being felt. One cause seems to be a kind of chain reaction that begins in the elementary and high schools, where teachers who have not been adequately trained themselves are trying to equip students with basic cultural and vocational knowledge by using systems that are outworn, competitive, and not geared to the changing world beyond the classroom.

This carries through to the university level, as a young woman who is an assistant professor at a local university comments. "Of course the incompetence gets passed on. It's built into the system," she explains. "Most of the kids I teach are really poorly prepared to do the work. I fail at least 50 percent of the undergraduates in my classes, and judging by their work, I should be failing more. I'm known as a hard teacher, but I also have a high teacher rating. So it's okay if I fail that many. But if I fail more, or if it becomes widely known that I fail that many, the department could get into trouble and so could I.

"You see, money and positions are given to a department by the dean on the basis of the number of students enrolled in its classes. If the kids stay away from your department's classes because they have the reputation of being too hard, the department gets less resources and cannot hire staff. The first to go, in those cases, are untenured people like me."

There are thousands of dedicated, highly able teachers and thousands of schools where real learning takes place. But the "pass along" system permits elementary school students to enter high school even if they are not educated to that level. High school graduates enter college, ready or not, and college graduates are eventually pushed out into the working world whether or not they are equipped to deal with it. One result: still another breed of activist.

"College students of the mid-seventies aren't following their predecessors in protest marches and demonstrations, but more and more are issuing the battle cry—'See you in court' to their universities," reports the *Sacramento Union*. "They hope to change the universities they attend by demanding accountability from the professors and the schools. The students, unhappy with what they are learning on campus, are filing consumer suits claiming that their schools are guilty of such shortcomings as negligence, fraud, and breach of contract. . . . Many students sue because their courses are worthless, aren't as they are described in the college catalogue or don't contribute to students' careers."

Even in academia, it would seem, everyone is a litigant, and students sometimes appear to have good cause.

There is much more that might be said about education, business and the human resources revolution, and we will return to the subject in a later chapter. Now let's look at another social catalyst.

THE UNIONS AND SOCIAL CHANGE

The union was yesterday's principal instrument of social change, whose sometimes violent advocacy of equitable pay and improved conditions of work on the production line has more than achieved its goals.

Today's union member is no longer identified with the spontaneous militancy of social activists. The union member is likely to be a middle class homeowner, with better working conditions than the nonunion worker in most industries, and enjoying better job security, pensions, and more leisure time. Often the unionized industrial worker does as well or better in pay and working hours than the white-collar boss.

But in the process of achieving their goals, the unions adopted or promulgated attitudes which are part of today's social concerns. For one thing, they have operated on the assumption that, like mechanical parts, all workers are identical units. Unions bargain on the basis of masses of working people, regardless of individual abilities. For another, unions appear to devalue work itself as something to be avoided as a necessary evil, or to be fragmented among as many people as possible.

A prize-winning 1977 cartoon was captioned: "This year, at least two labor organizations may try to organize the armed forces into military unions." The illustration showed "Typical Tank Today," with gunner, driver, and commander. Then it portrayed a "Unionized Tank," staffed with four drivers (one for right turns, one for left turns, one forward, and one reverse), a commander, assistant commander, union steward, supervisor, grievance committee of two, and no gunner—but a fire-fighter in the engine room. The cartoon effectively parodied the way in which the original union concerns for preserving jobs has sometimes decayed into featherbedding and other make-work practices. The old union rallying cry of "a fair day's work for a fair day's pay" has an ironic ring in the ears of some people today who feel it might better be replaced with "maximum pay, minimum work."

If the work ethic appears to be in decline, unions must take their share of the blame.

Social Change Hits the Unions

The unions, like business, are feeling the impact of accelerated social change and the human resources revolution. In the past they fought to reduce working hours as a way of giving their members leisure time. Now they are actively seeking to reduce hours further as a way of spreading available work among larger numbers. "Because of technology and automation," says Joseph Tonelli, president of the United Paperworkers International Union, "tens of thousands of workers have been displaced. If the free enterprise system is to survive, we can't have a third of the nation unemployed and expect the other two-thirds to provide support in the way of unemployment insurance and welfare benefits. . . . It's going to have to provide jobs for everyone. The work week now has to be reduced to 30 or 32 hours. There's nothing sacred about the 40-hour work week." A shorter work week, of course, will mean more leisure time, fitting in with current social trends.

Social advocacy movements are putting new kinds of pressures on the unions, sometimes directly, like the drive to introduce more minority workers into craft unions, and sometimes in unusual new ways. When the Communications Workers of America were considering a strike against American Telephone and Telegraph in 1977, for example, their president, Glenn E. Watts, attributed this to an unusual source. According to *The New York Times:*

> Mr. Watts insisted that the union needed gains matching contracts in the steel and automobile industry, or about 10 percent a year. And, in effect, he blamed the consumer protection movement for any strike. "If we are forced to strike I would also lay a great deal of the blame at the doorstep of the New York State Public Utilities Commission," he said. "That august body . . . commissioned a study which claimed that telephone workers are overpaid." State regulatory boards, now directed more toward consumer advocacy, often take a harder position against rate increases than in the past. The contention that the phone company overpays its workers is used as an argument against rate increases. . . . By resisting the union and taking a strike, Bell "will have demonstrated" to the state commissioners that "they are, in fact, hard bargainers with the union," Mr. Watts says.

The consumer advocacy movement, by this reasoning, can be held responsible for creating the threat of a major labor strike.

Like other institutions in our country, unions have been attacked from all sides. Among their critics are their own members and employees. The United Steelworkers Union is a case in point. The union entered into an "experimental negotiating agreement" with the steel industry which banned industrywide strikes. Rebellious steelworkers complained that the agreement took away their most effective weapon, the strike, and in the summer of 1977 some 16,000 to 17,000 steelworkers walked out, shutting down 85 percent of the nation's output in a dispute with their own union.

A 1973 report of a Special Task Force to the Secretary of Health, Education, and Welfare, *Work in America* notes: "The union strategy of only bargaining for extrinsic awards has begun to show signs of wear. Worker discontent with this traditional role of unions has left many union leaders bewildered and frustrated. . . . Young workers who are rebelling against the drudgery of routine jobs are also rebelling against what they feel is 'unresponsive' and 'irrelevant' union leadership."

The High Cost of the High Cost of Labor

Organized labor has a major economic impact on our society, more than most people, including union members, realize. Labor costs affect not only the way we live and the life-style we can afford, but also the fluctuations of the economy.

It may seem to an outsider that many of the present privileges and powers of unions are paid for out of the pockets of the unorganized majority. Whenever budgets are planned for almost any kind of institution, the largest item on it will be for labor, a "fixed" but no longer stable cost that is certain to increase. When the amount of the increase is in dispute between an institution and organized labor, there is a settlement—with or without a strike—that may adversely affect many people in addition to those directly involved.

"Without making any judgment about unions," one economist has commented, "they don't reduce wages; they push them up." The end result is usually a rise in the cost of doing business that is passed on to the consumer. Union economists decry the notion that labor's wage demands are a major element in inflation, but socially and economically the immense powers and pressures of unions, under very little governmental control, pose a major social dilemma. The plight of Britain today, with a labor-dominated economy, is an ominous signpost.

THE ECONOMIC ROLLER COASTER

The "affluent society" is dead, it can be reasonably argued. In the decades that followed World War II the economy assumed boom proportions under the stimulus of the cold war, the Korean war, and the space race. We had the resources to support not only a major military effort and a luxurious civilian economy but the most challenging technical goal a nation had ever set for itself. In addition, we could at the same time launch major social programs to protect our work force from economic shifts and bring hitherto neglected minorities into the economic mainstream.

This affluence, however, was not achieved without a series of painful economic adjustments along the way which have spurred the human resources revolution. The economy had been on a roller coaster, punctuated by a series of busts and booms, that on the whole moved steadily upward until the near crash of the early 1970s. We were hit then by a dangerously deep recession—a double recession, in fact. The first phase was apparently triggered by an economic slowdown resulting from the end of the space program and the drains of the Vietnamese war. The second was the result of the Arab oil boycott and the consequent steep rise in the cost of energy. These have adversely affected public responses to business. As a working measure of these economic highs and lows, let's take a look at how they affected one segment of the working population: the engineer and scientist.

These professionals are the key to a technologically oriented society like ours. They are the people who not only create new products and projects and keep the technology operating, but their efforts create new jobs for the workers needed to construct, operate, and supply new facilities. To a high degree it is the engineer who maintains the nation's capabilities in production, in defense, and in major social services that are based on technology, such as, for example, health care.

Since 1961 the Engineer/Scientist Demand Index maintained by Deutsch, Shea & Evans has been charting on a monthly basis the demand for these technical professionals. With the base year of 1961 equaling 100.0, the Index hit a high of 190.3 in 1966, the average for that year. Just five years after that, in 1971, technical demand dropped to 41.5. It took another five years to climb back to the level of 123.5, in 1976. This Index is pragmatic, based on the actual employment advertising directed to technical people. Its dips and rises relate directly to the job opportunities and security of this segment of the American work force.

What struck the technical community in the late 1960s hit the economy as a whole in the early 1970s, as many of us have good reason to remember. Mass layoffs shook the country. Unemployment reached heights unheard of since the 1929 crash, and this time the people in the unemployment lines were not only the technical specialists or the lower echelon and unskilled workers, always the traditional victims of economic fluctuations. Many were white-collar workers, middle managers, high-level executives: people who had assumed that they were immune to economic change, with years of service in their companies, mortgages, and kids in school. Often they were "company people" with good records and reputations for loyalty and service. Nonetheless, all these people found themselves unexpectedly unemployed in a depressed and shaken economy with no prospects for re-employment.

"I worked for the company for twenty-two years," one middle manager said during the 1972 recession. "They've always talked a lot about how important their people are to them. And I believed it. So why am I here on this unemployment line? I'll tell you. The only thing a big company is really concerned about is not its people and not its customers, but just that damned bottom line."

The shock was profound and the shockwaves have yet to subside. These, too, are shaping the new society which is emerging.

THE NEW SOCIETY

As a result of the changing social attitudes described here and many others that we have not explored, a new society seems to be emerging from the present bewildering ferment of change. What will it be like? It is much too early to characterize this new society in any detail, particularly while the change is still going on. But at least we can see some of the ways in which this social change is creating the human resources revolution. One is the deepening antagonism toward business itself. "In the Age of Uncertainty," John Kenneth Galbraith writes in the book of the same name (Houghton Mifflin, 1977), "the corporation is the major source of uncertainty. It leaves men wondering how and by whom and to what end they are ruled."

This uneasiness, which has persisted for a long time in American society, appears to be deepening, hardening from uncertainty to a decidedly negative attitude. The antibusiness syndrome is one of the readily identifiable new directions today.

Antibusiness People; Antipeople Business

Opinion polls report that the ordinary citizen has a much more negative attitude toward business today than a few decades ago. In fact, a recent survey of corporate chief executives found they consider declining confidence in business the major external problem facing corporate management and one they expect to persist for years to come.

From one observer's viewpoint, a key reason for this decline and for the general lack of confidence is that business is widely perceived to be grossly insensitive to human needs. Working people are painfully aware, for example, that when the economic balloon begins to lose altitude it is workers at every level, as recent events have demonstrated, who are seen as expendable ballast. Jungle-like hiring and firing are the norm rather than the exception in industry. People are too often acquired for their ability to deal with a given project and, in the

American tradition of waste, tossed aside when they are no longer needed, as expendable as a paper cup.

Older workers in particular are victims of this practice, at every level. The mass layoffs of the 1970s were simply a dramatic demonstration of this. Only recently have there been outplacement help or reassignment within the company for those whose jobs evaporate, and then only for a handful. There are angry reactions today not only to the practice of forced early retirement but to mandatory retirement in any form in an inflation-plagued economy.

The prevailing view is that business treats people like so many statistics, to be manipulated in the same way that engineering data are run through a computer. Pat Watters writing in *The New York Times* gives an example.

> One man told me about the one-two punch that almost floored him. He was laid off at age 48 after 26 years equally divided between only two companies. He went through the ordeal of joblessness for several months, then, happily, found a better job than he had had before. He worked at it for two months and then—blam! He was laid off again. What had happened? The new job was with a just-opened branch office. A computer at headquarters had miscalculated operating expenses and ticked out a new set of figures that meant one employee had to go. Since my friend was the last hired, that meant him. All impersonal. The computer sends down a number and destroys his life.

It is against this mechanistic view of themselves that many workers are asserting their rights through litigation and other forms of social rebellion.

Business: Legality versus Morality

Another aspect of the antibusiness syndrome can be found in media reports suggesting that industry is willing to tolerate lethal conditions in the work place until called to account by government, the courts, or activist organizations. Even then many companies resist to the last legal ditch. Only a few years ago a small chemical plant producing a dangerous chemical was found to have conditions that led to the crippling and death of a number of workers. The top executives were interviewed on a television program, and their smiling defense was that legally the responsibility was not the company's. This tendency to divorce the legal from the moral is a major factor precipitating antagonism to business.

While business is perceived to be ignoring dangers to people in the work place, it is seen to be actively destructive to the environment. The movement to reclaim and preserve the natural environment has done its share to fuel antibusiness feelings. It is business, as those concerned with the environment see it, that proposes to move into and destroy untouched natural areas; dump toxic materials into waterways, lakes, and seas; create major air pollution through manufacturing processes; waste natural resources; and promote human consumption of dangerous substances, if in doing so it makes a profit. Business profits, like the high costs of labor, are seen as not only excessive but inflationary, as are the salaries paid in the top echelons.

In this climate efforts to explain the business view of the economic facts of life to the public make scant headway. People are acutely aware of the prevailing business practice expressed by the phrase, "the cost will be passed along to the consumer." When business taxes go up, or the cost of business space increases, or unions win bigger contracts, or company costs increase for any reason including government fines for pollution or employment discrimination, the public sees itself the ultimate loser.

People are angry, too, at incessant add-ons to the costs of the products they buy, like the auto industry's "dealer preparation charges." They resent the declining quality of products and the high costs of repairing them, and express their anger by purchasing foreign products.

Business: Guilty till Proven Innocent

The shock of Watergate was particularly severe to Americans because they had elected to positions of public trust people who made conspicuously moral pronouncements and then were found to have consistently lied to the public.

Business involvement in the scandals of the Nixon administration and in high-level payoffs, corruption, and crime have had a similar if muted impact because they contrast sharply with the high moral posture adopted by top echelon business people. Adding to antibusiness feeling is public awareness that business people caught in crime, like the Watergate conspirators, are let off with a judicial slap on the wrist. At most they are given a light sentence at a country-club-like penal facility.

The result is a deepening cynicism regarding anything business may have to say, and increasing concern with business influence and involvement in the political life of the country. The public is aware, as never before, of the irresponsibility of Congress, the power of lobbies, and the sometimes intimate relationships between regulatory agencies and the industries they oversee.

Social change, then, and with it the revolution in human resources, would appear to stem in part from an altered view of the organization. For many today it no longer confers prestige to work for a major corporation. Often it may be the reverse. The smoke of the manufacturing plant is no longer accepted by communities as a desirable sign of progress, but as air pollution, symbolic of the malignant effects of industrial processes on people and the environment. As has been observed, "America is no longer a business civilization."

The Age of the Activist

One of the by-products of technological change has been that the population is exposed to more information than ever before in history. We saw and heard for ourselves the police dogs used against civil rights activists in the sixties. An Asiatic war was brought into our livingrooms in bloody color. We witnessed a Martian dawn. We have 1,811 daily newspapers, 8,342 radio stations, and some 35,141 books published annually. The total information output is awesome.

Further, increased leisure has produced what might be called the "multiplied person." We are workers, information absorbers, activists in organizations from PTAs to political groups, corporate shareholders, travelers, students, members of religious groups and professional associations, consumers, hobbyists, volunteer workers—the list is almost endless. Perhaps it is this combination of multiplied information and multiple interests that has been the genesis of the social advocacy trend.

For example, a woman who is director of communications for a New York consulting organization says, "I'm very upset about the recent Supreme Court decisions regarding women. So I've decided to work to get the law changed. I don't have much time, what with working here during the day, plus the house, my garden, the kids, and my writing, but if you believe in something, you have to work for it. You have to make time for it. Change never comes cheaply, especially social change."

As people have become involved in more roles they have come to value themselves and their interests more highly and to resent depersonalization. They have seen what can be accomplished by individual and in particular by group action. They have become more willing, even eager, to fight for causes in which they believe and with which they identify their interests.

The result is the development of a new constituency within our society, one that is of particular importance to business and that is a key to the human resources revolution. It is this frame of mind that has led to the toppling of a President elected for a second time with a landslide majority and which has created sufficient political pressure for its social aims to see many of these become the subject of corrective legislation. It is an audience, as will be explored in more detail later in this book, which is critical for business not only as a social force but as an element in the human resources revolution.

The Lotus Eaters

One further social development worth noting is the rise of the leisure ethic as a counterpoise to the decline of the work ethic.

On his homeward voyage from the Trojan wars Odysseus paused at the land of the Lotus Eaters. There some of his crew tasted the fruit, lost all memory of home and duty, and wished to stay there eating the lotus forever. The term has entered our language with the connotation of people who live for pleasure in a dreamlike state. That mythical kingdom, perhaps some early drug culture, has counterparts in life-styles today.

The phrase "doing your own thing" expresses a viewpoint widely adopted by the younger generation. It represents one of the basic new directions of our time: the trend to a strong concern for people as individuals and for individual values. It also implies a liberation from the conventional, from the accepted way of doing things. It leads to a healthy questioning of current values and existing rules. But doing one's own thing can also lead to abdication of responsibility, a high level of self-centeredness, and insensitivity to others. In particular, it is destructive to the self-discipline that is the key to any kind of accomplishment, and in our society and by the young in particular it is often interpreted as the absolute right to do what one chooses without regard for others. It can serve as a raison d'être for instant gratification and for opting out of responsible action.

Another facet of our society is the extent to which we are an "entertainment culture." We are deeply involved with entertainment purveyed largely as a commercial product. One highly visible result is the extreme wealth rapidly accumulated by successful rock stars, sports figures, or show business personalities.

Perhaps from a merger of these two elements, perhaps as an unconscious response to the nuclear threat that overhangs us all, or possibly for reasons that sociologists have yet to surmise, there is a related change taking place in this new society. We are substituting a leisure ethic for the work ethic.

If we are not always able to do our own thing in a society that still requires (to a degree at least) work in exchange for money, if we have no prospects for fame or fortune unless we get a hit in the spreading institution of government-sponsored lotteries, there is now a compensation available. We can devote ourselves to making the most of our leisure time, to making leisure, in fact, the focus of our lives. It is this leisure life-style that appears to be dominating the thinking of Americans, more than achievement through work or even the accumulation of money.

Everyone is aware of extreme examples. There is the young West Coast-based executive of a major computer firm, well up the corporate ladder with high-level prospects just ahead. He quits his job, divorces his wife, grows a beard, buys a houseboat, and begins a new kind of life surrounded by quadraphonic sound, low-pressure living, and amiable girls.

More of us, however, are like bass fisherman Barney C., more interested in having the time to pursue our leisure interests than in acquiring money. We spend what we make beyond the basics on boats or summer homes or sports cars or photographic gear or foreign travel— whatever expresses our real interests. We know we can never have the money of Onassis so we settle for more time and the satisfaction that, too often, we do not achieve from the work we do.

A Culture in Transition

The human resources revolution, as we are defining it here, is the product of these and many other changes that are affecting us as a people. To what has already been outlined, a good many other changes can be added, all of them contributing significantly to the society toward which we are moving. Among them could be included the decline of religious faith and the immense growth of our population over the past few decades.

Whatever the causes, it is clear that a significant transition is taking place. Its scope has been effectively delineated by Ian Wilson of General Electric who says in his monograph, *Corporate Environments of the Future:*

> We in the United States in the mid-seventies are in the throes of a major transition comparable, say, to the transition that took place when man the hunter and nomad became man the settled farmer; when life in the cities—

civilization, in its literal sense—became the norm; and, most recently, when agricultural society gave way to industrial society. Now our society is on the brink of becoming something different, a new form of society. In this sense, the United States is as much a revolutionary society as is Maoist China.

Exactly what this new society will be is still hard to say, though we can make out some of its outlines. Some futurists have labeled it 'the post-industrial' society; others refer to it as the 'technocratic age'; still others as the 'learning' or 'cybernetic' society. Whatever future generations call it, it will be a world radically different from our present world, not only in its physical properties, but also in its attitudes, its values, and its institutions. Small wonder, then, that we are experiencing such agonies of uncertainty, unrest and turmoil, such questioning of our social, political, and economic institutions—including, of course, business.

CHAPTER THREE

Heterogeneity Unlimited: The New Work Force

"If you want to really understand what's happening to the American work force," advises one economist, "just stand outside any office building or plant at quitting time."

It is advice that management, theoretically in the closest touch with American workers, has yet to take. Business certainly has a vested interest in change, but that concern has been directed almost exclusively to the effects of change on its marketing plans, not upon its work force. One survey suggests that almost 50 percent of the major companies responding have some kind of "early warning system" to alert management to social change, yet three-quarters of this group use their system only to project changes in consumer attitudes and demand for new products. Of the total sample, only 15 percent report using such a system to identify new kinds of human resources needs.

Business apparently still has to learn that the factors affecting the marketplace are also those affecting human resources—and vice versa. Toy manufacturers, in other words, are likely to be aware of the downward shift in American birthrates, but they associate this trend with a declining market for their products and not with a prospective short supply of new workers a decade or two ahead. This "manpower myopia" is one of the reasons why a human resources revolution is occurring.

As for other demographic factors, some are clearly apparent in observing the streams of people entering and leaving business establishments. The sheer number of them is impressive. There is a striking sexual and ethnic diversity represented, significantly different from a decade ago. These differences are of key importance, but beyond them are others not visible to the inquiring eye—educational levels, the nature of the work in which these people are engaged, and new ways of working that are a response to social change.

THE SIZE FACTOR

"The East Side Expressway is experiencing the usual traffic delays this morning. The Cross-City Freeway has a tie-up in the two left lanes and motorists are advised to divert to Grand Island Parkway south of. . . ."

Every weekday morning across America hundreds of such traffic reports bring the familiar bad news to long, slowly moving lines of vehicles converging on cities and towns. Other commuters in buses, subways, and trains are only aware of too few seats and unscheduled stops and starts as they make their way to offices and plants. Even in the midst of an uncertain economy and with several million unemployed, the nation's work force has grown so large that it clogs every means of transportation, twice a day, in simply getting to and from work.

Little more than a quarter-century ago that American labor force was about 64 million strong. By 1960 the total had jumped to 72 million. The 1970 census showed 84 million workers. Now there are some 100 million people in the labor force—more than our total population a few decades ago—and 17 million more to come by 1990.

Dr. Samson Tuchman, director of economic planning for the National Broadcasting Company, has been studying the impact of population changes on the American economy in the years ahead.

> The structure of the labor force has been changing. There is an increasing concentration of women and people under 25. Additionally, this labor force has been expanding at a relatively rapid rate—an important element in the strong growth in real GNP projected for the latter 1970s, since it provides the increasing manpower pool needed by expansion-minded companies.
>
> By the same token, however, we will have to run hard to create enough new jobs just to keep pace with the rapid growth in the labor force. While the number of people employed will be expanding substantially through the rest of this decade, so too will be the number of people looking for work, making it difficult to keep the unemployment rate below 6%.

Demographic statistics may be considered dull, but when they show that there will be two people in the work force in the near future for every one in the recent past, business needs to take note. These numbers indicate that population growth is far from a matter of adding more consumers. It means providing the jobs for these new millions because their wages will provide that "consumer spendable income" which figures so prominently in marketing plans.

THE HETEROGENEOUS WORK PLACE

The Major Minority

The flood of women into the work force is "the single most outstanding phenomenon of our century," in the much-quoted phrase of Eli Ginzberg, chairman of the National Commission for Manpower Policy and long-time student of shifts in the working population. "Its long term implications," he says, "are absolutely unchartable." *Ms.,* the noted feminist magazine, announces the advent of the age of the "pink collar."

From any viewpoint the demographic data are impressive. There are, for example, more working women in the United States now than full-time housewives. Some 28 million of the nation's children have mothers in the work force, and by the time you read this almost one out of every two American workers will be female. Moreover, as common experience tells us, women are taking on more and more occupations that once were labeled "for men only," and they are backed by the government as well as by women's rights groups.

The Alaska pipeline, involving the toughest kind of outdoor work performed in Arctic temperatures and rugged conditions, would have been an all-male enterprise a dozen years ago. But women migrated to Alaska to find jobs on the project both as office workers and in the field. They operated heavy equipment, performed highly technical tasks, and compelled male construction workers to accept them as equals. In an article entitled "Women on the Pipeline: Good Pay in a Man's World," *The New York Times* described some of these women. One was Mary Clove, twenty-four, a former medical student who had been a pipeline truck driver, driller, and riveter for two years:

> She's the only woman on a 30-man crew, and, now that the men accept her, she has few hassles; "But," she notes, "it all depends upon the crew you're on. . . ." Miss Clove laughs, tying a knot in the plaid wool shirt she's layered over a baggy white t-shirt, "After two years, my mother back in Texas still doesn't believe I'm doing this. I send her pictures and she writes back saying, 'But dear, you should dress like a girl.' My dad thinks I should get on with med school. But I tell them you're only young once."

Women are also joining unions as part of their working lives. The reason can be seen in studies showing that while more jobs are open to women than before, the pay differentials between male and female workers still persist. In 1975, for example, the median income of working women was 57 percent of the men's median wage. Julian Kien, director of employee relations of the American Paper Institute, sees some possible developments in union-management issues as a result of this pink-collar influx into organized labor:

> The increasing organization of the white-collar sector, coupled with the rising proportion of women in the civilian labor force, has resulted in a substantial increase in female union membership. In 1972, women accounted for about 22 percent of total union membership. Between 1964 and 1972, the rise in the number of women in labor unions accounted for 40 percent of the growth in total union membership. The increasing importance of women in union ranks can be expected to bring to the fore new issues for both management and labor. For example, day care facilities may become an increasingly important issue at the bargaining table. Other bargaining issues which may be emphasized as a result of increased female membership may include maternity leave and hiring and promotion policies, particularly in terms of their impact on placement and opportunities for women.

With more women entering management positions, some are headed for the top. The long male dominance of the executive suite will eventually be broken, with unforeseeable results.

The Two-Career Family

One demographic spinoff of this influx of women is the sharp increase in households in which both husband and wife have careers. This trend seems likely to continue. People who have become accustomed to living on two salaries are not likely to cut their income in half, especially with inflation an ongoing threat. That raises a new aspect of the human resources revolution: the two-career family.

A survey by Atlas Van Lines shows that 38 percent of the reporting companies have already relocated families in which women were the principal family breadwinners. *Business Week* recently told how companies, reversing conventional corporate policy, were encouraging couples to work in the same unit. Instances of men making a move to further a wife's career are becoming commonplace.

"I know a professor who teaches communications theory at a university here and who is also a computer specialist," a consultant observed when the subject of two-career marriages arose. "His wife is a research chemist. She's moved into new jobs twice in the last three years.

Fortunately they've been in the same area. When I asked her husband what they'd do if she got a good offer from another part of the country, he told me, 'I'd urge her to take it, if she wants it. My own skills are portable, I can find a position anywhere.'"

A Multiracial Work Force

"We've come a considerable way," says Ida Lewis, publisher of the black newsmagazine *Encore*, over a business lunch. "For one thing, I think white people have got used to the idea of working with black people and a lot of the tension of ten years ago, when the equal employment drive started, has tended to disappear on both sides. For another thing, and maybe it's the most hopeful sign, there are a lot of black youngsters in college now, with a good chance of getting into worthwhile jobs when they come out." She sighs. "But there is still a mighty long way to go, especially for black kids with no chance for college."

More than a decade of equal employment efforts has served to move the United States toward a multiracial work force. It has involved many companies in extensive programs to attract, train, and provide upward mobility for blacks, Hispanics, and even the most neglected of minorities, the American Indian. This effort has included support of educational programs to prepare young minority people for mainstream jobs. For example, universities like the Georgia Institute of Technology work with major corporations and liberal arts schools around the country to attract young minority students into engineering programs. Only 3 percent of all college students in the early 1960s were black, and although the recent recession curbed some growth in this area, the percentage has edged up to 7.5 percent.

By 1986 an estimated 100,000 minority students will have graduated with business or accounting degrees and some 33,000 will have gained engineering degrees at the bachelor's level—the kinds of training for which employers most frequently recruit at the colleges.

On the negative side, black youths have the highest unemployment rate of any group in the nation with no sign at the moment that this situation will be significantly changed for some time to come. Even those blacks who are at work, as the HEW report *Work in America* points out, "are to a striking degree disproportionately unemployed or working at bad jobs. This disproportion reflects the persistent, systematic discrimination and closed-off opportunities that racial minority persons experience in work, education, and other major institutions in our society."

Although we have begun to build a truly heterogeneous work force, and are systematically adding to the numbers of minority people at work at all levels within it, we are apparently not meeting the expectations of these groups in terms of what employment should bring them. "One might expect," *Work in America* continues in its comments on minority workers, "that a third of minority workers in middle-level blue-collar, white-collar and professional jobs would find their jobs as rewarding as their white counterparts do, but this does not seem to be the case. The most dissatisfied group of American workers, for example, is found among young black people in white-collar jobs." One result, this study notes, is that young blacks perceive work problems as problems of equality, and "therefore, the problems are not easily quantified and not easily rectified. Because of this, white employers (and often white co-workers) are becoming increasingly frustrated and intolerant as black demands accelerate almost in proportion to employers' concessions."

While reacting to one aspect of the human resources revolution—the drive for equal employment opportunity—we are extending its scope by adding increasing numbers of people who are dissatisfied with their working environment.

A New York company in the food industry presents another example of how this demographic change is creating difficulties that must be factored into the company's human resources practices. This company, like others, is required to provide upward mobility for women, and attempted to accomplish it by introducing women already on the payroll into blue-collar jobs like machine operation that had hitherto been the prerogative of male operators. But their effort came up against an apparently immovable cultural roadblock. The bulk of the company's workers at this plant are of Hispanic background. "When we try to encourage these women to take training for machine operation," the company's personnel director laments, "we get almost no response. Given the Hispanic culture's emphasis on male and female roles, women simply can't conceive of moving into or competing for what they see as men's jobs. It goes against the grain of their whole cultural pattern."

Dealing with the complexities of this multiracial work force is going to be one of the more difficult tasks business faces in the decades ahead.

The Age Factor

Newsweek called it "The Graying of America" and made it the cover story of its February 28, 1977, issue. The magazine quoted Philip

Hauser, director of the University of Chicago's Population Research Center:

> We are faced with the prospect of very drastic social, economic and political change over the next quarter century. . . . A prime force behind this transformation is the postwar baby boom, an explosion of births lasting roughly from 1947 to 1957. About 43 million children were born then—a fifth of the present population. They crowded the schools in the 1950s and 1960s, then flooded the job market in the 1970s. By the 1980s and 1990s they will be a middle-aged bulge in the population, swelling the 35 to 44 year old age group by 80 per cent—from 23 million people today to 41 million by 2000. And early in the next century they will reach retirement, still the dominant segment of the total population. It's like a goat passing through a boa constrictor.

At the same time two other age-related phenomena are in process that will affect work and the work force in the years ahead. One is the number of Americans over sixty-five, the traditional age for retirement. There are about 25 million now and there will be more than 30 million by the end of the century. The other phenomenon is the declining fertility rate, which will greatly reduce the numbers of young people entering the work force. These demographic trends are also part of the human resources revolution.

Older workers have been campaigning against forced retirement. One of them, Harris McMann, airline pilot who was retired at sixty by his company, has taken his case as far as the Supreme Court. "To me," he says, "I look at it and say, this is illogical, this is an injustice, this is a social policy that should be done away with." Pressures from older workers, many concerned with the impact of inflation on their retirement incomes, has resulted in a Congressional bill raising the mandatory retirement age to seventy.

Strong concern about this development is already being expressed, not only by business but by associations concerned with affirmative action like the National Urban League. Business sees a slowdown in hiring and promotions that will lead to discontent and turnover, especially among younger workers. Affirmative action supporters fear that the intake and upward mobility of minorities and women will be adversely affected.

Meanwhile, some major companies report a trend toward early retirement among their older workers. General Motors, for one, says the average retirement age in the company is about fifty-nine. This further confuses the issue and clouds predictions on the future impact of ending mandatory retirement. In the end, perhaps, it will not be the Supreme Court that dictates whether people stay longer on the job, but the demographics of the long-term falling birthrate. As the numbers of children decline so do the numbers of future eighteen-year-old entrants into the work force, and the numbers of college graduates business can recruit from to fill entry-level professional and managerial positions.

THE FADING BLUE COLLAR

Another kind of American Revolution took place at Valley Forge a few years ago. One day all of the hourly employees of General Electric's Space Division there were made salaried employees. General Electric, in effect, phased out the blue-collar worker and the division became a white-collar operation. The Space Division was able to make this move because of the highly specialized nature of its work and the limited size of the work force. The change was made for internal purposes of efficiency, but what happened is symbolic of a trend that is accelerating as we change from a primarily manufacturing economy to one in which other kinds of work predominate. The difference between "white-collar" and "blue-collar" work is gradually disappearing under the impact of technological change and the human resources revolution.

Modifying the Work Force

The impact of new technologies on the work force has been mentioned earlier, but the reasons and the extent of that impact are worth emphasizing.

Relatively simple machines, or improvements in existing machines, can have important effects on individual livelihoods. "Everybody makes the same joke about my job, 'It's an up and down business,'" the New York elevator operator says, drawing on a cigar. "But it's no joke. As far as work is concerned, this business is only going down. Everything's automatic today. Used to be a job you could get with no training. Now once this building goes, where am I going to look?" The elevator itself is an example of a technical advance that created literally millions of jobs by making the high rise building practical. But the number of elevator operators, once in the hundreds of thousands, had dwindled to scarcely 25,000, and that figure is going down as automatic elevator systems become the norm.

The *Wall Street Journal* carries ads for 12-ounce tape recorders an executive can carry in a pocket. Such advances in business recording systems from the machines that inscribe dictation on a plastic belt to the latest high technology word-processing instruments have resulted in reducing the United States steno pool from 275,000 in 1960 to fewer than 100,000 today.

The computer has caused massive change in the work force in a thrust that is still in process. Computers have displaced uncounted thousands of clerks and other paper workers, but they have also created hundreds of thousands of jobs that never existed before. There are some 250,000 programmers, for instance, and almost as many systems analysts. More than 50,000 people work in the repair and maintenance of the machines and their peripheral equipment, which other thousands build, ship, and install. There are computer designers, computer scientists, computer consultants, and so on down an extensive list of specialists. Beyond these, computer technology has brought into being or drastically modified hundreds of thousands (more likely millions) of individual jobs, from that of the Oregon sawmill operator to the clerk who rents a car.

The essence of this technological change is that it is unpredictable. Who could have forecast the transistor or the integrated circuit with their far-reaching consequences. This is future shock in the work place.

The Post-Industrial Work Force

As manufacturing and processing industries grow more automated, they are simultaneously dwindling in importance as employers. Agricultural workers were once the most numerous and economically important part of the economy in terms of their contributions. Since the tractor replaced the horse and farming became automated, these workers have become the smallest element within the total labor force. The same pattern is occurring in blue-collar manufacturing, which is also becoming highly automated.

The key characteristic of a post-industrial age, as defined by Daniel Bell and others, is that the basic nature of the national output changes from manufactured products to information and services. In a post-industrial age, therefore, white-collar information workers and service workers increase in number and manufacturing workers decline— precisely what is now taking place. Within the past decade the white-collar worker has become the most numerous group in the economy, comprising 50 percent of the work force. Manufacturing workers are second with 33 percent, service workers are now 14 percent, and agricultural workers have stabilized at about 3 percent of the working population. This trend is projected to continue in the years ahead.

NEW WAYS TO WORK

Most American workers may be only vaguely aware of the current transition from a manufacturing to a post-industrial organization of society, but they have been reacting to the changes they perceive in their working environments in several pragmatic ways.

The Career Changers

The government in a routine check of employment trends during a recent five-year period found that Americans had been changing not only their jobs but their occupations on a grand scale. Nearly a third of all workers in the United States switched careers during that period, and career changing was the single largest reason for workers quitting their jobs. Follow-up government research has confirmed that this massive career shift continues. In retrospect we can identify such career shifts as reactions to a rapidly changing technological and economic environment. Career changes, however, are made not only from necessity in our society but increasingly as a means of finding working satisfaction.

Charlie E. is an example of this "second-career syndrome." "As a teacher," he says, "I used to have to work during vacation periods and in the summer at odd jobs just to maintain a decent income for the family. Well, a considerable number of this state's school systems have had to restrict their educational budgets, including the one in the town where I work. That resulted in my being on a shortened schedule, at still less pay, so I got a six-hour evening shift job at a local manufacturing company. Within a few months, an opening in their marketing division was posted, so I thought, why not try for it? I ended up with a new kind of career that pays a lot better than teaching, is more interesting and has a good future."

Sometimes second careers are forced on people. During the recession of the early seventies many of the people who were thrown into unemployment set off in new directions. A different kind of necessity motivated the research director of ·a major chemical company. His doctor advised him to find a less tension-ridden occupation after he had suffered a mild heart attack. He took a severe cut in salary to accept a job teaching chemistry at a small college, and within a few years was happily combining teaching and administrative jobs at the school at a comfortable income. "Technical obsolescence" is a perpetual hazard for engineers. It is said that ten years after graduating, the data and skills engineers acquire are outmoded; many thus aim for the managerial ranks rather than a lifetime professional career.

In a survey of career switching, *The New York Times* cited the case of Tudor Leland:

> Two years ago, Tudor Leland, a 52 year old Transworld Airlines pilot, flew a 707 jet back from his usual Athens run and quit. He had been with the airline 29 years, mainly in supervisory capacities. Remembering how he had felt squeezed by the "nitpicking" of the Federal Aviation Agency, management and craft unions, he says, "There is no longer a way in most big business today of being able to produce and give your thoughts in a way which might be of value to your company." Now he is struggling— optimistically and with three partners—to navigate a boat yard and a charter boat business in Beverly Farms, Mass., into the black.

A Columbia University research project suggests, too, that more and more people in middle age are shifting to the nonprofit sector, redirecting their skills rather than making drastic changes in occupation. Many people find their financial pressures ease in middle age, due to their children reaching an independent age, or perhaps to an early pension such as is provided by the military. This makes it financially easier to begin a second career. Thus one problem that management may increasingly face in the future is how to hold onto experienced people who seek new satisfactions from different kinds of work. Internal company systems that would help people make career changes within the organization may be one method of handling this. Educational institutions also need to learn how to serve a new kind of student—the second-career person—whose backgrounds and needs will be very different from those of the conventional undergraduate.

The New Entrepreneurs

In a classroom on the campus of Transylvania University in Lexington, Kentucky, a student asks, "Would you go over that part about portion control again?" The instructor nods and turns to the diagram beside her, while the students follow a duplicate of the chart in their blue binders as she explains once more. They don't look like the ordinary undergraduate class, and in fact many are beyond normal college age. They're learning something a college doesn't usually provide—the nuts and bolts of how to manage a small restaurant profitably. The course isn't given by Transylvania but by the Long John Silvers restaurant chain which operates its own management course on campus. Many of the students represent a new kind of entrepreneur: the franchisee.

Franchising has already become a major part of the national marketing system. There are more than 900 franchising companies in the United States with at least 400,000 franchised businesses. They account for nearly 30 percent of all retail sales or nearly $160 billion. When the associated services are added in the overall figure approaches $180 billion. Some of these franchises are of the traditional kind—automobile dealership, gasoline stations, and soft drink bottlers—but nine out of ten franchising companies are less than twenty years old and represent new businesses.

Franchising is already providing jobs for 3,300,000 Americans. We see them every day in McDonald's more than 4,000 restaurants, in the 2,000 or so Holiday Inn hotels. Not as visible are such operations as Manpower, whose 706 offices throughout the world are franchised employment agencies, and Century 21 Real Estate, the franchised land-brokers who expect to have 10,000 offices across the country by 1980. There are franchised accountants, franchised flower growers, and some well-established manufacturing companies have recently turned to this system. Blue Bell, Inc., producer of sports and casual wear, is breaking new ground by bringing franchising to the clothing industry, with their Wrangler Wranch stores now numbering into the hundreds.

It seems likely that the concept of franchising, a kind of corporately encouraged entrepreneurism, will continue to spread. Reports of new franchising operations appear almost daily: there are even franchised camping grounds for people who want to tackle the great outdoors under standardized conditions. Certainly this industry has already made a substantial impact on the demographics of today's work force and represents still another aspect of the post-industrial changes now taking place.

The Part-Timers

One reason franchising has become so successful is that many franchise operations need a minimum full-time staff and can use part-time workers to handle periods of high volume. This kind of work was once done primarily by students who worked after class and on weekends for spending money. Now part-time work has become a way of life for a substantial segment of American workers including more than a million who "moonlight" by taking second jobs. A recent estimate puts the number of part-time workers at more than 15 million people. Everyone seems happy about it.

"They're productive and plentiful and many companies couldn't get along without them," declares a front-page story on part-timers in the *Connecticut Business Journal*. "The majority of the part-time labor force is made up of women; about 25 percent are teen-agers and the rest are men. But women dominate the part-time labor force and most of them are married. Some of their reasons for working are obvious. They need the extra income; they like to get out of the house; they want to be home after school. They use part-time employment to re-enter or enter the labor force. Part-time workers are not limited to retailing (though about half of the employees at Sears, Roebuck are part-timers) or food service (90% of McDonald's 250,000 restaurant people work part-time). They also work in banks, in insurance companies, for manufacturers, and in just about all types of service businesses."

Marilyn D., who has held a part-time job with a major New York bank for eleven years, says, "I like part-time work for a lot of reasons. For one thing, it's stable. Even during the recession, the cutbacks here were mostly among full-time workers. I don't earn a big paycheck, but it helps out and it doesn't put the family in a higher tax bracket. I see my kids off to school and I'm there when they come home. I just like to work, you know—do something other than housework. It keeps me on my toes."

The same kind of motivation apparently accounts for people who do another kind of part-time work, the temporaries, who fill in for a day or a week wherever a need exists. For the most part they work through "temporaries" agencies who place them, pay them, provide benefits, and bill those who use their services.

Many have skills that could readily win them a regular job and some use temporary work as a search for an ideal place to work, but a great number are like Jane D. "I'm perfectly capable of holding down a full-time secretarial job," Jane says, "and I have. But I prefer to work as a temporary. I meet more people that way. I've never worked at a company long enough to get bored. I don't get involved in office politics. If I don't like the place, I just don't go back. If I feel like taking a few days off to spend at the beach or go skiing, I do it. No hassles. And I split an apartment with two other girls, so money is no real problem."

Part-time work, then, far from being the mark of a person who can't get a "real job" as it was in the past, may be the wave of the future. It combines the increased leisure important to many people with the stimulus and reward of working. Management may do well to remember that the seven-day week ("If you don't come in on Sunday, don't come in on Monday") has given way to the five-day week and numerous long weekends. The four-day week has come up in union negotiations as a way to spread the work; several hundred smaller companies are already on such a schedule.

As the human resources revolution rolls on, the time may come when we're all part-timers in a working world in which two work forces alternate half-week shifts.

OTHER DEMOGRAPHIC DEVELOPMENTS

Careers and Education

"Among the best publicized trends of the 1960s was the increased educational achievement of Americans," Dr. Sam Tuchman of NBC recalls. "Young people were clearly staying in school longer than students had in earlier generations and college enrollments more than doubled in that decade. But recent data suggest that the educational wave will create only a slight increase in the median level of schooling, from 12.3 years in 1975 to 12.5 years in 1985. High school and college graduates will comprise a larger part of the population. But more schooling is not necessarily the equivalent of more education. It is not at all certain that a high school education means today what it has in the past."

Philip Farish, editor of *Industrial Relations News,* says that those who recruit the relatively unskilled for entry-level jobs agree with Dr. Tuchman's observation. "They shake their heads over the job applicants that turn up." Farish says, "Millions of young people with high expectations and not a great deal in the way of skills are heading toward the job market. Not too many of the young have a realistic idea of what the real facts of the job market are." Nor are these youngsters prepared for even relatively simple tasks. Farish cites a study by the National Assessment of Educational Progress which reported that tests given to 100,000 children and young adults showed that fewer than half of the seventeen-year-olds and young adults could measure a $3\frac{3}{8}$-inch line accurately. Only half of that age group could solve a simple arithmetic problem involving finance charges, and 74 percent couldn't write a job application letter.

Another piece of data with implications for the human resources revolution occurs in a federal study showing that almost 80 percent of recent college graduates have taken jobs that were previously held by people with less education. While a part of this shift may be attributed to the increasing complexity of some jobs, one commentator suggests the larger implication is that the jobs will not provide the opportunity or challenge that young people seek, and the result will be broad, prevalent job dissatisfaction in the years ahead.

Stephen P. Dresch of the Institute for Demographic and Economic Studies in New Haven also points out that the high-education job market is already saturated, and he predicts a significant decline in the rate of college entries that could reach as high as 50 percent in the next decade. As a result of this persistent saturation, Professor Dresch sees limits to vertical mobility and economic achievement among this group. "Deep and pervasive frustration will infect large segments of the American population," he concludes.

Government and Employment

One demographic fact of life that corporations will be living with is competition with government for the available talent on the job market. Public sector employment in the United States more than doubled in the past twenty years, reports a Conference Board study entitled *Road Maps of Industry*, (June, 1977) increasing from 7.4 million to 15 million with most of the increase concentrated at the state and local level. "Over the years," the report noted, "there has been a shift to a larger share of total non-agricultural employment going to the government sector; while only 13.3% were in public employment in 1950, the ratio rose to 19.2% by 1975, declining slightly thereafter."

One reason for government's ability to attract workers was also evident in the study—pay that is five times greater than it had been twenty years earlier. The average pay at the federal level, according to the report, was $15,000 in 1975, more than $4,000 higher than in the private sector. Another reason, as other studies show, is that aside from good salaries, government workers enjoy substantially higher benefits and vacation privileges than their private sector counterparts. Along with this is a high degree of job security.

A psychological factor is also involved. In the sixties government employment was perceived by many young people as providing a lever for creating social change to an extent not possible within the corporate environment. Many of these during the sixties and seventies rejected the traditional career route into and up through the corporation as a way of life.

Looking Ahead

The operational word for demographics through the turn of the next century is "dynamic." Changes like those discussed briefly here will be occurring in every part of the American economy to an extent we are only beginning to comprehend. There are other factors as well. Significant changes in the family structure as a basic social unit include two-job families, fewer children, more divorces, and many more single-person households.

Population, at least during the next decade, will be exhibiting a geographic shift as it grows, centered in the South, Southwest, and West. These regions during the period from 1970 to 1975 accounted for about 85 percent of the country's population expansion. According to current projections, even more people will be living in suburban, exurban, and nonmetropolitan areas rather than in major cities.

As with other demographic changes, these shifts will affect the distribution, makeup, and goals of the American work force. To cite one example, the pattern of employee benefit programs will undergo further changes to accommodate the changed life-style. Benefits programs have traditionally been structured on the conventional family group and have had a generally rigid framework. Already the pattern is being challenged. Arthur H. Burton, Jr., a vice president of Prudential Insurance Company of America, foresees a "smorgasbord" type of benefits program emerging in which employees will be able to select from a broad spread of benefits those that best suit their needs and fit within their particular compensation levels.

Dead ahead, as Dr. Sam Tuchman of NBC points out, is "a dramatic change in the growth rate for the civilian labor force. Labor force expansion will fall off sharply after 1981." Recent declines in American investment in research and development may slow the rate of technological change to some degree by reducing the number of new technical breakthroughs. But powerful new technical tools already exist, like the "computer-on-a-chip" microprocessors, which can be expected to make more jobs obsolete and create others at a rapid pace in the years ahead.

We have yet to grapple with the implications of the post-industrial society with its emphasis on white-collar and service jobs and de-emphasis on manufacturing. But an increasingly urgent need to deal with the aging capital equipment which characterizes the United States economy, particularly in its basic industries, can be expected to lead to extensive modernization. When this occurs it will mean a more automated, less labor-intensive national manufacturing complex, further decreasing the blue-collar segment of the economy. At the same time it will increase the already extensive capital investment in the individual worker, hasten the trend to "white collarization" of the work force, and create new problems and new conflicts within organized labor and between labor and management.

On the basis of demographic trends alone we can expect the human resources revolution to roll on unabated during the next decade or more. But there is another factor that must be considered: how the social attitudes and trends that now characterize our society are being translated from personal life into the work place.

CHAPTER FOUR

New Attitudes
in the Work Force

A full-page, four-color ad for *Psychology Today* shows two young people cavorting in the surf in wet bathing suits, in a leisure scene typical of today. The ad's headline puts their attitude succinctly: "Our parents lived to work, we work to live." Consultant Fred E. Lee agrees with the idea and adds: "Make way for the Spock generation."

He sees an increasing emphasis on personal pleasures and individual satisfaction, not only characteristic of our new society but as an element in the work place that is taking many companies by surprise. "Perhaps the work place is the last to feel the pressure of the changes that have taken place around us," says Lee, who heads Fred E. Lee & Associates, a Dallas management consulting firm. "Or, it's the last place trying to hold out against new values and new approaches to living."

What has Dr. Spock got to do with it? Lee answers:

By 1980 42 percent of the labor force is going to be in the twenty- to thirty-four-year-old age group. This is the group whose parents brought them up on the ideas that Dr. Spock recommended in his famous book on child-raising, and consequently business is now having to deal with people who have a psychologically different approach to work from any generation preceding them. For one thing, they were raised in an environment of participation. They've taken part in decision making almost since they were old enough to talk. They've learned to ask *why?* They've grown up to question things—ethics, quality of life, the meaning of work. If they don't get answers that satisfy them, they keep asking, sometimes in disruptive ways. As a result, they've got different values from those of their parents and their bosses.

Because these children have been involved in decision making, they have grown up much more open than previous generations. They tell it like it is, as the saying goes, and they expect others to be equally open and honest with them. This can be disconcerting to people in the business environment who don't have that orientation. For another thing, they are very *time* conscious.

This means that time is high on their priority list. They want time for self-improvement, leisure, and so on. It works in two ways. They value money less than time, for example, but many think you can buy more leisure time by working harder and making more money. They emphasize the immediate present and make decisions for *now*, with little concern for past or future. You might say the generation gap has hit the work place.

As Lee and others are pointing out, the new attitudes toward work which are part of the human resources revolution have their genesis in both the social changes and the new demographics of the work force that have been outlined in previous chapters. Not only are there psychological factors affecting the new attitudes that business is encountering, but economic ones as well.

The old fear of losing a job or being catapulted into instant poverty has dwindled if not disappeared. Dickens' Bob Cratchit, blessing himself for having a job and thanking his boss for his wage, is no longer a character on the working scene. Even with the devastating impact of a deep recession still fresh, the attitude that jobs will be there for the taking still exists, even if the attitude is slightly battered by circumstances. Today's workers are prone to think not what they can do for the company but what the job can do for them.

Jack M., for example, is shop foreman for an aerospace parts manufacturer. He makes good pay, but he knows he'll never be company president or even make middle management since he hasn't a college degree. Rather than be concerned with the traditional upward climb, therefore, he has a new attitude: To get as much security as he can on the job and as much free time as possible when he's off.

Jake's cousin Robert has an engineering degree and ten years of experience. "But I'm wondering," he says, "if I'm ever going to make it to that hallowed ground of $40,000 a year. Managers make it; engineers don't." He's becoming an activist about engineering salaries, working through the local chapter of his technical society.

Then there's Abigail R. Married with two children, a homeowner, Abigail wants to go back to work. But she wants a job on her own terms, which include worthwhile pay, security, and a chance for advancement in a kind of work she would like. She's turned down two offers and is content to go on looking. "I don't see any sense in working if I can't enjoy it," she says. "My husband makes a good salary and so there's no pressure on me. I'm going to take my time and see what comes up."

New attitudes like these, relatively mild instances of changed thinking about work, are pushing ahead on two tracks through the entire structure of our working society. On one track, skilled, often unionized workers are increasingly satisfied to remain in their positions for all of their working lives. They press now for more job security, preferably on a lifetime basis, a shorter work week, and benefits that move further and further away from the traditional economic protection. The lower white-collar echelons are adopting the same kind of attitudes and goals.

On the other track is the college-educated, upwardly mobile worker who can fit into the ranks of middle management and who sees prospects for greater opportunities. While the brightest or most highly educated command and get comfortable salaries, others fit into a mix of management and workers that isn't what it used to be. Women, blacks, and now middle-aged men are all contributing to a new activist environment.

RISING EXPECTATIONS

"During the next ten years or so, the population will be younger and better educated on the average, less satisfied with the status quo, seeking to develop their own individualities and abilities, less tolerant of accepted beliefs and more anxious to control their own destinies than ever before," says economist Dr. Carl Madden, of the United States Chamber of Commerce.

Already it is possible to see this pressure of rising expectations in union-management negotiations and in the spread of benefit programs that have moved away from simple increases in pay and improved working conditions.

In the work place these social attitudes are expressed in demands for more "social" rather than economic benefits, for better and more interesting jobs, and for conditions at work that parallel "the good life" outside the office or plant. Union leaders sitting down at the bargaining table in 1977 were talking about lifetime security guarantees for their members. Management's unofficial response to this straw in the negotiating wind was that even this—what might be called an "ultimate benefit"—was not beyond reason. This union move also suggests that union workers have acquired most of the benefits that really interest workers; the guaranteed job is a step beyond the current elaborate packages that have been developed.

Burgeoning Benefits

Employee benefits already run to a third of the total payroll in most companies, *Business Week* reports, and have risen at a faster rate than salaries in a number of organizations. Robert Heinz, compensation manager of Hercules, Inc., says that his company expends fifty cents in benefit payments for every dollar it pays in wages and salaries, when social security is included.

Fringe benefits that were considered generous by management twenty years ago are today standard items that employees take for granted—so much so that many companies try ingenious means such as mock "benefits checks" in pay envelopes to jar workers into an appreciation of their value. Even the two-week vacation period is being expanded to meet rising expectations about leisure time. Arthur H. Burton, Jr., vice president of Prudential Insurance Company of America, expects that within a few years nearly half the American work force will enjoy thirty-day vacations every year and get fifteen scheduled paid holidays.

This leisure trend is already well under way. A survey of 200 large companies turned up the fact that half had recently added more paid holidays and some were already planning or providing three-week vacations in place of the traditional two-week program. One California aircraft manufacturer gives its entire work force paid time off between Christmas and New Year's. A four-day Christmas and Thanksgiving holiday is becoming commonplace. In high-pressure businesses like publishing, law, and advertising, the four-week vacation is often given after a minimal time with the firm.

The Social Side of Work

Parallel with the national trend toward more time off the job is another, much newer development: making life on the job more palatable. This is the effort that some companies are making to provide amenities in the company facility that workers can use in leisure time during the working day or after working hours. These include swimming pools, recreation rooms with indoor sports equipment, attractive and inexpensive food service, and for many corporate headquarters facilities, landscaped rural surroundings. Some of these attractions were originally created for top and middle level managers, often a product of an exodus from urban surroundings where restaurants and health clubs were readily available. Now they are being extended to white-collar clericals and blue-collar production people as well, though still on a limited basis.

The move to onsite recreation rooms where lunch hour ping-pong, gyms, jogging paths, and swimming pools are available is the beginning of a new era. Attitudes of workers who spend free time at the plant working out and enjoying leisure facilities are inevitably going to be different from those of people who see the work place as simply a necessary and unpleasant site to earn money.

"The organization is becoming more a 'living atmosphere' that grows and evolves in an open-end style in order to satisfy or in response to the rising expectations of workers," observes Philip Farish, editor of *Industrial Relations News*. As a result, he believes, "Leaders and managers will more and more arrange for their organizations to be self-organizing and self-adaptive. They will be 'process-oriented' and they will derive their authority from exercising responsibility, influence, expertise, creativity, and the design of process."

This reflects another element in the rising expectations of the work force. Workers have decided they want jobs that are meaningful to them, and this is occurring across the board, from the unskilled laborer to the middle manager, but in different ways.

"There are just some kinds of jobs you can't get people to take these days," the employment agency executive says, gesturing toward a stack of job descriptions. "I get people in here every day who've been out of a job for a month, for a year. No real skills, like welding or typing. So I show them these openings. People desperate for janitors and dishwashers and maids and that kind of thing. No dice. Even when the pay is good. If people think it's a dirty dead-end job, they'd rather not work. House work? It isn't dignified. Even secretaries. Business in this town is screaming for secretaries, but to a lot of women today, that's a dirty word. They want to be executive assistants or whatever. I tell you, it's a different world than when I started this business twenty years ago."

Emerging attitudes seem likely to generate substantive changes in the working world. The monotony of the assembly line is in the process of fading out, although it may take years. Business will have to adjust to workers who want a greater choice in what they do, a voice in how the work is done, an opportunity to relate to workers around them. We already see such adjustments taking place.

The same sort of adjustment is in prospect for middle management. Business is finding that it must provide not only challenge and opportunity to hold their best people on these levels but a new kind of working climate. As the human resources revolution spreads, the distant, authoritarian boss, for example, is proving less effective than the personable teamworker who succeeds in motivating by example. Younger managers (often educated in behavioral psychology as well as in business) are coming into the work place with their eyes wide open, working in ways that widen their comprehension of the new attitudes that baffle older managers.

The human resources revolution is, in fact, compounded of all these elements: new attitudes in the work place adapted from those developed outside, rising expectations for a more rewarding, more human working experience, and a greater "democratization" of the working world in response to the tides of change. These new attitudes are rising at the same time that comfortable old assumptions about behavior at work are crumbling—the work ethic, for example.

THE CHANGING WORK ETHIC

"The guys in plants nowadays, their incentive is not to work harder. It's to stop down the job to the point where they can have some time. . . . A guy wants to keep himself occupied at something else than being just the robot they schedule him to be." The speaker is an official of the United Auto Workers local in General Motors' Lordstown plant. "Assembly workers are the lowest on the totem pole when it comes to job fulfillment. They don't think they have any skill. Some corporate guy said, 'A monkey could do the job.' They have no enthusiasm about pride in workmanship. They could care less if the screw goes in the wrong place."

The union official's voice is one of many in Studs Terkel's book *Working* (Random House, 1974) which echo this conception of work. Many people experience the feeling every day, both in their own jobs when they are dealing with others who care little about what they do and show it in their work, and in their personal lives. It's common now to take a car back to the dealer because the fault it was taken in for wasn't corrected or the work that was done created a new problem.

What seems to be happening is a reversal of the values that had prevailed since the beginning of the nation. From the time early colonists proclaimed "he who does not work shall not eat," work has been viewed as the predominant and essential element in everyone's life. We have called it the "Protestant work ethic," reflecting an earlier attitude that equated work with religious ideals. As colonists of other faiths came to America and became part of a growing country in which people had to depend mostly on their own efforts to wrest a living from what had recently been a wilderness, the idea was readily accepted. By the nineteenth century work was elevated to the status of a secular religion, here and abroad, and idleness was thought of as a social sin, a notion often exemplified in Dickens' novels.

These traditional attitudes toward work are being rapidly turned around today. The work ethic once considered an immutable part of the "American Way" has proven to be as susceptible to change as the rest of the social fabric. It could be said with an ironic echo of Churchillian rhetoric that never before have so many asked so much for doing so little. Work, as a quasireligion, appears to be going the way of the passenger pigeon, except for a few individuals whom business magazines castigate, interestingly, as neurotics and call "workaholics."

The reasons for the decline of the work ethic may be left to the speculations of sociologists, although possibilities spring to mind. The nature of blue-collar work is a far cry from the sense of craft that once gave a worker pride in a job. Until recently, workers at most levels in a company have been seen as expendable, interchangeable elements in the semimechanistic, semimilitary structure that has characterized business philosophy since the industrial revolution. As unions have become more powerful they, too, have acted to segment and control jobs; their orientation is like that of business in treating workers as a mass, not as individual people. In the process, through featherbedding and other practices, they have downgraded work and stifled initiative while obtaining financial advantages for their members. Too many companies in turn have demonstrated that in the crunch people don't count against the cold figures of the bottom line.

It could be argued, in fact, that the basis for the whole human resources revolution is the conflict between the mechanistic practices that characterize industrial economies and the new perceptions held by people in the work place of themselves as individuals with rights of their own. A recent article in *The New York Times* spotlighted this issue under the title "Wanted: A 9 to 5 Bill of Rights," and in which David E. Ewing of Harvard points out that the only place in the nation where people are deprived of the human rights they otherwise have is when they step through their employers' doors.

Employees in Management?

"Japanese managers and executives have learned the value of listening to their employees and capitalizing on the wealth of knowledge that every worker has about his job," says George Sherman, vice president of industrial relations for Midland Ross Steel. His comment, and what his company is doing, suggest ways in which the human resources revolution is leading business and workers alike to reach for new ideas. Workers and their unions are looking for more say in company actions that affect their jobs. Companies are looking for ways to resurrect the work ethic by providing more motivation for involvement and productivity. Developments in other countries provide some cues.

The labor efficiency of Japanese workers has impressed management, and their lifelong job security impresses labor here. Several years ago the new approach to automobile manufacturing by the Swedish Volvo firm which allowed workers to perform as teams and greatly increased worker satisfaction attracted considerable attention. Though a union team came back from Sweden unimpressed, the idea of job enrichment continues to spread. American workers are not yet asking nor are American managements thinking about workers on company boards, but with some assistance from government this too is becoming a familiar phenomenon abroad. Will it spread here? Companies are already adding women and minority people to their boards, so the possibility exists.

Meanwhile, a more direct approach to employee involvement is being instituted experimentally by companies like Midland Ross. This organization has revived the Scanlon Plan by which workers get dollar incentives on a monthly basis when the plant's productivity exceeds a standard level. The result has been a 16 percent increase in overall productivity, absenteeism lowered by half, a substantial decrease in turnover, and approval of this new working approach by 87 percent of the plant's workers. "I happen to believe that all of us involved in industry are sitting on an untapped gold mine and that we have a huge reservoir which is only waiting for us to draw from," says Sherman in talking about his company's experience with this kind of worker participation plan.

Another approach is being taken by Rockwell International. A new facility at Battle Creek was planned by the company's director of education and training, Dr. William Snow, and the assistant secretary of the United Auto Workers Union, Donald Rand. The working units were designed to permit workers to take responsibility for their own tasks and job functions. They were integrated, whole units. Teams of workers were created to plan their own schedules, processing, vacations, and overtime. Production workers, renamed "manufacturing specialists," also did their own inspecting of finished products.

One of the most comprehensive work participation plans, according to *The New York Times,* is the design of a $5 million facility for Carborundum Refractories Division, near Jamestown, New York. Using some 150 suggestions from assembly line workers, the designers put in a smoothly flowing U-shaped production line that involves broader worker responsibility for the finished products.

These experiments suggest that if employee attitudes toward working are significantly changing, there are opportunities for companies to restructure their own approaches to what working should be and to do it profitably.

Horatio Alger Bites the Dust

"We have broken down the ethic that a successful life must be spent in one enterprise or corporation," a Michigan State business professor observes. "We no longer believe in the gold watch theory."

If the work ethic is altering, the Horatio Alger legend seems dead. That legend, as it came to be interpreted, asserted that with loyalty, hard work, and clean living, an American boy could start at the bottom and work his way right to the top. The pyramidal structure of most organizations fostered the idea of unlimited upward mobility based on merit. Just before the turn of the century, when the Alger myth flourished, there were highly visible examples—role models, we call them now—to sustain it. There was Marshall Field, sleeping on the counters of the Chicago department store where he began his career because he couldn't afford lodgings. There was Andrew Carnegie, a poor immigrant boy; Simon Guggenheim, selling lampblack; butcher's boy Peter Widener; and dozens of others.

What we are seeing today, however, is a far cry from the Alger phenomenon. Rather than putting their faith in "Luck and Pluck," today's entrants into business depend on a high level of education, including the coveted MBA degree. They do not start for pennies; $20,000 a year is not an uncommon beginning salary for the right degree. Rather than working their way up, the new graduates are immediately part of middle management, generally with no working experience at lower level jobs. As for loyalty, turnover among new college hirees, during their first three years of work amounts to about 50 percent, and executive recruiters advise managers that job hopping rather than staying in one organization is the way to get ahead both financially and in terms of advancement.

Does hard work bring success? Not according to *The Changing Success Ethic*, published in 1973 by the AMACOM Division of the American Management Association. It's author, Dale Tarnowieski, surveyed 2,600 executives. Promotion, this group concluded, is "largely subjective evaluation or arbitrary." An automobile company survey of middle management came to a similar conclusion. More than half the salaried employees responding believed that "job performance" would not help their chances for promotion.

Out of this disillusionment with the Alger tradition have come several problems and changes of attitude. The midlife career change that is becoming common within our society, and is especially visible among business executives below the top, is one. Plagued by long hours, a never-empty briefcase, the frustrations of commuting, and work that is increasingly abstract and decreasingly satisfying, they quit the corporation for entirely new and different roles as professors, franchisees, photographers, or owners of small businesses.

Further, a great many workers at all levels have none of the traditional aspirations. They will settle for a good living without the responsibilities, insecurities, and lessened leisure that go with higher-level work. These people see executives working far longer hours than they do themselves—or than their unions would permit. They know that these workers have no more protection against losing their jobs than do the lower echelons, and perhaps less. The greater financial rewards do not tempt such workers, who see the tax systems dissipating much of the difference between their own wage packets and the higher-level paychecks. Sam G., who is a machinist for a Norwalk, Connecticut, manufacturing firm, says, "Every afternoon in the summer, I take my boat out into the Sound for a little fishing after work. It's nice to get out on the water, you know. And as I come home in the evening, I go under the railroad bridge. I see these commuter trains go by. They're full of guys who get up before I do to get to the station to get to the city, work like hell, and then get on a train to come home again. I've had two or three hours fishing before they even get home at night. So who's making out better?"

Goodbye to All That

The lessons of the mass firings of the recession, the disruption of the familiar education-work-retirement cycle, the forced exile of corporate transfers, and the parents worn down by a competitive work environment who must still open their briefcases every evening have not been lost on the young. One expression of this is evident among the new middle-management group. For years American business has produced its legions of corporate nomads whose alumni joked wryly that IBM stands for "I've been moved," but now the human resources revolution is resulting in new attitudes. "Sorry, we don't want to move. We like it here," is the answer more companies are getting in response to offers of greater opportunities with the company elsewhere. Business is losing out to a much more glamorous, more modern version of Horatio Alger: the Beatles.

The prospect, if it is still a prospect, of climbing rung by painful rung up the corporate ladder may have turned on the silent generation of the fifties, but in the seventies we are living in an entertainment culture in which rock stars and sports figures earn astronomical and well-publicized figures. Hence a new kind of American Dream, in a sense Alger's "Ragged Dick" is transposed to another, unimagined level. Most of these sports and show business figures started out as obscure and struggling people who made it to the top of the economic heap virtually overnight. This happens even to writers. At the turn of the century only two writers in America were millionaires: Harold Bell Wright and Gene Stratton-Porter, both popular novelists who wrote many books to achieve that status. Now it is possible to make a million dollars on a single book.

With examples like these before them, what young person still dreams of becoming a fire fighter or nurse (doctors, of course, remain staples of the TV screen), much less entertains a burning vision of making it to a corporate presidency?

The human resources revolution, then, is in part a product of today's different aspirations and a willingness to opt out of conventional career paths and develop a noncompetitive life-style.

"You moved up here from the city?" the reporter asks the young unmarried couple who are working a Canadian farm. "How come?"

"There was nothing there, for us," the young man replies. "It was a big hassle. Up in the morning, get to work, come home dog tired, watch the TV. That's no kind of life."

"You were working an eight-to-four job, though," the reporter pursues. "Farming now, you're up at five and not finished till after dark. Isn't that as bad as your office job?"

"You don't understand," the girl says. "This is hard work, sure. But it has some meaning to it. In the office all I did was handle a bunch of papers. I was a way station for papers. Nothing really connected with life, just figures. Up here, we're doing something worthwhile, something basic."

"And, we're not trying to compete with a lot of other people for a raise or an office with a window or any of that jazz. This is something more human. We'll never go back."

It was only the other day, in the sixties, that this kind of flight, so new to America—and yet harking back to our own early history—was filling the columns of newspapers and magazines. Young people were dropping out of school and going back to the soil. The older ones tossed up promising jobs to do their own thing away from corporate routines and urban frustrations.

What is happening now is not so much a reaction as it is an evolution. The legacy of the flower children of the sixties, with their different drum, appears now in a widespread tendency among workers who would never identify themselves with flower children to plan how they can best leave their jobs and live a life devoted to their own interests. There are many who discover they can live as well on unemployment benefits, part-time work, or welfare as they could on low-paying, unsatisfying jobs. There is not much incentive for them to return to a work force that can offer them neither security nor a measure of enjoyment in their work.

The erosion of the work ethic, in other words, reflects an America in which the monolithic view of people's roles in life, which the nation was founded on and which was accepted for almost two centuries as an immutable order of existence, has been found wanting. Like the Wizard of Oz, it has been exposed as a humbug. We are reaching for and finding new values, confused as these may be at the moment. How far this evolutionary process will take us no one yet knows.

Making It: The Mixed-Up Salary Situation

Fueling the negative attitudes toward business careers, undermining the work ethic even among the most loyal and conscientious of company people, and creating rebellious attitudes among older workers, is the present confused situation involving pay, the most basic reward for work.

"Ten years ago, I started here at what I thought was a pretty good salary, $10,000 a year. Every year I've been getting merit raises—nothing spectacular, but enough to make me think I'm getting ahead, or at least staying even with inflation and all. Now they're bringing a kid into my department, right out of business school, and they're paying *him* eighteen-five to start! He'll be up to $20,000 in a couple of years, then he'll move someplace else that will offer him more. Where does that leave me? Where's the payoff for that ten years I've stuck by the company and my experience here? Those consultants are right when they tell you to move if you want to get ahead."

That quotation and variations on it constitute another factor in the human resources revolution. It concerns the constant erosion of the value of pay not only by inflation and taxes but by the factor called salary compression. *Business Week* observed, "Some companies may have been complacent about compensation problems, because, by and large, managers have not been hard to come by in recent years. . . . Still, there are enough complaints coming to the surface, enough compression problems arising, and sufficient turndowns for promotion and defections of superior managers, to make senior executives anxious."

With inflation, the escalating cost of living, and stiffer federal, state, and local tax burdens, plus sales and community property taxes, middle managers and even top executives are finding that the traditional pay-reward system isn't working. Companies caught in profit squeezes and forced to give across-the-board inflation-correcting increases find it increasingly difficult to reward top performers. The influx of new talent at the bottom at salaries rivaling those of more experienced people worsens the situation.

In a recent survey by the Employment Management Association and Deutsch, Shea and Evans, 69 percent of the responding executives reported salary compression a problem at their companies. Studies by the Engineering Manpower Commission show that this is a problem among technical people in industry. Other data suggest that the normal increases companies give are swallowed up by taxes and sometimes result in an actual reduction of take-home dollars.

The problem is compounded on the shop floor, where supervisors often earn less than skilled workers with overtime opportunities. Offering salaried overtime to supervisors and lower middle management has resulted in reducing the differential between higher and lower management.

While managerial salaries in the white-collar ranks are tending to reach plateaus, hourly wages with built-in cost-of-living increases bolstered by energetic union demands are not. Further, in high-cost labor areas like Chicago and Detroit the problem is more acute, since hourly wages are based on regional pay scales but salary levels for middle management tend to be ranked against a nationwide scale.

"Some of our engineers and administrators," says an executive of a design-construction firm, "go out to a construction site and find that, degree or no, a lot of the people they are supervising—hard hat construction types—are taking home bigger paychecks. Not only that but the college-trained guys take home a briefcase full of work every night—cost estimates and materials bids, things like that. You've really got to put in a sixty-hour week if you're going to get ahead in this business. But the union guys, a lot of them, are on a six-hour day. Period. They've gone fishing when our engineers are sweating out paperwork. So they wonder, 'Who's got the better job?'"

Caught in an institutionalized framework that has been buffeted by economic change and the human resources revolution, upwardly mobile, college-educated workers find the path to the top is not only unclear but increasingly confusing. A young MBA with a major New York City bank put it this way to *Business Week* reporters: "Salaries of incoming MBA's are a function of the market. But once here, your salary is a function of internal policy." Even with the high starting salaries of a couple of years ago, and later increases, new recruits are within close range. "We are at a point now where we are really contributing and taking on a great deal of responsibility. But we get the feeling that we are expendable, that they feel we can be replaced with new MBA's. It's causing a lot of people to re-evaluate their position in the organization. My own superior is complaining about his differential over me, because he started at an even lower level than I did. On it goes throughout the organization."

Apparently it is not only the work ethic that is eroding, but the whole basic relationship between output and rewards appears to be in jeopardy. Here, too, is one of the urgent causes of the human resources revolution, and a major cause for the more militant attitudes of employees against their employers.

EMPLOYEE ACTIVISM: WORKERS AGAINST BUSINESS

Little more than a decade ago Ralph Nader was a lonely, ascetic, somewhat Quixotic figure bent on attacking the serene and righteous structure of big business. His first book, *Unsafe at Any Speed,* (Bantam,

1975) impaled the automobile industry for pushing on the public tail-finned, gas-eating automobiles that he claimed were not safe. Television beamed in on the Nader phenomenon when he defended himself before a congressional committee. Business called his rise "media hype," seeing him as an irresponsible folk hero whose notoriety was shallow and transient.

But the "media hype" turned into a general epidemic, whether it was the man who made the history or the idea whose time had come. Nader and "Naderism" is now a symbol for activism in every aspect of business—pollution, safety, testing standards, financial ethics, in fact, all the activities of the work force that spill out into society at large. When he advanced the idea that workers themselves should be the "whistle blowers," he alerted the public to be aware of deception, discrimination, or danger—to look for injustice of any kind in the work place, and people are doing just that.

When several engineers from a nuclear reactor company in California quit their jobs to protest what they believed to be hazardous radiation conditions, it was a direct result of the whistle-blowing concept. Such scenes are happening with growing frequency. A safety engineer files suit against his company for not complying with the safety standards in testing they had publicly stated they would enforce. A government employee reports that coworkers are taking under-the-table payments. A security analyst reports the frauds in an insurance company and an entire business comes tumbling down. These moves are not directed simply toward products, process, or environments—they represent a growing disenchantment with employers who engage in questionable practices.

There are hazards for those who "tell all." The case of a thirty-five-year-old executive, a research manager in a large company, underscores the point. Realizing that his company was not complying with its asserted position on pollution, he began to speak out at meetings. The reaction was cool and fatal. Besieged by silent harassment, a reduction in responsibilities, a curtailment of parking privileges, he eventually quit and moved to another city. One observer of the incident called for an employee bill of rights to secure free speech. Noting the appearance of several corporate underground newspapers exposing unethical corporate practices and alleged violations of law, David Ewing, a member of the Harvard Business School faculty, asserted in the pages of *The New York Times:* "There is no freedom of the press in American organizations. In effect, therefore, United States society is a paradox. The

Constitution and Bill of Rights light up the sky over political campaign-
ers, legislators, civic leaders, families, churches, people, and artists. But
not over employees."

The human resources revolution is based in part on an attempt to
solve this paradox. Its shock troops are the activists of the rights
brigade.

Feminist Activism

A chic, fiftyish woman with sun-streaked hair leaned back in the swivel
chair in her California office. "They were all waiting to see how the
Bakke case came out," she says. "They would just love it if affirmative
action and quota systems went by the wayside. They won't hire more
women unless they are forced to." As one of a handful of successful
women executive recruiters, Jenny S. knows her subject and her clients.

Her listener, a thirty-eight-year-old lawyer stymied in her administrative post with a large aerospace company, had come to assess the
chances for better opportunities. "I'm not trying to discourage you,"
the recruiter says. "We do get openings, but only to fill a special niche
and most often in a highly visible position in a company."

Women's activism made many gains in the sixties and seventies, but
movement leaders now report a backlash and a stiffening resistance to
more gains. Every court case won sets another precedent, and so
companies are tending to dig in and fight, often at great expense.

But the pressure remains and the activism reflects all the new attitudes involved in the human resources revolution: the stronger role of
the female in family life, including that of (sometimes sole) breadwin-
ner; more widespread education and the drive to put it to use; heightened competition to enter professional and middle-management jobs;
and the rising expectation that a woman can go after any job she
chooses.

Large numbers of women have entered the work force, but equal
opportunity for achievement lags. In the years between 1974 and 1976
approximately 2 million women found jobs, so that by 1977 nearly half
of the total work force were women, and a good portion either supported themselves or their families.

As women have moved ahead, demands have become louder for
equal opportunity in promotion or entry into male-dominated fields.
The files of the National Organization for Women and other watchdog

groups are filled with complaints by women forced out of jobs or underpaid because of sex discrimination. The backlog of cases, and consequent resentment, grows every year.

One landmark case lost by the American Telephone & Telegraph Company (AT&T) gave many women back pay for promotions they might have had if no sex discrimination had existed. Sixteen women employees of the National Broadcasting Company in New York got a $2 million settlement out of court which provided for programs for better on-the-job progress, increased new hiring of women, and back pay awards. The expense and time involved in fighting a sex discrimination case—and sex discrimination is usually subtle and difficult to prove—tends to create a situation in which the largest companies with potentially the greatest gains for women become the targets. Carol Parr, political director of the Women's Equity Action League in Washington, D.C., says: "We do seem to have more women in middle management posts—the barriers have broken slightly. Ten years ago, women were stuck in secretarial jobs, but today they have broken through. However, they are not getting beyond middle management." She adds that the government has assumed a posture of "benign neglect," mainly because affirmative action for new recruits seems to be working.

Fully a third of the seventies business school graduates are women, and their numbers in engineering and law schools are growing. The continuing gap, however, between career objectives and realities is underlined by a median income that is about half what it is for males. The average income for a woman college graduate is less than the average income for a male high school dropout.

We can see this in the case of Anne Branigan, reported in the *Chicago Tribune*. A graduate of Northern Illinois University, she was unable to find a good paying job, or any job, in her chosen field of marketing. She did not want to be a secretary, and instead took a job as a telephone line splicer. "I like it. My work is my own. I make my own schedule, and since I'm the only college graduate in my crew, chances for promotion are good."

She recognizes that if she were a man she probably would have found a white-collar job with a future—and she is still looking, she says—but meanwhile her new attitude has shown her a way to a new solution: blue-collar work. Women carpenters, mechanics, truck drivers, and plumbers are increasing, and even in the face of job harassment are showing a persistence that baffles their coworkers. A woman bricklayer, often asked by coworkers what she is doing on a job like that, replies: "I'm a working woman, a wage earner, and I have to pay rent, gas, electricity, and telephone like anyone else."

While the new activism may have cooled slightly since the early years, it is nonetheless firm and watchful. Despite the backlash, the significant fact is that sex discrimination lawsuits are costing organizations hefty amounts of money. Moreover, women are showing more and more political clout, winning male adherents in Congress to legislation meeting special instances, such as the exemption of pregnancy from disability insurance plans, and electing representative women to public office. They hope for more human resources commissions in state governments.

Black Activism

"The political civil liberties we won in the sixties were easier," says a correspondent for a black newsmagazine in her thirty-fourth-floor Manhattan office. "We marched in Washington in 1963 for jobs and freedom. We got the freedom, now we want the jobs."

The new mood in black activism holds that with the diminishing of support for civil rights more must be done in the private sector, especially in business, or blacks will face worse unemployment and consequently more social repression than they have already experienced.

In spite of gains in the average household income of blacks in comparison with whites, the unemployment rate of black youths in inner cities runs as high as 40 percent. Such youth joblessness, which is likely to add to the permanent underclass of disadvantaged, is a major cause for alarm.

Speaking to a meeting of black leaders, Donald MacNaughton, chairman of the Prudential Insurance Company, called for black activists to shift their strategy from a reliance on more government programs for income redistribution to one of helping business enlarge the total economic pie so that the black slice will be larger. The struggle in the seventies, he said, has been to implement the rights won in the sixties.

The new attitudes in black activism are in no way isolated from the human resources revolution. While whites are seeking ways to enhance their rising expectations in the work place and relating it increasingly to their personal needs, blacks are seeking from a less advantageous standpoint to do much the same. As Vernon Jordan, the executive director of the National Urban League, put it: "They want more and better jobs, housing and education—in short, full economic and social parity."

Benjamin Hooks, executive director of the National Association for the Advancement of Colored People, asserts: "The new fight is not to sit in front of the bus, but to own the bus company." A few black business executives are doing just that. There was a recent meeting in Houston of six millionaires, all black and self-made heads of their own companies: a rather unusual gathering.

But for many blacks whose rising expectations put them in competition with white management, these expectations are meeting an equivalent measure of frustration. A young, black, talented marketing expert hired by a New York advertising agency was called in during his first day on the job by the agency's president. "Well, you will never be president here," the boss said. "Now what else can we do for you?"

While it is still difficult to fight the racial barrier in the upper management ranks of some businesses, it is being done successfully on the lower rungs. A major airline found itself in a legal snarl when a fired black airline stewardess brought suit. Although the company officials said that she was dismissed for excessive tardiness and fainting once while on duty, the court found that the real reason was discrimination based on her color. Her lawyer forced the airline to produce volumes of time card records to prove her point.

The notion that blacks cannot represent white business institutions would seem to be woefully misguided when viewers look at Ed Bradley, CBS's Sunday night anchorman, a highly visible person seen by millions of viewers. Asked if Bradley's success had inspired fear in CBS executives, Bill Small, news director for the network, replied, "You mean concern about having a black anchor? No. It never entered into the decision. At this time, the American people are long past the stage where they will turn off their television sets just because there is a black man anchoring the news."

Yet for every black making a gain in the upper reaches of business, more are living in what has been called the permanent underclass— ghetto blacks lacking education and opportunity. Their only hope is more activism, and their cost to society will only climb higher until their problems are finally addressed and ameliorated.

Fully aware of its mandate in getting business to resolve the problem, the National Urban League's "State of Black Amercia" paper for 1977 called for full employment as a matter of national policy. Such a policy would include incentive to private industry to hire and train workers, a modernized federal works program, and a vastly expanded public service employment program that would improve the nation's schools. Adding a new dimension to discrimination, they are saying that young people should not be barred from jobs because of age.

Ironically, the same argument is used for middle-aged workers, usually white.

Middle-Aged Anger

Permanently furloughed in 1972 from his $30,000-a-year job as a sales-engineer manager for a chemical products company, Bill W. took it in stride. After some disappointing tries at new employment, he found a job pumping gas and kept looking. Three years later, depressed and given to angry moods, he realized that at fifty, with a successful career behind him, he could not land a job.

Job change over forty has become a perilous and costly game, for whatever reason—being fired, laid off, or looking for promotion. Many of the long-term unemployed casualties of the troubled economic climate of the early seventies came from the older middle-management ranks as the result of cutbacks. They were often the first to go in companies of all size. An advertising salesman who had a meteoric career in his thirties found that when he was laid off at fifty his old connections soured and the answer was usually the same: "We'd hire you in a minute, but we want someone who will give us 25 years."

White, successful, and angry middle-aged men have become a new and surprising segment of the human resources revolution. They always believed in the hard-work reward system, and their disillusionment was only recently defined. Not wanting enforced early retirement, some have moved into drop-out, career-switching patterns, seeking more satisfying if lower-paying work. The broker has turned farmer, the engineer gone yachting for hire; others have stayed to fight, using the laws against age discrimination in employment.

"An increasing number of managers," a *Wall Street Journal* article says, "are hiring lawyers to challenge their companies' personnel policies. Usually older men, they find themselves caught in the middle management glut due to over-hiring practices of the Seventies."

A case involving Standard Oil of California settled in 1975 was a harbinger of things to come. The company lost a class-action suit brought by 120 middle managers who had been fired from their jobs, the court found, because of their age. They got $2 million in back pay, and of the 120 asked back into the company, 25 accepted. A similar action was initiated against American Motors Company by a group of middle-aged salesmen claiming they were fired to pave the way to promotion for younger people.

In another twist on the age factor, Westinghouse Electric Corporation got embroiled in a lawsuit with a group of laid-off employees who charged that they were deprived of pension benefits because of their age. They were in the forty to fifty-five age group, and the company had denied them benefits given to older workers who had also been laid off. The court awarded the group of forty-four a total of $1.5 million in back pension benefits.

These and other legal actions indicate that age discrimination, also an issue with women activist groups, may emerge as the next major arena for affirmative action. Even a professional group, the Institute of Electrical and Electronic Engineers, has rallied to the cause. In a friend-of-the-court brief filed in a lawsuit involving Sperry Rand, it is asking the court to decide whether experienced engineers are better qualified and hence more employable than recent college graduates.

Without the support of union programs, older middle-management males who have always believed in the exchange of hard work for good will and rewards from their employers find that they have nothing to lose when that good will is gone. It happens in government civil service as well. Dr. John Droger was an over-forty economist with the Environmental Protection Agency when he joined in an age discrimination lawsuit that alleged younger personnel were promoted to ranks denied him because of age. Although he told a newspaper reporter that his superiors had warned him he would get a demotion if he went ahead, he persisted.

"Filing charges is rather common nowadays," said the employee relations vice president for Armstrong Rubber Company, Robert Miller, in a *Wall Street Journal* article. "Terminated employees can file under the National Labor Relations Act, the Civil Rights Act or some other regulation pertaining to age, sex, race, or religious discrimination. . . . There is almost always some avenue open to an individual who is terminated."

The human resources revolution is not the prerogative of the Spock generation; clearly, it prevails across the board and on into retirement-age employees. The great debate, whether to work or not to work, to retire or not to retire and at what age, is only beginning.

One measure of the extent of these changes, which have only briefly been reviewed here, was the issuance in 1977 by the *New York Times Book Co.* of a new book entitled *The Changing Character of Work.* Advertised as providing "over 1,500 concise summaries" compiled from articles in sixty-two foreign and domestic publications, this "summary" of the situation runs to two volumes and more than 600 pages.

CHAPTER FIVE

Beyond the Work Force

T he public relations counselor looks up from his eyeshade, a rem-
nant of his long-ago days as a city editor. He gestures at the
reports, data sheets, color transparencies, and layouts that clutter his
desk. "More and more," he says to his client, Elwood Marvin, the chief
executive officer (CEO) of a medium-sized manufacturing firm, "these
annual reports are beginning to look like apologies for being in
business."

Marvin nods. Among the dollar figures of this new annual report
being prepared are sections on environmental compliance, explanations referring to rulings of the Federal Trade Commission, discussions
of the company's consumer-responsiveness program, its recruitment
policies and affirmative action programs, new retirement policies, and a
short piece on the company's philosophy toward resource and energy
conserving manufacturing practices. At the end there is a very successful earnings statement. "I wonder which section matters most today,"
the CEO muses.

"All of them," the counselor answers. "Every move the company
makes today impinges on one or another of your markets or affects your
image or can affect your operations. It's a wild, wild, world out there
now."

The human resources revolution, like the energy crisis, affects today's
corporations both internally and externally. It relates not only to their
own workers but to a broad range of audiences that are important to the
organization's marketing success and institutional image. There is a
"new scorecard" for management, as Peter Drucker has said, in that
management is no longer concerned solely with the bottom line, but

must also respond to changing social factors. The new social concern with human resources, therefore, has created a whole new set of audiences—a phalanx of outsiders concerned to see how the company hires, promotes, utilizes, compensates, provides working conditions for, dismisses, and pensions off its people.

The company's own retirees, for example, are likely to be part of what *Newsweek* labeled the "gray revolution." Its professionals, on whom the company leans strongly—engineers, lawyers, accountants—are adopting new attitudes toward their employers, and so are their professional associations. Activists of many persuasions, re-energized unions, federal gadflies, all have new concerns related to the company's human resources programs. Militancy has risen, too, in such unexpected places as local communities where a company has facilities, and among shareholders who see human resources policies as affecting company profitability—and who themselves may be company employees, past, present, or future.

Let's take a closer look at a few of these groups whose emerging concern with people in the work place are part of the human resources revolution, noting at the same time that many of these external audiences can affect the bottom line.

RETIREES

In the coming decades there will be a substantial increase in the percentage of the population over sixty. This older group will dominate in terms of voting power, market needs, and employment. It represents an about-face from the youth-oriented world of the sixties to an economy centered largely on the "geriatric set." Among this group with growing clout will be, for better or worse, the company's own retirees.

Ambassadors or Antagonists?

The attitudes that people take into retirement concerning their companies and business itself seem likely to undergo the same sea change that is affecting other elements of society.

Concern with the stability of social security as a source of retirement income and the inroads that inflation is making into the fixed pensions and other resources of retirees is affecting the question of retirement and retirement income. Retirees are beginning to see this as a question of survival, and no longer think of themselves as grateful recipients of largesse from the company.

Meanwhile, companies are finding that their retirees are useful image-builders in the communities where they live. They can contribute to the company's aims in varied ways. "Retirees are the forgotten influentials," says Henry Wallfesh, executive vice president of Retirement Advisors, Inc. "Most companies have yet to realize that it is personal reactions and reports about a company, by someone who has had actual exposure to it, that contributes most strongly to company image. That means an organization's ex-employees can be a potent factor for or against favorable opinions concerning the company."

Asked what he considers the most common mistake managements make in thinking about retirees, Wallfesh has a ready answer.

"Not thinking about them at all. In too many companies, retirees are merely an abstraction, the group that gets a check in the mail every month and should be properly grateful to the company for it. But that term 'retiree' is misleading when it is interpreted as a homogeneous, over-the-hill group of TV watchers. Like the company's current employees, it represents a broad cross-section of people, many of whom have had high levels of responsibility. Ex-managers and division heads and engineering executives are retirees, too.

"It means that retirees are, among other things, a variegated group with contacts and influence at all levels, locally and nationally. Many of these people are not only active, they are activists, stimulated by the example of how women, for example, have been fighting for and winning rights. The whole mandatory retirement movement is a good example of older people in action. Retirees are often in a position to aid their companies if the rapport is there.

"I know of one company—my own—that very effectively uses retirees as sales people. That's not a fair example, of course, because we're involved in the retirement field. But I'm aware of instances in which retired people boost company products, if they don't sell them directly. Retirees have helped their companies recruit people in a tight job market, sending younger friends and relatives to the personnel office. Some come back themselves to work part-time. Retired people are often active in local politics and end up on zoning boards and town councils where their knowledge of the company and its practices can sometimes make a difference to company plans. They may be leaders of professional associations, civic groups, advocacy organizations. Probably the most valuable role that retirees play is ambassador. With activism increasing among older people and with many retirees involved in a variety of advocacy movements other than age—environmentalism, for example—these people can be roving ambassadors. They know from first-hand experience what business and industry are all about. They know a lot about your company and the attitudes that exist there. If you keep them informed, they know about the company's problems and goals and programs. So, whatever they're involved in, if something's going on that can affect the company, they're likely to speak up and add a perspective that your public relations people, for example, couldn't readily get over."

Thirty Million Influentials

With a consistently expanding population of people sixty-five or over in the United States, if present trends are maintained—23 million as of 1977 and an estimated 31.5 million by the end of the century—retirees can be regarded by corporations as a big part of an influential audience. This is an audience, furthermore, which is organizing, as did women and minority groups before them, into such groups as the American Association of Retired Persons and the National Council of Senior Citizens. "Seems to me there are a lot of things that need to be done in this country," one retiree observed recently, "and the way things are going, it looks like a lot of the doing is going to be up to us."

From a different viewpoint, those numbers are also significant to companies marketing consumer products or services to older people. A company's human resources practices regarding its older employees and those in retirement could affect the purchasing preferences of this over $200 billion market.

THE PROFESSIONALS—NEW
PRIORITIES IN THE SOCIETIES

Like the retirees, the professionals—engineers, accountants, lawyers, and chemists—are showing definite signs that the old established ways are changing under the impact of the human resources revolution.

Consider Tom B., a chemical engineer in his mid-thirties, who takes his standing among his peers more seriously than he does his position in the company he worked for. At the last meeting of his professional society he presented a paper on process control. Afterward he told colleagues about a conflict with his company. "They wanted me to run a batch without quality control, to meet a deficient schedule," he said. "I told them I wouldn't do it. I didn't leave the company, although that choice was suggested to me, but I wouldn't do it."

A survey of professionals employed in business, both MBAs and engineers, turned up facts showing that they are more concerned with ethics and their professional responsibilities than was heretofore assumed. Only a handful of those responding—8 percent—said that when they were asked to do something unethical, they agreed to do it.

Thus they are putting their employers on the spot for not innovating, for not complying with environmental and pollution regulations, and they are also finding it easier to criticize the employer off the job if need be.

A Consciousness of Liability

A consciousness of liability is invading the professional consciousness. "While adherence to high professional standards has always been there, in the new environment of business, more open to inspection for governmental sources, and forced to comply more with government regulations, the professionals are being held accountable; this is having an attitudinal impact."

In an article in *Business Week* entitled "The Troubled Professional," the reasons for the changed attitudes are forcefully documented, and with them has appeared a fundamental revision of the client relationship.

"Today that assumption (client protection) has collapsed," the magazine says. "In working for large institutions, from corporate law departments to research laboratories, professionals help to set in motion events that spread far beyond those who come into immediate contact with their clients. Mass production of complex but defectively designed machinery can injure millions. And complex business institutions can multiply the effects of fraud, seriously injuring people who have no direct connection with it. . . . Society is increasingly charging professionals with the job of preventing harm, at the risk of their own necks. Professionals, that is, are now being held responsible for the acts of their clients."

For corporate lawyers this is being translated into direct accountability for any illegal acts by clients and, increasingly, legal weight is falling on the side of eliminating the confidentiality of relationships as an excuse. If a client wants top-level representation he must comply with the law. The same is true in the accounting profession. The spurt of litigation against certified public accounting (CPA) firms for overlooking client's missteps has produced a backlash, and accountants themselves admit to being under pressure.

Not only is this true, but with the proliferation of government compliance procedures and regulations, also spawned by the human resources revolution, the CPAs are being asked to oversee a longer list of company activities than in the past, a trend that will exert pressure on management to do what it says it will do.

The professional societies are backing their members in this new climate, and they are themselves changing. The presidency of the American Banking Association was contested for the first time in 1977 by advocates of social issues. At the Institute of Electrical Engineers, a leadership issue centered on whether or not the society should work to limit numbers of engineers graduated and raise educational standards.

The pressure is for professionals to maintain and follow through on ethical standards established by their societies, a pressure apparently exerted by the issues-oriented younger generations who came to maturity in the whistle-blowing era of Ralph Nader. They are saying that professionals have a duty to put ethics ahead of the client or corporation that employs or retains them, and if they do not, they can be named as coconspirators in any wrongdoing.

The friction that results from changing old confidential and sometimes questionable patterns into the new ethic about work and professionalism is already creating more litigation. Three Bay Area Rapid Transit (BART) engineers fired from their jobs complained to the board of directors about defective safety standards on the new subway. They sued and won an out-of-court settlement for loss of compensation and reputation. Their defense fund was paid for by the state professional engineering society. The American Chemical Society and the American Association for the Advancement of Science have also provided members with legal assistance.

Muted Militancy on Human Resources

Professional associations, particularly in the technical fields, have gradually become involved with human resources over the years, particularly by providing assistance to members seeking jobs. Many societies also conduct annual salary and benefits surveys among their members to provide a picture of national pay scales for a given field. Now, in these more militant times, some societies like the American Chemical Society (ACS) are pushing beyond the liaison and information roles.

In 1977 the official publication of the ACS, *Chemical and Engineering News,* printed a six-page report, one of a series, on layoffs involving chemists and chemical engineers. This included a graph which named specific companies and indicated the extent to which they had complied with ACS guidelines for employers regarding giving advance notice, severance pay, assistance in finding new employment, pension vesting, protection plans, and rehiring privileges. The actual data on these points, as provided by both company and the people terminated, are given in detail and reveal some interesting discrepancies.

> One company stated, "None of the chemists terminated at the G——— facility had more than five years service." "Six of the eight terminees responding reported that they had more than ten years of service," said the ACS.
>
> "The company has a policy of rehiring those terminated before new employees are recruited. This policy was explained to the terminees," said another company. "One terminee indicated that rehiring rights were explained to him. The other terminees did not report being informed of a rehiring policy," reported the ACS. "The terminees were given two days advance notice of the impending separation," the company reported. (The ACS guidelines call for a four-week minimum of advance notice.) "Advance notice ranging from no notice to two days of notice" was reported by the people terminated.

The impact of this information (and the refusal of some of the companies involved in the layoffs to provide the information requested) on the images of the respective companies as employers has yet to be felt, since this is a fairly new program. But it does set out, in black and white, the "good guys" from the "bad guys" in terms of their compliance with ACS standards. More importantly, perhaps, it provides a preview of the ways in which the professional societies can take action regarding a company's human resources practices.

Obviously these new attitudes toward their working responsibilities by both professionals and their societies are a result of the changing social attitudes that have triggered the human resources revolution. This is, as yet, a muted militancy, but one which has important long-range implications concerning the relationships between corporations and what is probably the most valuable single element in their work forces.

But there are other significant implications as well. Professionals, as a group, are in the highest-earning echelons. As such they constitute a target market for many high-tagged consumer goods throughout their working lifetimes. They are also, as a consequence of their earning power, frequently involved in investing for themselves. Beyond this, engineers, for example, are highly influential in purchasing decisions for many of the products of the original equipment market (OEM), and for services relating to engineering projects. Accountants and lawyers may also be involved in company purchases and investments. Professionals also have a strong influence on corporate image in terms of employment practices, quality of products, and investment. For corporations, this is a critical audience, in more than one sense of the word.

GOVERNMENT GADFLIES

Though many people in business will groan at the thought, part of the external audience concerned with the company's human resources is a broad spectrum of government employees in federal, state, or local regulatory agencies and political leaders at all levels. There need be no recounting here of the problems and costs of dealing with the federal regulatory agencies concerned with human resources. Unhappy experiences with agencies such as the Equal Employment Opportunity Commission (EEOC) and programs like ERISA have created still unhealed scars in the business community. A 1975 Deutsch, Shea & Evans study of business attitudes toward equal employment opportunity agencies summarized the survey results in these terms:

> Briefly, an uneasy and, at times, confusing relationship exists between business and government in the area of equal employment. The confusions seem to be generated to a great degree by what business perceives as unnecessary redundancy of government bodies charged with equal employment enforcement, marked lack of coordination within and among these agencies, and serious inefficiencies in the ways the agencies operate.
>
> Further, most respondents perceive the agencies as pursuing goals other than those set down by Executive Orders and civil rights legislation. This perception, and its fundamental causes, surely adds to the difficult nature of the government/business interaction.
>
> One aspect of this relationship is essentially disturbing—the impact of government agencies' power on the willingness of companies to comment publicly about these bodies, including possible abuses and inefficiencies. More than half the respondents said that they would hesitate to criticize the agencies, many stating 'fear of reprisal' as the cause.

That report was an opening gun in a series of attacks particularly on the EEOC which has led toward reform in that agency, now under the new leadership of Eleanor Norton. There has also been a sweeping denunciation of government paperwork resulting in efforts to lessen the flood—for example, the Commission on Federal Paperwork. At this writing, we still await improvement.

Whatever the problems, government in a broad range of programs has been and remains one of the major forces behind the human resources revolution. Government people from presidential advisers to local zoning boards can affect company operations and goals. As an offshoot, the paperwork web relating to human resources is largely intact even though, as in the case of ERISA, it is in the service of perpetuating unworkable rules toward unreachable goals.

Government as Customer

Government, as an external audience, is doubly important to most corporations. It can not only punish them, expensively, for infringements upon human resources legislation, it can also affect their ability to do business. It should be noted that the AT&T case in which the company was accused of discriminating against its female employees was prosecuted by the EEOC, not before a federal court but before the Federal Communications Commission.

Further, the government is itself a major customer for many industrial organizations producing defense products, office equipment, and a variety of services. Here, too, human resources can affect the bottom line. As personnel people know, one of the key equal opportunity agencies is the Office of Federal Contract Compliance. That agency, it is generally understood, has the ability to deny government contracts to organizations that do not meet federal standards in complying with such programs as equal opportunity employment.

This is one of those laws "more honored in the breach than in the observance," but the *Wall Street Journal* in 1977 reported on one organization, a bank in the Southwest, to feel its effects.

> For the first time, the federal government is using its economic clout against a bank in an effort to force it to hire more minority workers. Dusting off an enforcement mechanism used only rarely under the Nixon and Ford administrations, the Labor Department threatened to bar the National Bank of Commerce of San Antonio, Texas, from holding government contracts unless it changes its hiring policies.
>
> The labor agency said in Washington the bank currently is a contractor to the Treasury Department, for which it issues and pays out U.S. Savings Bonds and notes and serves as a federal depository. Last year, the agency said, the bank's federal deposits totaled more than $139 million. The department said the bank had "refused" to set goals and timetables for hiring and promoting women and minorities and to correct what the department contends were hiring inequities. The government said the bank took the position that the federal contracting rules amounted to "reverse discrimination" when no court has found job bias.

Even if it is rarely exercised, the power is there for government to affect an organization's profitability as a means of achieving mandated human resources goals.

"We can expect the government to be looking over our shoulder, from now on, in terms of what we do in personnel and human resources," one employment executive observed at a national meeting. "And I don't think filling in the forms and arguing with the agency representatives is enough. We should not only be complying with the laws, which is damned difficult because many of them are so muddled, but we need to be very visibly doing so. That way, we're not only less of a target to the regulators, but people like our local representatives and senators can point to us as good examples. And we can get in a few words on improving the situation."

BUSINESS AND THE EDUCATIONAL COMMUNITY

"If American education were a conventional business supplier," a vice president of a multinational company mused over a lunch spent discussing the company's college recruiting problems, "we'd be looking elsewhere for our supply of new people, on the grounds of lack of quality control, failure to meet specifications, and unsuitability of the material for the environment in which it is to be used. We have to depend on the educational system for our recruits, but the quality of people being graduated really worries me. You'd be surprised at what we have to spend in re-educating a lot of the people we hire at all levels."

In San Francisco the executive vice president of a major design construction firm makes a speech expressing concern about the anti-technology attitudes surfacing among new generations of college students, and echoes the complaints of other executives about negative attitudes toward work and responsibility on the part of recent high school and college graduates.

There are further concerns. Competition among companies and other organizations for such skilled people as engineers and accountants involves intensive recruiting, not only costly in itself, but one of the contributing factors to the critical problem of salary compression, with inevitable effects upon the company's productivity and bottom line. Another nagging point of controversy between business and the educational establishment is the conviction on the part of many business people that schools are a principal and continuing source of negative attitudes toward business. It is true, that some of the most eloquent and influential critics of business have come from the academic community—but so are some of its stronger supporters. The spirit of the university is to encourage free inquiry, wherever that is practiced there will never be a monolithic body of opinion.

While business may be critical about some of the end products, it is generally strongly supportive of the educational system, concretely expressing its support in financial gifts, awards, grants, fellowships, equipment, sponsorship of university chairs, underwriting the construction of new facilities, and similar aid. Further, there is a constant interchange between business and academia on a variety of levels, from the co-op systems whereby students gain paid on-the-job experience while they study, to the employment by business of academic consultants and the use by universities of business people as guest lecturers and teachers.

The complexities of this long-established love-hate relationship need not concern us here. It should be kept in mind, however, that it is a relationship built to a very high degree on business as a consumer and education as a producer of trained human resources. This interdependency is being strained as perhaps never before.

The Hang-Ups in Academia

There is growing apprehension that the educational system is not doing its job. The spiraling costs of higher education and the financial strains on both the schools and the students are raising hard questions. Too much theory and not enough practice is a general complaint of recent graduates. "We are finding," a business school professor in a highly regarded graduate school lamented, "that we need to teach more enterprise." The problem is compounded in the technical fields and others by the speed with which technologies and the fields they affect, including business, are changing. Not only business but the newly militant professional associations have begun to act on their concerns. The Institute of Electrical and Electronic Engineers, for example, is beginning to look critically at the accreditation process in terms of the standards of training their members, now at work, feel are needed for adequate professional preparation.

The problems of education are not limited to the higher levels but begin in the backyard of every business, in local high schools and the training and academic preparation these institutions are providing.

The Educational Audience

The human resources revolution has re-emphasized the relationships between business and education. The educational community is a highly important, multilevel audience capable of affecting business in several critical ways.

The first of these is the role of education as a source of trained people. If not enough are produced, business will find it expensive, not only in competing for those available but in not being able to expand in new directions for lack of the people with the desired skills. Inadequately trained people are costly because they require training on the job and have long-term effects on a company's productivity and ability to innovate.

Second is the role of the educational community in creating attitudes toward work and working, toward business as a whole, and toward individual companies. The people who emerge from the American educational system today will tomorrow be in a position to influence the political and social direction of the country and the extent to which business has freedom to operate.

Finally, as the pages of any periodical directed to college audiences will show, the educational community is a major market to which many companies direct sales appeals. It is a tenet of marketing that the impression an organization makes on a school-age audience is likely to persist for years to come. This is an area in which the interrelationship of human resources with the company's marketing and institutional goals is particularly clear.

THE ADVOCATES

"The closing down by the South African government of newspapers, the Christian Institute, student groups and other organizations is regrettable," Control Data Corporation observed in a 1977 story in *The New York Times*. "We hope this action will be reversed. At the present time, our company does not consider it appropriate to enlarge our investment in South Africa." The same story reported that Stanford University had reexamined its portfolio of investments in companies doing business in South Africa, a move prompted by student protests when the school refused to vote its Ford Motor Company proxies over the issue of that company's investment in South Africa.

That single news item suggests the complexities of today's human resources relationships in the world scene. It indicates the problems multinational companies face, the extent to which the decisions they make are monitored by special interest groups, and the power that the advocacy approach has.

If the educational community is the oldest of the external audiences involved with human resources in business, the advocacy groups and activists are the newest. Their impact, mentioned earlier, scarcely needs reemphasizing. It was civil rights and equal employment advocacy that marked the beginning of the human resources revolution. We have seen airline cabin attendants strike because they felt their company's advertising exploited women, we have seen boycotts of companies and products in support of human resources goals, and we have seen litigation emerging as a major weapon in forcing social change on business and other institutions.

The impact of the advocates upon the bottom line appears nightly on television where corporate commercials now are careful to include minority people and working women in their ads, showing an awareness of the value of these markets. One estimate puts black buying power, for example, at $77 billion annually. *Grey Matter*, a commentary published by Grey Advertising, one of the major American agencies, notes that, "Now more and more discretionary money is making women, even teen-age girls, more and more influential in choosing what to buy. In the United States, while registration of only about one-fifth of autos is in women's names, more than half the driving is done by women. They buy 60% of the gas sold and have emerged as a major factor in what type and make of car to buy. . . . It is not unreasonable to expect that, as publications are edited more pointedly for emerging interests of women, ads deemed demeaning of them could have a tough time running."

Activists, then, present both a problem and a potential in their dual but related roles as litigants and consumers.

WHO NEEDS YOU? THE NEW ATTITUDES OF COMMUNITIES

At 8:15 P.M. on a Tuesday evening the town board supervisor of a suburban New York village rises to announce, "We have decided to reject your application for a zoning change, six to two. We felt that we did not wish, and could not in all conscience, given our responsibilities to the community, consent to the requested change to allow your company to establish a facility here which would re-structure our town government, affect the quality of life we enjoy here, and possibly have a deleterious effect upon our natural environment." There is applause from the audience, many of them commuter employees of corporations similar to the major company whose bid for a new headquarters site has just been turned down.

In another town, not much bigger, in a Southeastern state, the town officials announced in a similar meeting that they had successfully convinced a corporation to establish a new electronics manufacturing facility there. "We've held discussions with the company over the past eighteen months," the chairman of the meeting says. "We know that this is a low-profile kind of industry that won't have any adverse effects on our environment, but will provide local employment and eventually give our tax base a real shot in the arm." Much applause greets this announcement, too.

Both decisions reflect a changing local environment for business. No longer can a company quietly buy parcels of land and set up facilities at will or expect to be greeted with open arms by local government. Communities have become aware that corporate facilities can be a mixed blessing. The more affluent towns, whose residents have seen the adverse impacts that major new facilities can have on environment, traffic, and the economy when a town's workers depend on a few major employers for employment, may turn down the most prestigious of potential corporate citizens. Even communities that need industry are likely to demand that it conform to predetermined standards.

Local communities have thus become part of the human resources revolution. In granting company rights to build, for example, towns are taking into consideration the extent to which the new facility will actually contribute to local employment. "There's a lot more exchange of information among town governments now than in the past. So we're more aware of what to look for," one selectman explains. "That means we're kind of wary when companies talk to us about moving here. We want to know, do they plan to import a lot of the people from their present location, for example. This has happened and a town that expected a new company to provide work for a lot of local people found that only low-level jobs were open, once the new plant was built."

With the growing concern for human resources, communities are also more closely involved and more critical of work practices within their own locales. They may complain about heavier traffic, forcing a company to set up new time schedules at the plant. There have also been bitter legal battles between companies planning to relocate their plants and the towns they are leaving. "It's a bad scene," says a young corporate lawyer. "Our plants in smaller towns are sometimes the major employers in the area. When rising costs of taxes, energy, and other factors lead to a decision to relocate, the community' just doesn't accept it and we find ourselves in court."

Most of us are aware of other instances in which community and company fight together against, for example, environmental advocates who would force a plant closing. Strikes, emergencies, and other work disruptions also affect relationships between communities and companies in ongoing ways. When New York City's lights go out, Con Edison is promptly in the news media to respond to concerns and complaints. Conrail commuters into that city find written apologies on their seats the day following any major disruption in service, with an explanation of what happened. Scaled-down versions of this are becoming standard practice throughout the country.

The local community is both an environment in which the corporate facility has to exist and, in today's world of electronic news, a section of the general public. What happens locally can affect the company's image before a broad audience and stimulate advocates into action.

TOMORROW'S EMPLOYEE

Perhaps the one thing any company can be sure of in this changing world is that tomorrow it will need new people. Increasingly the people a company needs are likely to be experienced, well-educated, or with training in scarce skills—and sophisticated in terms of employment. Hiring today is no longer a matter of hanging out a sign that says, "People wanted" and standing aside as applicants stampede through the doors. Instead, even during periods of high unemployment the company is involved in a complicated process of wooing qualified and probably already employed people.

The corollary, inescapably, is that there exists another and very extensive audience outside the company which has a personal interest in how the company stacks up as an employer, the conditions of work at the company, and many other job-related factors. This phenomenon has been demonstrated by studies of people in relation to employment, ranging from professionals to white-collar clericals. Just as marketing people have had to be aware of "brand image" and financial specialists speak of an organization's "financial image," both of which affect potential customers for company products or securities, there are also, as any personnel executive will tell you, "employer images." This is expressed in dialogues like the following:

> "Hey, Conrad, you're back on campus."
> "Yeah, just finished a co-op session at XYZ company."
> "Oh? You know, I've kind of been thinking about taking an interview with them this spring. They've been doing a lot of interesting things with computers in their marketing department. What kind of an outfit are they to work for?"
> "Al, you wouldn't believe it . . ."

Research suggests that dialogues like this one are the most persuasive in determining an employer image; so are second-, third-, even fourth-hand reports on "what's the company like," attributed to people who have been there or talked to someone who worked there or was interviewed there or had some other personal contact with the company.

The personal touch applies both on and off campus. "Ben, you work there, now what's the company really like? I get the impression from some of the people I've met at the American Society of Mechanical Engineers (ASME) convention that it's really oriented to us engineering types." That method of assessing a company as a place to work is regularly employed by professionals in a kind of grapevine that is extremely efficient. Woe to the company that shows up negatively, because professionals are a sensitive lot with long memories.

In the mid-fifties, for example, the president of an Eastern aerospace company made an offhand remark that "engineers are a dime a dozen." Not only did that company immediately have an increasingly difficult time recruiting technical people thereafter, but as much as ten years later in research on employer image among engineers the "dime a dozen" remark was quoted and identified with the company.

Companies and even entire industries have images. The on-again, off-again, hire-again, fire-again image of the defense and aerospace industries, for example, turns off stability-minded prospects. It takes the lure of higher pay—considerably higher these days—to lure skilled people into such organizations. A study of secretaries in Manhattan who had recently changed jobs indicates that more than half had an "employer image" of companies for which they would like to work, and more than 90 percent of these had followed up by applying.

Women and minority people are vitally interested in a company's human resources record and practices. Here, too, the grapevine and a substantial number of minority and feminist-oriented publications spotlight companies as potential employers and affect their ability to meet affirmative action goals.

From the company's viewpoint, the attitude of this audience of potential employees can mean dollars and cents simply in terms of recruiting. The most characteristic statement that emerges concerning a company with a poor employer image is, "You'd have to pay me a lot to work there."

Recruiting and the Public

Given the wide range of openings that a corporation has to fill in the course of a year, from high-level management candidates to entry-level production workers and white-collar clericals, communicating job opportunities to those who may fill them may mean reaching most of the general public. Certainly it means that the recruitment effort is going to reach some of the company's key consumer and industrial markets and the financial community as well. ("I check out the employment ads every day," one broker comments. "It gives me a good realistic idea about what companies are growing and in which direction.")

The audience of tomorrow's employees, therefore, includes business people, professionals of all kinds, especially those in the company's own fields of activity, and specialists such as computer programmers, salespeople (including the competition's), technicians, production workers, secretaries, machinists, construction workers, and on down the line.

This audience includes women who are not only job candidates but also one of the largest segments of the consumer and financial markets; minority people with their buying power; students who are a market of their own; government people who scrutinize the company's employment advertising—in general, a healthy and important cross-section of the general public.

THE SENSITIVE SHAREHOLDER

It is shareholder meeting time. The company's top executives are seated on the dais, the mikes are working, and the public relations director is in the wings, clipboard under elbow, instructing a photographer. The atmosphere is cool as the question-and-answer period comes; the auditorium is packed. "You're on," the chief executive says to himself, sensing his adrenalin rising. He looks for Lewis Gilbert, the well-known corporate gadfly, but the first question comes from a middle-aged woman.

"Mr. Chairman," she says, grabbing the microphone, "the West End Feminist Association, which I represent, wants to know how the company is complying on female employment, and what programs you have planned."

The chairman has the figures at his fingertips, but says the company does not have daycare centers, adding, "yet." He glances at his public relations counselor for approval, but that helper is talking earnestly to a business reporter.

The scene is repeated over and over. A questioner at one meeting presents a resolution calling for putting minorities on the board and gets 20 percent of the vote. At another someone asks what a product recall for defects due to careless assembly will cost the company. Someone else asks what the company is doing about a legal matter involving bribes. Union shareholders heatedly criticize management for "unresponsive" labor relations, and so it goes.

Shareholder Constituencies

All are examples of the new and growing presence of what is called "shareholder constituencies." Often dissidents, sometimes not, these are people who take their ownership in a company seriously and raise questions as to how the company is coping with the external social forces that are more and more seen to be part of operations. The target is management where it is most vulnerable—in the postures it takes toward government, markets, and investors.

Under the Securities Act of 1933, companies must disclose any pending or threatened legal actions that may cost them money. The potential sources for such conflict have multiplied over the past two decades, with the accent on such human resources-related areas as employment discrimination. The increasing pressure for public disclosure from the Securities and Exchange Commission (SEC) is self-reinforcing as other government agencies get involved and advocacy groups, religious organizations, unions, and political groups assert their interests.

The more sophisticated, informed shareholders are relating these public issues to the bottom line. Sensing the interconnections between social conflict and the ability to do business profitably, they are asking the hard questions. Does a discrimination lawsuit alienate a share of the female, black, or middle-aged market? What about loss of government contracts, or even the ability of the company to hire top people?

Effective complaints can lead to costly litigation and expensive compliance, a balance that is making shareholders more alert to conflict with the public. An article in *The New York Times* headlined "Dissident Stockholders Begin to Get Somewhere at Last" reports that corporate management is tending to meet some of the objections, and sometimes it agrees to shareholder resolutions. Exxon management, for example, agreed to disclose its strip-mining activities when a church-sponsored group asked it to do so. Mobil acquiesced in having all of its outside directors sign conflict-of-interest statements, but in another action managed to defeat a resolution that would withdraw its products from Rhodesia and South Africa.

Charles Luce, head of New York's Consolidated Edison, was asked to explain layoffs of supervisory personnel before a group of unionized employees at a public shareholders meeting. In Racine, Wisconsin, a group of union shareholders, angered at the company's stand on a strike issue, raised the question at a meeting and got 6 percent of the votes, considering this a moral victory.

Such union shareholder participation is getting more encouragement from Washington as part of the continuing controversy over who owns what part and how much of American business. The fact that almost half of the $871 billion in securities in 1972 was found to be in the hands of pension and trust funds has led to a drive to spread ownership among people in middle- and low-income brackets. While many of these are beneficiaries of company pension trusts, the thinking now is to encourage employee owned and operated funds, and more employee stock ownership.

Corporate Response

A Conference Board study on international board practices points out that in the United States more companies are establishing committees of outside directors who audit the company's "social responsibility and ethical conduct." Such new policies are being used to shore up the board of directors' authority. "The overall trend is being propelled by directors' fears of lawsuits springing from their board duties, a loss of public confidence in big business and its leadership, and rising skepticism over the ability of boards to govern modern, complex companies. Many firms are taking such action to stem growing government intervention into business operations," the report says.

If management compromises with shareholder groups, together they are more likely to defuse flash points, since both have in common that they are interested in the bottom line. With the SEC now allowing a higher rate of disputed resolutions to reach the floor at shareholder meetings under a ruling mandating shareholders' rights to disclosure, shareholders are becoming more sensitive to and more interested in what their companies are doing. Business today, by and large, is also being "demystified"—its activities are reported in the general news columns and no longer confined to the business section. Any kind of outside activism, changes in trade, or social conflict are less relegated to the specialist and more to the public-at-large, thus creating a new climate for shareholder interest.

THE AUDIENCE OUTSIDE

The confrontation between employees and management is no longer a one-on-one situation. The human resources revolution reveals that how business utilizes people is of concern to all of us in our varied roles as workers, managers, advocates, consumers, and investors. This chapter has attempted to suggest the diversity of external audiences concerned with human resources and their relationships with other aspects of the company's operations and goals. Companies have responded to these changes with new policies and practices, among which has been the emergence of a significant new dimension in a basic corporate activity: communications.

CHAPTER SIX

The New Dimension in Corporate Communications

In the auditorium of a United States Army base in West Germany, a group of soldiers soon to complete their military service listens attentively to a speaker in civilian clothes who is filling them in on job opportunities with his company, a major East Coast manufacturer of automated machinery. He is one of some twenty corporate recruiters who have been airlifted to Europe by the Department of Defense to tell people leaving service about job openings and how to find them when they arrive back home.

In a manufacturing plant in Iowa, Jerry K. is part of a group of production line workers intently watching a television set during working hours. It isn't a world series game they are watching, but a report from the president of their company about its profit-and-loss performance during the first nine months of the year. The videotaped report is being shown simultaneously at other company facilities around the country. Afterwards Jerry says, "It looks to me as if we're in for some tough competition. I hadn't realized how difficult it's getting to sell our equipment overseas."

One of the country's leading feminist spokeswomen looks out at an all-male audience. "Whether you like it or not," she begins, "a few years from now about half of this audience is going to be women." Her audience, middle-management executives who work at the New York headquarters of a major financial organization, listen stolidly. They are attending at the order of their company, which is determined to develop good working relationships between the increasing number of women executives it is adding and their male counterparts.

At the same time in the auditorium of a small high school several hundred miles south in Anderson, South Carolina, a rapt audience of teenage girls watches a movie in which women are captaining airliners, operating bulldozers, participating in an undersea archeological dig, and tracking down criminals. It is a documentary about women at work in nontraditional jobs, prepared and distributed by one of the country's largest corporations.

Bessie M. is one of an enthusiastic group of older people who have gathered at an Atlanta airport. "I never in my life thought to be doing this," she says. "A trip to the Holy Land. This tour is going to take us to all of the places mentioned in the Bible. When I told my friends, they just couldn't believe the company would arrange something like this. I told them, 'why I worked 30 years for that company before I retired, and it is a company that thinks about its people.'" Bessie M. is a retiree off on a charter flight arranged by her former company, a Georgia-based conglomerate. A company newsletter to its retirees told them about the travel opportunity.

Disparate as these events may seem, they have a common denominator: the extent to which the human resources revolution has led corporations to reach out in new ways that involve them in new relationships with their own people, the media, government, schools, and other groups within a fast-changing society.

As a result the communications load within the corporation has been multiplying. Each new development in human resources seems to require a response that involves the company in some type of communications program, whether aimed at an individual in a personal talk or at a broad audience using media that are relatively new on the corporate scene.

So extensive has the communications web become, so varied are the new corporate audiences and so changed are the conventional ones that what was once a relatively simple function tagged "employee communications" has undergone a major metamorphosis.

From the impact of the human resources revolution an important new kind of corporate communications is emerging, but one of which most corporations are so far unaware.

THE CASE OF THE FRAGMENTED PRINCE

The Canadian humorist Stephen Leacock once wrote about a prince with a problem who rushed out of his castle, flung himself on a horse and went riding off in all directions. This classically fragmented approach to a crisis aptly describes how business has been reacting to the growing momentum of the human resources revolution. As one personnel executive admitted, "I'm so busy putting out fires that I don't have any time for long-range thinking."

The speed with which the human resources revolution is creating fresh and unprecedented problems engenders similar reactions at the top level. The response there has been to toss these problems into the lap of the personnel department as the only group within the company knowledgeable about what is going on.

"My value to the corporation," says one chief operating officer, "is primarily my financial know-how; we've got major problems in raising capital and maintaining cash flow. These people problems are something I'm not equipped to cope with. So I have to rely on my personnel people . . . but I'm getting the feeling they don't know how to cope either."

Back in April 1975 *Dun's Review* was saying, "Complex new company problems in human relations have become the top priorities for management, and the employment executive, as a result, has become one of chief executive officer's key troubleshooters." Because business has yet to recognize the change identified here as the human resources revolution, "troubleshooting" is an apt description of what is now going on.

There is no question that business is reacting on a large scale to a broad variety of human resources problems. But so far it is doing so in a fragmented way; few companies appear to have a coherent set of programs and policies based upon identifying and reacting to human resources as an area of major concern to the company. Nowhere is this more apparent than in communications.

A corporation's marketing communications is a highly structured internal system organized to develop and disseminate an immense amount of information to carefully researched audiences. In addition to the company's own marketing people whose heads have ready access to the chief executive officer (CEO), there may be a variety of external support organizations, notably advertising agencies handling various company products or services.

In sophisticated corporations the marketing organization is directed toward well-defined corporate goals. It operates within tightly planned marketing strategies, with budgets related to the importance of the function to the corporation's bottom line.

Examine the human resources area, however, and the picture is vastly different. Yes, there is an immense amount of communications directed to the work force and to outside audiences, as later chapters will show. But this communications web was created under the exigencies of the moment and assigned to whatever agency within the corporation was judged able to handle the particular load—usually the personnel or public relations departments. Sometimes research is done; more often it is not. External support organizations are sometimes utilized; often they are not. Some aspects may be under the eye of the CEO; many are not.

In most organizations there is no one responsible executive comparable to the vice president of public relations or the financial vice president, for example, who report to the CEO. There are no specific budgets for human resources communications in most companies, nor a strategy or planned objective, nor a means of meshing these with the corporation's other communications programs.

The initial response to the human resources revolution, of jumping on the corporate horse and riding off in all directions, still prevails within most companies.

Yet paradoxically, so extensive are such communications in most major companies that they constitute an important new dimension. In scope and importance, they are becoming comparable to corporate marketing and institutional communications.

Expanding the Communications Mix

So far most organizations have responded to the exigencies of the human resources revolution by improvising programs, particularly communications programs, as the need for these become apparent. They have expanded their recruiting efforts in response to new technologies and government requirements. They have attempted to communicate with audiences like advocacy groups who are totally new to corporate experience. They have opened up dialogues with minority workers, with women, with communities.

The government itself, as we have seen, requires not only a great deal more paperwork from businesses but compels them to deal on many different levels with federal, state, and local administrations to an unprecedented degree. Concurrently unions demand bargaining table consideration of issues transcending time and money and ultimately affecting the very nature of the management-employee relationship.

Companies have begun to respond to these audiences and to others mentioned in previous chapters sometimes by greatly broadening old communications channels and sometimes by inventing new ones.

This expansion and enrichment of the corporate communications mix has occurred under the pressures of urgent need, in response to a continuing flow of new developments in the human resources field. In the space of a decade, for example, we have seen the implementation of the civil rights act in terms of employment for minorities, the emergence of the feminist movement in pursuit of similar goals, a spate of legislation that has affected corporate employment, pension programs, safety, and a revolt against mandatory retirement.

Resulting new programs have been adopted and implemented with minimum attention to their relationship with other company communications programs. New audiences have been added in response to problems or in an effort to head off problems.

Only now, as one begins to analyze these developments in relation to the social changes occurring simultaneously, is it becoming evident that they have a common denominator. The extent to which such programs have become a part of the corporate scene, and are likely to continue into the indefinite future, is becoming understood. Their function and importance to the organization is unfolding.

What has occurred, in fact, is that a new dimension of corporate communications has emerged—human resources communications.

PUTTING IT INTO PERSPECTIVE

It is one thing to claim that a new form of corporate communications has come into existence but quite another to prove the case. One way is to put this new form into perspective in terms of its objectives, its audiences, and its media as these compare with the two major long-established areas, marketing and institutional corporate communications. Of these, marketing communications is probably the most clearly defined, and the one to which people are most frequently exposed.

Looking at Marketing Communications

On the television set the curtains part and a glamorous tap dancer begins her routine, moving across the tops of giant soup cans, ending with a spectacular finale. To paraphrase a show business phrase, that isn't just entertainment, it's marketing.

Television commercials are probably the best known of a spectrum of company communications that sell a company's products and services to a huge and diverse audience. Every individual is a multiple target.

First we are consumers of general kinds of goods—automobiles, food, beer. Then we appear on the marketer's computers as homeowners, and thus potential purchasers of grass seed and floor tiles. Our subscription to a tennis magazine places us in the category of buyers of sports equipment, while a passport indicates a target for travel services. These are only a few of our marketing classifications.

Again, we may be business or professional people, or otherwise gainfully employed. Marketing people want us to consider new suppliers for our organization, new products or materials it can use, new ways of doing things, even new locations. "What do you think it's like to live in Dallas/Ft. Worth?" an ad asks in the pages of a business magazine, where other messages invite us to consider computers, air freight services, and office furniture.

But advertising, as everyone knows, is only the tip of the marketing iceberg. Press releases on new products appear in trade publications; trade shows and exhibits unveil new models; volumes of literature go to buyers, distributors, and dealers. American corporations send armies of salespeople into the field armed with audiovisual presentations, catalogs, sales pieces, and samples. There are sales seminars, and even spectacular musical productions rivaling Broadway by which companies stimulate their salespeople to consider this year's revamp of last year's version of whatever the company is selling. These changes themselves probably originated in the marketing department.

A simplified definition of marketing communications might describe it as creating product ideas, presenting new products, defining product advantages, and informing about product applications, with the aim of selling the products and creating an image that will enhance future sales. The audiences for such communications are consumers, the people who stock and retail the product, original equipment manufacturers who may use it in their manufacturing processes, the purchasing organizations within industry, and those who may influence their choice, that is, company engineers. The communications media employed would include advertising, public relations, trade shows and similar exhibitions, sales literature, and the person-to-person element provided by sales staffs.

Because the success of marketing communications determines in large degree the company's financial health, corporations regard it as a crucial activity and therefore an area of high priority. It has the ear of top management, is buttressed by very large budgets, and is supported by an extensive roster of outside support organizations such as advertising, public relations, and marketing research organizations.

Research, in fact, is one of the key elements in the marketing program. "Everybody knows by now," says Theodore Levitt writing in the *Harvard Business Review*, "that marketing and selling are not the same thing. Selling tries to get the customer to want what you have. Marketing tries to have what the customer will want—where, when, in what form, and at what price he wants." In the process marketing communications runs the gamut from the TV commercial to feedback provided by the potential consumer.

Institutional Communications

Though not practiced as extensively as marketing communications, corporate institutional communications is also of primary importance to management. This is a complex, many-sided activity involving areas vital to company survival, including the task of informing various audiences about the company's profitability, growth, achievements, future prospects, and activities contributing to all of these. Another aspect is making the company known as a responsible "corporate citizen" in supporting social goals and aims. A third area is that of reporting on the diversity of the company's products, services, and economic interests. Institutional communications is also an element in the company's defense mechanisms, presenting the company's side of issues, national or local, in which it may be involved.

The objectives of this flow of corporate communications are also many sided. One is to maintain the flow of investment capital into the company, vital in enabling it to grow. Thus, institutional communications is employed both to transmit information to the investing public and financial community, and to establish and maintain a corporate image that will attract investment and confidence. This kind of image building in turn reinforces the marketing effort by drawing attention to some of the company's products and capabilities.

Olin Corporation, for example, directs a two-page, four-color ad to readers of the major business journals with the simple headline, "Who is Olin?" Eight brief paragraphs illustrated by colorful and attention-getting drawings answer the question in ways that even busy readers are unlikely to miss. Under an illustration depicting cruising crocodiles the copy reads, "Olin helps keep your backyard pool from becoming a health menace. HTH pool sanitizer is the largest selling dry chlorine in the world." In another double-page spread, "We're Union Camp," reads an ad, "Look at us this way . . . as a major producer of paper, paperboard and packaging."

Another aim of this kind of communications is to influence public attitudes. Sometimes this takes the form of professing support for the free enterprise system or viewing with alarm the inroads upon it. It may be educational, aiming at indoctrinating a particular public with the basics of economic theory. From time to time some corporations attempt to defend their own industries, counter or influence the actions of government or of regulatory agencies, or try to obtain public support for or against pending legislation. Atlantic Richfield, for example, at a time when oil companies were under fire on many fronts, created an extensive ad campaign that invited public ideas on improving transportation in the United States, resulting in a massive public response. Another ad of this kind, part of a series by Deere and Company in business magazines, featured one of the many road-building machines it manufactures at work excavating a site for new bridge abutments. The copy read:

> More than 80,000 large and small bridges on our secondary road systems require this kind of improvement or complete replacement. The choice is one of paying directly for this needed construction work, or paying indirectly in terms of accidents, recurring repairs and expensive detours for motor freight, school buses, local farm products and today's modern agricultural equipment. Adequate funding for preservation and renewal of our transportation system should be one of our nation's first concerns.

The audiences for institutional corporate communications are broad, varied, and shifting with the nature of communications objectives.

If advertising is the archetype of marketing communications, public relations could be said to occupy the same role in institutional communications. Traditionally the public relations function in industry has had the ear of top management as being most tuned into public and special economic interests, trends, and concerns.

Although it is not as neatly structured nor as clearly defined in its operations as the marketing area, institutional communications is nevertheless a familiar, flexible instrument of high sophistication. In recent years it has expanded considerably in proportion to the extent to which business has come under fire from a variety of external sources. As with marketing, this form of communications utilizes advertising, public relations, mailings, exhibits, audiovisual presentations, and an extensive roster of other means of transmitting the corporate message.

Defining Human Resources Communications

Much of what has been said here about marketing and institutional communications is likely to sound familiar. The concept of human resources communications, however, is new, since it stems from massive social changes that have occurred in a short period of time and are still happening and unpredictable.

One way to understand the concept of human resources communications is to compare its function within the corporation with that of the marketing and institutional communications we have just examined. Marketing communications is concerned principally with achieving sales for the company. Institutional communications could be characterized as a form of corporate environmentalism, concerned with maintaining an economic ecology of investment, regulation, and public attitudes in which the company can grow.

Human resources communications has a much different objective. Its basic function is to maintain an organization's ability to operate. Unless an organization is able to hire, motivate, and maintain an adequately trained work force, it cannot fulfill its basic economic purpose which is to produce goods or services. If its people will not work, that is, if they go on strike, or cannot work due to government restrictions or community objections, or can work but not sufficiently well to compete against other organizations for the available market, the organization cannot exist. Human resources communications are a means to achieve the one end and avoid the other.

This kind of communications is also aimed at avoiding restrictions on operation—boycotts by outside groups, class-action suits by employees, unfavorable local regulations by communities. Inevitably, all three communications areas overlap and affect each other.

Marketing communications, in strengthening the company's bottom line, also contributes to a heightened financial image of the company. Marketing messages—TV commercials, for example—have an impact on the company's own employees in demonstrating the products, roles, and goals. Many companies today feature employees in their ads, for example, the Sears Roebuck and its Allstate commercials about "the good hands people." Marketing concepts, however, sometimes suggest the company's negative attitudes toward its own employees. "Fly me. I'm Karen," triggered a strike by National Airlines' cabin attendants that lasted several months.

Institutional communications aimed at attracting investors may have a favorable spillover effect on potential job applicants. A recent United Technologies ad makes the point that the company is number one in research and development expenditures in relation to sales, and documents this over a five-year period. Such information is likely to influence a creative technical person to pursue a career there.

Human resources communications can also affect marketing goals. Internally, for example, they contribute to productivity, morale, and such programs as "zero defects" which enable the company to compete more effectively in the marketplace. Externally they help the organization acquire the qualified people needed to keep growing and avoid the alienation of important consumer markets.

THE ELEMENTS OF HUMAN
RESOURCES COMMUNICATIONS

Some elements of human resources communications have been around a long time—employee communications, for example—but they too have undergone radical change in recent years. Others, like the trend to provide stockholders with information on the company's human resources programs, are very new.

Basically human resources communications are concerned with four different though interrelated functions: One of these is staffing. Another relates to morale, productivity, and motivations in the work place. A third function has to do with adjusting to change—the need both to acclimate employees and prepare them for various kinds of job-related change, and the necessity of dealing with outside audiences of importance to the company in terms of the changing scene in human resources. Finally, human resources communications are employed by companies as a means of expressing or reaching some special goals related to employment, like affirmative action.

Recruitment Communications

Recruitment communications is a convenient starting point to describe these various elements. Since at least 1950 most major corporations have been engaged in a variety of communications programs having to do with acquiring entry-level people and trained or experienced specialists.

It was in the early fifties that the supply and demand situation and the attitudes of people about work began to change. Unlike the depression-struck thirties, no longer were people desperately seeking any job that would produce income. Increasingly recruiting has been not simply announcing that jobs are available and opening the door, but a sustained and extensive wooing of people to join the company. The wooing has been required because there often have not been enough people with the desired training to go around.

The kinds of communications involved in the extensive, widespread, ongoing search for people that is now an accepted element in our society will be detailed in a subsequent chapter. For the moment it is enough to note that the scope of recruitment communications ranges from the classified pages of newspapers to recruiting trips to other parts of the world, elaborate audiovisual presentations, brochures, and other literature.

Recruitment communications, like its marketing and institutional counterparts, aim not only at "selling the company," in this case as an employer, but creating for it a favorable employer image. It is estimated that the overall expenditures for recruitment communications is approaching a billion dollars a year.

Recruitment communications reach a range of publics almost as broad as marketing communications. They are a product of the personnel department, and a form of corporate communications independent of other major communications functions.

Employee-Directed Communications

"Employee communications" conjures up for many of us the image of the traditional house organ with its columns of births and weddings, reports on the company bowling teams, and some edifying comments from the Top on the importance of hard work and punctuality. A vastly changed landscape of employee communications now exists, as we shall see in more detail, in which workers not only have special television presentations directed to them but they may have personal dialogues with top management.

This change, another result of the human resources revolution, is indicative of the broadened function of this aspect of communications. Employee-directed communications aim at multiple goals in relation to the work force:

1. They meet the new demands of the seventies-style employees for more information—a great deal more information—on what is happening in the enterprise in which they are taking part.
2. They serve as a vehicle for influencing an increasingly alienated work force to identify with the company.
3. They supply a variety of practical communications needs stemming from day-to-day work that, given the size of the typical corporate facility, would be difficult to achieve except through such channels.

4. They provide a medium through which management can attempt to gain the interest and cooperation of the workers in a variety of work related projects, from safety practices to production goals.

These by no means exhaust the purposes of this aspect of human resources communications, but they do suggest how it is an information source, an element in morale, and an interface between management and the work force.

Nor do the new employee communications still deal with only a broad and undifferentiated mass of ciphers. Today they involve not only the total employee population but in the manner of marketing and institutional programs, they include particular "publics" within the company to whom special kinds of media are directed and specific kinds of messages are sent—middle-management, for example, and corporate professionals.

Affirmative Action Communications

One of the most conspicuous elements of human resources communication is its application in equal employment opportunity. The need to take affirmative action in hiring has created still another broad range of communications efforts from recruiting ads in minority media to motion pictures aimed at providing new role models for minority youngsters and young women. It has also involved companies in dialogues with advocacy groups, with community leaders, and with educators at all levels. The aims of these communications range from acquiring the people necessary to meet federally imposed "affirmative action hiring goals," to creating an environment within the company in which these newcomers to the corporate scene can work and achieve.

Training and Development

A variety of factors, both social and economic, have dictated the need for still another aspect of human resources communications: the training and development programs for which corporations spend billions of dollars annually. Like recruitment, this area of communications is chiefly involved with staffing company operations with people able to handle the growing complexities of modern day work. Training also serves to help increase upward mobility within the organization, to adjust workers to the technological changes affecting the work place, and often simply to introduce people to the world of work at the entry level. In recent years training has also remedied the deficiencies of many of the young people who have been entering the work force from both high schools and colleges lacking basic skills necessary for working.

As ham goes with eggs, so in the world of business, development goes with training. The function of development, as most of us know from our own experience, is to enable people to do a better job in the positions they hold, and to prepare them for better jobs to come. The extent of this effort, particularly in "management development," is remarkable. Few achieve or move beyond the middle ranges of management without exposure to seminars inside and outside the company, lectures, literature, and lately, a generous supply of audio and video tape cassettes. Development programs aim at increasing various kinds of business skills, but in recent years many programs have had a strong human resources orientation. People have been learning to manage more effectively through sensitivity training, transactional analysis, and other techniques. Other development programs aim at enabling more conventional executives to cope with people from very different backgrounds, with different ideas, and with a militant concern for their own rights.

For many companies union relations are an aspect of human resources communications. Although workers and management often meet in the role of antagonists over the bargaining table, common recognition of joint human resources problems—the need for training employees to handle new kinds of equipment, for example—has also led to cooperative programs between company and union.

Educational Relations

As another aspect of human resources, corporations are engaged in the process of shaping the future work force through a variety of communications programs aimed at college campuses, community colleges, and to a more limited degree, high schools. The interrelationships between the corporation and the college are long-standing and range from one-on-one personal meetings between university heads and their corporate opposite numbers to extensive financial support extended by companies to schools, including campus recruitment and co-op programs whereby students alternate between company jobs and the campus.

The obvious reason for much of this activity is the corporate need to obtain trained people. Less obvious, but implicit in the communications programs we will be examining later in the book, is the objective of influencing career choices and thus the makeup of the work force in years to come.

Other Aspects of Human Resources
Communications

A new development gaining ground, perhaps in response to the grow-ing strength of the older population as an advocacy group, is retiree relations. This is the communications link between the corporation and its former employees, not only passively by pension check and mecha-nized Christmas cards, but in new and positive ways.

Community relations, a long-time company concern, is taking on a new frame of reference and is engaging many businesses in dialogues with community leaders concerning employment practices, working conditions, and other human resources topics.

Finally, new modes of communication between the company and its more sensitive, socially aware stockholders are beginning to alter the nature of stockholder relations, focusing more and more on the social factors of corporate leadership.

A UNIQUE NEW COMMUNICATIONS
FUNCTION

When this broad pattern of communications by companies is consid-ered as a whole, it clearly represents a new departure, a new dimen-sion. No other kind of corporate communications serves the same ends. Only human resources communications focuses on the critical task of staffing the organization to meet changing needs, training and develop-ing employees at all levels to deal with technical and social change affecting the work place, and motivating that work force to achieve company goals.

It alone is directed to complying with the multiplying government legislation affecting the makeup of the organization's work force. It alone maintains the essential dialogues with the multiple communities involved in affirmative action, professional employment, and local human resources concerns. No other element within the company is involved in stimulating the national output of trained people the com-pany needs, including women and minorities, through in-company programs and extensive relationships with schools and communities.

Human resources communications as a field has developed in response to clear-cut corporate needs to deal with people not as con-sumers or investors but as workers. Companies must now deal with militant, litigious, and alert people, both inside and outside, who care how the company treats its people.

Organizing the Human Resources
Communications Function

Clearly in today's social climate this new kind of communications serves a variety of immediate and long-range needs vital to corporate survival. Yet in most major corporations, though they are involved in almost all of the various kinds of human resources communications programs cited here, there is no recognition, no perception that these programs are elements in a larger and important whole.

What is needed is a central focus for this activity in the way that marketing and institutional communications have developed policies and goals that give coherence and direction. As it now stands, human resources communications are highly fragmented. Recruitment, for example, is the function of the personnel department. College recruiting may be a function of individual divisions, and college relations a corporate function under the direction of the public relations area. An affirmative action executive may have responsibility for in-company communications relating to affirmative action, while the personnel department conducts affirmative action recruiting. Employee communications, according to a survey of the International Association of Business Communicators, can fall between several stools: "Only 38.9 percent [of these employee communications executives] report public relations/public affairs the title of their department. . . . Nearly 22 percent report their department title as a separate communication or publications department. Another 8.4 percent are in the marketing/ advertising departments and 5.9 percent in personnel."

In practice this means that unlike marketing and institutional communications, there are no carefully developed and researched long-range programs. There is no commonality of concepts, no agreement on images to build outside the company or on the nature of the overall information needed by the corporation's people. Just as important, there is no organized means by which human resources considerations can make themselves felt in other elements of corporate communications. For example, one major chemical company is heavily involved in college programs to interest women in engineering careers and vigorously seeks hard-to-find female chemical engineers through advertising in technical journals. Recently one of its divisions placed ads in the chemical journals that these engineers, female and male, read, proclaiming that its new product was "X-rated" and illustrating the idea with a photograph of an unclad young woman. Because of this lack of interchange on the vital subjects of human resources and communications, companies are unwittingly destroying their credibility by presenting contradictory faces and alienating those who influence purchasing decisions.

The human resources factor has become too important in today's world, and looms too large in tomorrow's, to continue as an orphan of the storm, split among numerous corporate divisions and pursued on a catch-as-catch-can basis. The time has come for companies to establish cohesive human resources communications functions.

CHAPTER SEVEN

Tapping Human Resources

R ecruiting is basic.

"For many years it has been said that capital is the bottleneck for a developing industry. I don't think this any longer holds true," says Fred K. Foulkes, professor of business administration at the Harvard Business School, writing in the *Harvard Business Review*. "I think it is the work force and the company's inability to recruit a good work force that does constitute the bottleneck for production. I don't know of any major project backed by good ideas, vigor and enthusiasm that has been stopped by a shortage of cash. I do know of industries whose growth has been partly stopped or hampered because they can't maintain an efficient and enthusiastic labor force, and I think this will hold true even more in the future. . . ."

Every organization, whatever its size, is constantly involved in tapping the available pool of human resources in the process of replacing or adding staff. Even during major cutbacks in the past, companies that were releasing employees by the thousands were quietly adding new people at the same time to fill new jobs that were developing, or to fill existing jobs more effectively. A company must get the people it needs with the training it needs in the numbers it needs and when it needs them, or it cannot continue to exist.

Though managements in general have had a lively awareness of the importance of obtaining the necessary human resources to remain competitive and operational, most have also displayed an extensive lack of interest in the recruiting function and the communications it involves. The human resources revolution has acted to alter that situation to some degree, which is fortunate. For in many ways recruiting is a prototype for the whole new field of human resources communications.

RECRUITMENT COMMUNICATIONS: WHY IT IS A PROTOTYPE

Though the "Help Wanted" sign on the factory fence and the classified ad in the employment section of the local newspaper may date back to the Industrial Revolution, recruitment communications as a system had its origins in this century, during the early fifties, a by-product of the guns-and-butter economy of the Korean war era.

World War II had taught us the value of concentrations of technical people in creating new weaponry and how to organize industrial resources into huge and efficient units of production. When a new need arose for technical people in large quantities, the three-line ad and the sign on the plant gate soon gave way to ads that took up whole pages of newspapers' classified sections, and the use of other media from billboards to extensive brochures to meet the competition.

From that time onward recruitment has been a major element in corporate personnel programs, and recruitment communications have become an increasingly broad function. Newspaper advertising alone is estimated to average about a quarter of a billion dollars a year for "help wanted" ads. This has led to a new trend in newspaper editorial matter as well. Papers like the Chicago *Tribune* and the Boston *Herald American* feature extensive career editorial material in their employment advertising sections. The Seattle *Post-Intelligencer* and other papers, even the venerable *The New York Times*, have added weekly career columns.

Recruitment has been a prototype for human resources communications in that it reaches extensive audiences outside the company with messages related to human resources. Day after day, in newspapers throughout the country, corporate logos appear in thousands upon thousands of messages that not only invite qualified readers into personal contact with companies, but extol and demonstrate company virtues as an employer.

Recruiting also involves internal audiences in certain aspects of human resources communication. For one thing, recruitment ads are read by the company's own people. "Yes, I do read my company's recruitment ads," one employee replied to a survey on the subject. "They tell me what's happening in the company." One company reports that when its recruitment program was halted for a time while a new campaign was being readied, company managers got worried inquiries from employees who feared that the lack of such ads meant the firm had suffered some serious financial reverse. Company people may be personally involved in hosting an open house recruiting project, in recommending friends for employment, or by volunteering to model for recruitment literature or ads.

Again paralleling human resources communication, recruiting involves the government, activist groups, academia, and the community. Corporate recruitment materials must meet EEO standards, for example; recruiters often work with minority, feminist, and other groups to locate job candidates. They are heavily involved with schools for the same reason. Since much recruiting is local or regional, it is a human resources activity with strong roots in a company's home communities.

Recruiting is conducted under the aegis of the personnel department, like a number of other aspects of human resources communication. It rarely interacts with marketing or institutional communications functions. A recruitment manager in a recently formed fast-growing software organization remarked, "We tried to get some help from our marketing department, but they not only knew nothing about recruiting, they weren't interested."

That's a fairly accurate description of the usual situation that human resources communications of any kind tends to encounter. Marketing and public relations departments in most organizations have other, larger (and to them more important) tasks to do. This situation also tells us why specialized communications organizations have sprung up outside the company, concerned with helping organizations meet such human resources problems as recruiting. Given the complexities of today's recruitment efforts and the extent and the size of the audience for this kind of human resources communication, the need for that assistance is understandable.

THE CORPORATION'S RECRUITING AUDIENCES

Most of the American work force is the target for recruitment-directed human resources communications. To fill their needs for people, companies must reach out again and again to varied audiences (who may also be potential customers or stockholders).

One of the ways in which recruiting differs from most corporate marketing communications is that its aim is to selectively screen the potential audience, rather than reach the largest number. A consumer ad aims at attracting audiences in the millions for the company's toothpaste or automobile. The recruitment effort may be directed to a virtual handful of people who meet the given job requirements.

The Specialists

Dr. Lawrence L. provides an example. He is part of a major corporate recruitment audience—engineers and scientists—of whom there are roughly two million in our economy. Dr. L., however, is not a workaday electronics engineer or chemist, but a selenologist. "I was puttering happily away at a university," he says, "and, I guess, planning to stay there for the rest of my working life. I just never thought, you know, that any organization other than a university would be looking for me. Then, a few years ago, I was looking through *Planetary and Space Sciences,* and found a recruiting ad. Sounded highly interesting; the company had more advanced facilities than I'd ever have at the school for my line of work, so I applied. And here I am." Dr. L.'s specialty is the lunar equivalent of earth geology, and at the time the ad appeared, there were perhaps two dozen people with a similar background.

Whether they seek highly specialized individuals like Dr. L. or the more commonly sought electrical, mechanical, chemical, and civil engineers, corporations in their recruiting programs reach large segments of the professional technical community on a regular basis, to satisfy their needs for experienced people and to build an image for future recruiting efforts.

Sally M. is a member of another major specialized audience for corporate recruiting, the half-million or more EDP specialists. "As far as I'm concerned," she told an attitudes researcher, "we're invisible people in this company. We're nowhere, you know—isolated. Management doesn't understand EDP so they make believe we don't exist." Sally has a high school education, plus computer training in a local community college. "I got into programming because I thought it would be interesting work," Sally says. "Some of it is, except for maintenance. I hate doing maintenance work; it's so cut and dried. But in this company, there's nowhere you can go if you're a programmer. Here you can be a programmer and then maybe a project manager and then a program manager—and that's it. So I'm looking around. A lot of jobs open now. Wherever I go, I'll get more money. But what I really want is a chance to go higher, to make a real career. Because the time will come when programmers at my level won't be needed; we'll be replaced by more sophisticated software, and I want to be far enough up the ladder by then so I won't be the one out of a job."

Sally M., with one eye on the recruiting ads and another on the future of her field, is typical of the recruitment audience today—sophisticated "consumers" of employment opportunities who have particular goals and directions for themselves.

Harry J., an MBA with a good job in international marketing at his company's corporate headquarters, is representative of still another audience, the millions of business specialists and executives. "I've got five years with my company," he tells a seatmate on the morning commuter train into the city. "As things go today, that's a little long in one place, but there's a department manager spot coming up, and I'm in line for it." His companion asks what happens if he doesn't get the job. "Well," Harry says, "I've got three companies in mind. I know people who work there; I check out their annual reports, and talk to my broker—you know, do some research. All three of them look to have a good growth situation. The compensation packages are good. And these are companies where they really believe in the importance of good people; they don't just *say* it, either. They've got career pathing, counseling programs, profit sharing. . . ."

Harry J. is not only sophisticated in his approach to employment; like many people, he has a few companies in mind that he wants to work for, companies whose advantages include their attitudes toward their people. This employer image plays an important role in recruiting, right through the ranks.

Mike C. represents another kind of specialized recruiting audience. He, too, holds a critical position, of a considerably different kind. His job is to keep his company's business machines, leased to other organizations, operating at top efficiency. If there are too many breakdowns customers will look elsewhere for equipment in a highly competitive market. On the job specifications for his position, Mike is listed as "technical representative." In practice he is one of several million technicians and other technical specialists who maintain and troubleshoot machinery that keeps the economy rolling, from massive automated assembly lines to delicate laboratory equipment.

"I got into this job," he says as he carefully repacks the tools he's been using back into the black leather kit bag, "because of a friend of mine who worked for the company. He said 'Hey, Mike, they need people like you.' I said, 'I haven't got any training to work on a business machine.' He said, 'Don't be crazy, man, they're going to train you for nothing and they're a darn good company to work for.'" Mike fastens up his bag. "You know, that guy was right. The company trained me and it's a pretty good job. Next week I start a new training course because we're coming out with a more advanced machine and I've got to learn how to work on it." He pauses on his way to call in to his office. "My friend Ralph, who got me into this job—you know what he got? He got a $50 United States Bond for recruiting me."

White Collar, Blue Collar

A July 8, 1977 *Business Week* article entitled "Suddenly, a New Shortage of Secretaries" examined one of the perennial problems in recruiting: the shortage of qualified secretaries. In the past quarter-century major cities have rarely failed to report the high demand and low availability for this skilled work. Recent events have exacerbated the problem. The secretarial job has acquired a tarnished image, both from the feminist insistence that these are positions which exploit and downgrade women and a residual tendency among some executives to treat secretaries as a kind of corporation-provided personal servant with steno skills.

Clerical white-collar recruitment, therefore, is an ongoing, bread-and-butter chore in almost every organization, not only for secretaries but for file clerks, typists, and products of the new technologies such as computer operators, word processing specialists, and positions involving management of offices and office functions.

So, too, is the search for skilled blue-collar workers. The cover of the August 29, 1977 issue of *Industry Week* depicted a statue of such a worker on a pedestal in a museum, a fitting illustration for the lead article, "The Extinction of the Skilled Worker." Machinists, welders, tool-and-die makers, shipfitters, and a roster of other skilled workers represent one of the most frustrating aspects of the recruitment effort for many organizations. The supply of these people, as the *Industry Week* article documents, is already small and continues to dwindle because of prevailing attitudes about blue-collar work, restrictive apprenticeship programs, and other problems. Further, skilled workers as a class are among the least mobile in our society, according to various studies. Most choose not to move to other locales even when they are unemployed because of a recession or the closing of a plant.

Still, in desperation companies needing such skilled people make nationwide or regional sweeps to fill available openings. When a Southeastern manufacturing company received a contract to fabricate liquid natural gas (LNG) tanks for new tankers being built, it beat the bushes in the region for welders and other skilled tradespeople. Daily and weekly newspaper ads were combined with radio spots in three nearby states to report on the blue-collar openings, and enabled the company to meet its commitment.

Entry Level: Starting from Scratch

General Dynamics' Electric Boat Division, which builds nuclear submarines in Connecticut, has made similar regional recruiting sweeps from time to time to fill its working ranks. Electric Boat utilized a technique characteristic of many corporate recruiting efforts today. It recruited unskilled, untrained, entry-level people, established its own training facilities, and turned these recruits into workers capable of the demanding tasks the technology of nuclear submarines requires.

The "train them from scratch" technique is not limited to manufacturing. Fast food service organizations like Hardee's recruit entry-level people with little or no background in the field, train them on the job in a company course, and place them as assistant managers in their growing chain of fast food restaurants. "We decided early in the company's experience that our recruiting would focus on the entry-level person," says Hardee's employment director Richard Nelms. "For one thing, we get out of the 'musical chairs' situation in which we recruit people from one company and another recruits them from us. We're growing our own. For another, it enables us to maintain a strict promotion-from-within policy that both attracts good people to us and is a strong factor in internal morale."

Entry-level recruiting involves companies with still other audiences of potential applicants. Local and regional general publics, as in the case of the shipbuilding organizations, are targets for recruiting communications of this kind. So are high school students. Many companies, as we'll see later, maintain a working relationship with local high schools as sources of entry-level people. The military, as the periodicals directed to high school students disclose, also see this group as a major entry-level audience and recruiting target. Business, in turn, recruits from people completing their military service, finding both those with applicable training for civilian jobs and a large pool of entry-level applicants.

The Academic Audience

"What courses did I like best?" The student, neatly dressed for the job interview, had obviously been expecting this question and quickly listed the chemical and business courses that related to the corporate recruiter's company.

"What kind of a career goal have you set for yourself over the next few years?" the interviewer asked.

"Well," the student answered, "I think that the energy field is going to be one of the most important in our economy for some time to come. And I think one of the most challenging areas there, technically, is the development of really low-cost methods of tapping shale oil resources, like your company's Wyoming operation. As a chemical engineer, I think I could. . . ." The interviewer smiled to himself. This was a student who had come well-primed to win a job offer from the company.

The yearly crop of college graduates constitutes one of the most important recruiting audiences to many corporations. Companies see the new generation as having up-to-date training and as a source of talent that will shape the companies' futures. Organizations are also keenly aware that these workers are considerably less expensive to acquire in terms of salaries than experienced professionals. The whole college communications scene is a highly organized, almost ritualized effort, ranging from the highest of high-level interchanges to a spate of specially designed literature that aims at impressing the undergraduate with the charms of Company X as the place to begin a career. We'll examine this later in more detail. In today's college recruiting world, few audiences are as avidly sought as those whose credentials include a black skin, an Hispanic surname, or the Ms. that means feminine gender rather than Master of Science.

The Protected Groups

In the legalese of EEO guidelines, they are called "protected groups," the people for whom equal employment laws exist. To business and industry, they are people to be recruited as evidence of affirmative action, with stiff financial and image penalities attached to lack of success.

The result is a further broadening of the audiences for the company's human resources communications, as well as for the recruiting effort itself. These audiences include the black community both nationally and locally, plus the predominantly black colleges which graduate about half the nation's black students every year. It also includes the Hispanic communities, growing in size and number in the United States and incorporating varied national backgrounds, including Puerto

Ricans, Cubans, and Mexicans. American Indians are a protected group, as are the handicapped, Vietnam war veterans, older workers, and, of course, women. The roster of protected groups continues to expand. Symbolic of this was *The New York Times* headline, "Bill on Alcoholics is Signed. Measure Prohibiting Discrimination Against Former Drinkers Hailed as 'Landmark' Legislation."

Once again the recruiter is charged with exposing the company as employer to large and critical audiences. The black population of the United States is more than 25 million alone; Hispanic-Americans are variously estimated to number from 11 to 16 million and women today, as we have noted, constitute nearly 50 percent of the work force, and more than that percentage of the total population.

The Career Influencers

"It's kind of a love-hate relationship," explains an employment agency head. "We can't do without each other, but a lot of the time we just don't understand the other's problems or points of view." The occasion had been a meeting between a local branch of a personnel association and the local members of an employment agency association. The objective was to improve communications. "We send them people we think will fit. They call us and say, 'Hey, didn't you read our job specs?' We figure that the kind of job descriptions they develop are unrealistic. They say, 'The agency gets its fee without doing any work for it.' That's why sessions like this are worthwhile. We get reminded that we're working toward the same goal—getting the right people into the right jobs."

Employment agency people are "career influencers"—though the ungainly term "sourcing agencies" is also coming into use. Such people, who can steer job applicants to the company, are another recruiting-related audience. Many of them are professionally involved in placement—employment agency people, executive recruiters, and outplacement specialists. Others are advisors and counselors involved in helping with career decisions, such as high school career and college placement counselors, together with some of the commercial organizations that have sprung up to do the same kind of work with experienced people who want to change careers or jobs.

The company's own employees, responding to programs in which they are asked to refer people they know, are sources of influence. So are teachers who take students on class visits to company facilities, or who get special tours of their own. Local associations are often involved, formally or informally, in helping to place people in jobs. The Urban League, for example, has long maintained a placement service as part of its national and local work in the black community. Churches, rehabilitation groups working with addicts and ex-convicts, young peoples' organizations like the Young Men's and Young Women's Christian Associations—all these may be career influencers. So, too, as some companies find, are ex-employees—the company's retirees, who may refer younger relatives and friends to the company as job candidates.

The recruiting audience, then, like the audiences for other human resources communications, is much broader than many managements think. Overall it reaches not only most of the nation's work force, but goes beyond it to involve high school students before they have made their career decisions, and at the opposite extreme, the company's own retirees who have left the work force but can still assist in locating recruits the company may need. Recruiting communications has evolved from a sporadic, hit-or-miss adjunct of the employment process to a complex, smoothly operating system for meeting the basic corporate needs for human resources.

RECRUITING: THE MEDIA AND THE METHODS

Football fans jammed into the Yale Bowl a few autumns ago to watch the traditional, emotion-laden struggle between the New York Giants and the New York Jets. As the pregame festivities built up and the time for kickoff neared, the attention of the huge audience was suddenly distracted. Flying low across the stadium was a small single-engined plane, towing behind it a banner with a strange device. The legend rippling in the autumnal air behind the slowly cruising aircraft read; "Electric Boat Has 767 Jobs Now!"

Air-towed banners are not a standard recruiting medium, but Electric Boat's unconventional approach suggests the range of communications media that have come to be employed in the perennial search for talent.

Basically, recruiting today utilizes four major methods, each of which involves its own patterns of communications. The most widely used and most familiar of these is the recruitment advertisement, appearing in an extensive range of publications and using, upon occasion, such odd media as the air-towed banner.

The field interviewing trip is another key method. An interviewing team travels from market to market setting up meetings with interested prospects; college recruitment interviews are a variation of this technique.

A third method is the use of recruiting events, such as the technical seminar, to attract groups of qualified people to a single spot to learn about the company and, directly or indirectly, about its job opportunities.

Finally, there are a variety of person-to-person methods to make the openings known to qualified people: executive recruiters, employee referrals, employment agencies, and so on.

The scope of recruiting can be purely local. Much of it is, in fact, since it is not economical for companies to relocate clerical people or production workers. But when special staffing problems arise the recruiting program is expanded to cover whole regions, to be national in scope, and not infrequently to include international recruiting, with field trips into foreign markets.

The Print Media: Newspapers

Jobs are news. Like daily news headlines. They are here today and gone tomorrow. This urgency—and the general impression, as one employment executive puts it, that "every manager in the division wants job openings filled yesterday, if possible; last week by preference"—is one major reason why the daily newspaper is the cornerstone of recruiting communications. Another is that newspapers provide the broad local coverage that recruiters seek and do it, as radio and television do not, in the context of an existing job marketplace, the employment pages where people are conditioned to look for new openings. Papers like *The New York Times,* for example, may run a thirty-page classified help-wanted section every Sunday, plus a twenty-five-page spread of recruitment ads in the Sunday business section.

Readership surveys suggest it is not just the unemployed job seeker who reads the newspaper employment sections. Consistently such studies have shown that about 70 to 75 percent of a publication's readership will check the employment ads at least once a month. Daily newspaper ads tend to reach a large segment of the adult readers in any community. "Browsing through the help wanted," one respondent noted, "gives you news of what's happening in terms of employment— who might be looking for *you.*" "It's kind of an ego trip," said another. "I see all those ads directed to programmers and I think, sure I like my job now, but if I ever want to move, there's a lot of people would like to have me."

While daily newspapers dominate the recruiting picture, other kinds of newspapers are in regular use. The *Wall Street Journal*, for example, has a Job Mart feature that has made it a major recruiting medium, unique in reaching the national business community. Much recruiting use also is made of its regional editions. The *Army Times, Navy Times,* and *Air Force Times,* weekly tabloids read by military audiences throughout the world, are extensively used to reach people leaving service. Lesser known but also used on occasion are the base papers which many military facilities publish and circulate to service people.

Many of Europe's distinguished newspapers are also notable recruiting media. The London *Sunday Times* and the *Daily Telegraph*, the Frankfurt *Algemaine Zeitung;* the Paris *France Soir;* and the *International Herald Tribune* all carry American employment ads, some for openings in the United States, some for positions in Europe or the Near East. In the Far East, the English language *Asahi Evening News* in Japan, the *South China Morning Post,* and more recently the Asian edition of the *Wall Street Journal* are among the numerous papers that carry similar advertising.

Weekly newspapers ranging from the sophisticated *Village Voice* in New York's Greenwich Village to neighborhood and small town papers are frequently included in recruiting programs, particularly with the movement of industry out of major metropolitan areas and into smaller towns and suburbs. Stauffer Chemical, one of these companies, moved its headquarters to Westport, Connecticut, from Manhattan. Headquarters now uses the twice-weekly local Westport paper and those of small surrounding towns, such as the weekly Weston *Forum*, to fill its local jobs.

The need to demonstrate affirmative action has brought another kind of newspaper into use by some companies: the minority press. By one count there are almost 250 black, Hispanic, and American Indian newspapers being published that are geared to carrying recruitment ads. Some are daily like Detroit's *Michigan Chronicle*, but most are weeklies, and they span the country from Boston's *Bay State Banner* to the *Navajo Times* in Window Rock, Arizona, and from *El Informador* in Chicago to the Sacramento *Observer*, a black newspaper which each year publishes an extensive series of careers issues distributed throughout California.

"If a company is really serious about affirmative action," says Ken Wilson, vice president of Afro-American Newspapers, Inc., a chain with publications in several East Coast cities, "then that company should be advertising to the local minority communities, and doing it on a regular basis. That's what is required by the Civil Rights Act, which spells out the point that organizations should be using minority media, and it is what the minority community looks for. It wants to know that a company, if it is serious in calling itself an equal opportunity employer, uses the publications created for that community to get its message over.''

The Afro-American group reinforces this point by issuing two careers supplements each year which attract considerable recruitment advertising.

In the context of newspapers alone, recruitment communications are reaching millions of readers daily, getting the recruitment message to the business community, minority communities, the military, and even carrying the company's name abroad.

Beyond this, however, as the story of the lunar geologist suggested, is still another broad group of media extensively used for recruiting communications: the journals.

The Print Media: Journals

From JAMA, the acronym for the *Journal of the American Medical Association*, where corporations and hospitals vie for medical talent to staff their facilities, to *Nation's Restaurant News*, where McDonald's seeks managers to manage the people "who do it all for you," there is scarcely a profession or trade for which people are in demand that doesn't have one or more journals providing recruiters with national coverage of the field, with a special job marketplace set aside for career ads.

"We tend to use newspapers a lot for recruiting because of the time factor," says Ben Jeffries, manager of professional recruitment for the Atlantic Richfield Company. "But journals often have advantages newspapers don't, time aside. For instance, I can use a weekly like *Oil & Gas Journal* to cover a good segment of the whole petroleum industry. Or I can narrow my reach to technical people in the field through vertical publications like *Petroleum Engineer* or the *Journal of Petroleum Technology*. Or use a very broad, across-the-board kind of journal like *Science* or *Technology Review* if we have a variety of technical openings to fill. Or we can get to some highly specialized types through publications like *The Journal of the Association of Petroleum Geologists*. This kind of pinpointed national coverage is the special advantage of the journal in recruiting."

As Jeffries' comment suggests, a single corporation is likely to be using many trade and professional journals simultaneously to meet the varied demands for people occurring within a company, from *Advertising Age* for corporate marketing specialists to *Waste Age* for environmental specialists.

General consumer magazines have not developed as a market for recruitment advertising due in part to the high cost of space (in terms of the recruiting budget, $25,000 a page is exclusionary) and the undifferentiated audiences counted by number and income rather than by job function, nor have special interest consumer magazines proven productive. But there are a handful of familiar newsstand names which also show up on recruiting schedules. These are the minority magazines like *Ebony, Encore, Black Enterprise,* and *Essence,* a publication directed to black women, plus *Ms.,* the feminist-oriented magazine, and *Working Woman.* The objective in using these publications, obviously, is to implement the organization's affirmative action efforts by reaching national minority audiences and working women.

Recruitment print communications in journals carry a human resources message to audiences within a company's own field and industry, messages that are read by job seekers and non-job seekers alike, thus contributing to the company's image as an employer. The affirmative action advertising in national magazines is seen not only by those interested in career opportunities, but by many who are activists and advocates in the field of equal opportunity. The message that comes over in these recruiting ads is, as Ken Wilson suggests, that the company is not just talking equal opportunity, but implementing it.

The Broadcast Media

During the recent recession a few television stations around the country experimented with a video version of employment pages. These focused on "positions wanted" rather than "jobs open" by interviewing unemployed people seeking work. A city-owned radio station, WNYC in New York, broadcast for a number of years a daily listing of job openings supplied by the local state employment service.

But perhaps because the broadcast message is so ephemeral, neither radio nor television has responded to the human resources revolution, either editorially or by creating new channels of information for the job seeker and the company with positions to fill. Radio is occasionally used to supplement newspaper advertising ("See our ad in the classified pages of Sunday's *News-Gazette*"). Minority radio stations have proven effective in publicizing entry-level jobs in some instances, and college radio is sometimes employed to announce campus interviews.

No one has been able to measure the impact of television's "General Hospital" or "Perry Mason" on enrollments in medicine and law, though it is said that the impact of the investigative reporting of the Watergate scandals has had the effect of jamming the journalism schools. But commercials that present women as scientists, business people, and entrepreneurs, and minority people as part of construction teams, airline operations, and professional groups, seem likely to make an impression on youngsters who have yet to set career goals.

Recruiting Events: Best Foot Forward

Back in the fifties General Electric was urgently in need of engineers and scientists to staff its new Special Defense Projects Department. Competition for technical people was high and the company needed a new approach to attract the level of people needed. Consequently one April evening a group of the fledgling organization's top technical people were in New York City taking part in a unique technical seminar. One of them was Dr. Yusuf Yoler, a featured speaker on the program, discussing and demonstrating the results of "shock tunnels," something new in the infant field of missile research. Other General Electric people spoke on state-of-the-art topics dealing with systems engineering and the new field of aerophysics. Their remarks were directed to a carefully selected audience of engineers and scientists.

The evening was a rousing success as technical seminars go, and was repeated later in Washington, Buffalo, and Boston. This seminar was not sponsored by the American Institute of Aeronautics or the American Physical Society, however, but by General Electric itself. It was intended to be and succeeded in being a highly informative technical session. It had the parallel objective of impressing the technical audiences it reached, and motivating some of the people attending to consider working with this new organization. As such it was probably the first state-of-the-art technical recruiting event ever staged, and it was extremely successful. From the four sessions came enough qualified engineers and scientists to staff the new facility.

Although technical seminars have remained relatively rare as recruiting devices, the idea emerges from time to time in new forms. Merrill Lynch Pierce Fenner & Smith, for example, has developed seminars on "Careers in the Financial Field" as a means of introducing this to people for whom stocks and bonds and puts and calls are pretty much a mystery. Various companies have utilized career planning seminars to attract college seniors to learn more about starting their working careers and, incidently, about the company as an employer.

The seminar approach, a communications device in itself, is supported by other kinds of communications. Special advertising (outside of newspaper careers sections) is used to attract the audience; direct mail is employed to screen applications and provide tickets and information to those who will attend, and as a follow-up, to remind those attending of career opportunities with the company. Within the seminar itself, as in some of the other recruiting events, generous use is made of audiovisual presentations, reprints of articles about the company, and other print material to reinforce the impact of the meeting.

The career "open house" is a widely used variation on the seminar idea. This is a technique used at all levels and in varying degrees of complexity. "I really had no idea of all the kinds of jobs that are open in a bank, or how nice the atmosphere is," said Sheila G. after attending a Saturday afternoon open house at a major Chicago bank. "All I ever saw of a bank before was just the customer section, with the tellers and so on. But there is so much more to it than that. And this bank has several women who are branch managers. One of them was talking about the training programs they provide. I was really impressed."

The open house communicates by inviting people in, usually through ads, with no need for the ticketing system used in seminars. Often light refreshments are offered. The program usually includes a tour of facilities, an audiovisual presentation about the company and its field, plus some talks about the kinds of jobs available and special advantages the company might have.

Some technical firms in attempting to attract engineering talent go further, setting up a program designed for the whole family including lunches in the company cafeteria, entertainment for the children, and special tours and presentations on subjects that it hopes will appeal to the spouses, since research suggests that, in families, selecting a new job is seldom a one-person decision. One New England firm, Electric Boat, took the idea a step further and chartered a train from New York, carrying a large group of designers and drafters and their families to visit the plant as a day's outing. The highlight was the launching of a new submarine the company had built. The idea was so successful it was repeated, this time bringing people from the Boston area to the shipyard.

When Deutsch, Shea & Evans developed the Jobs for Veterans program for the government and the Advertising Council in the early seventies, among its recommendations was the use of job fairs, which proved to be one of the most significant sources of employment for veterans at that time. These events, along with plant tours and open houses, emphasize the person-to-person aspects of recruiting. They involve a variety of communications techniques, not only to attract people and inform them during the course of the event, but in preparing the events themselves. They bring people into personal contact with the company's own people who take part as hosts, speakers, and guides; that contact is one of the key elements in building employer image.

Recruiting Literature and Audiovisual Materials

Attracting job candidates today involves both personal meetings and the reinforcement of the printed word and the visual image. No organization seeking to hire college students on even a modest scale, for example, can do without the indispensable college recruiting brochure, shelves of which are the familiar trademark of the college placement office. Many of the brochures rival the corporate annual report in glossy, four-color impressiveness.

Some companies make a practice of mailing their house organs to prospects, particularly when these are magazine-style periodicals that offer lively and informative articles on company projects and achievements. The annual report is often an addenda to a mailing, or is handed out at interviewing sessions in recognition that the sophisticated job seeker is data-oriented. Some companies like utilities and department stores include flyers in customer billings from time to time to indicate the availability of employment at the company. One organization in desperate need of executive secretaries resorted to handbills given out on the streets near the office building—and got the people it needed. Probably the most unusual piece of recruiting literature on record was handed out at a technical convention in San Francisco: Chinese fortune cookies, each of which carried a slip indicating the reader would find good fortune and a fine professional career at a noted aerospace corporation.

Some recruiting literature is for internal use, in conjunction with "employee referral" programs. This is the most widely used of all recruiting methods other than advertising. Referral programs aim at stimulating current employees to make job openings known to qualified friends, relatives, or acquaintances. This is sometimes a highly informal process of passing the word that a position is open. Increasingly, however, it involves a structured, formal communications program involving posters, direct mail to employees, coverage in the company house organ, and awards to participants ranging from dollar payments to drawings for grand prizes that may include a week's vacation trip at company expense.

Many companies use job posting, which is usually a bulletin board on which positions in the company are described and the qualifications listed. Employees interested are urged to make application for the openings. Some organizations reprint their recruiting ads in the employee publication, a variant of job posting.

Audiovisual presentations have been far less prominent in recruiting than have print materials. This situation is changing, however. More companies have assembled slide and tape presentations to show at recruiting events and during interview situations. Several years ago one Washington employment agency began videotaping interviews with job candidates and offering them to companies for review. Another organization is using a two-way approach, taping interviews with graduating college students and preparing tapes on companies to show to the students. Some attempts have been made to provide audiovisual recruiting materials to college placement offices to supplement or replace the traditional brochure, but this has been stalled by lack of equipment and supervision for showing films or tapes.

"I think audiovisual techniques are the coming thing in recruitment communications," says Sanford Browde, vice president of administration and personnel of Litton Industries' Monroe Company. "When we're dealing with generations that have been raised on the tube, we need to make more use of the technology that can really 'show and tell' what the jobs and the company is all about." One company having problems recruiting for lower-level jobs because it is in the midst of an industrial complex where it is overshadowed by better-known firms has been circulating a short film within its immediate locality to gain recognition as a potential employer. Another, utilizing a company film made for a different purpose, shows it on low-cost, late evening time on nonnetwork television in markets where it is recruiting. Newspaper ads call attention to the program, and a voice-over tells where to call for an interview.

The introduction of videotapes and closed circuit television in internal company communications suggests that recruiters, with more facilities to use, may become more visual in the future.

THE RECRUITMENT MESSAGE: THE
CHAIRMAN'S SHOES

"It was really unusual. We had seniors who were practically fighting to sign up for interviews," recalls Frank Cousins of the Bendix Corporation. The cause of the campus commotion was a Bendix college recruiting ad which was headlined, "14 Years Ago the Chairman of Bendix Was Looking For A Job, Too." The ad's copy explained that Bendix understood the problems of young people starting out their careers because only fourteen years before, the company's chairman, William Agee, had had the same kind of choice to make. "The idea of someone becoming a corporation head at such a relatively youthful age," said Cousins, "was one that apparently appealed strongly to students and impressed them with Bendix' potential as an employer. The ad also neatly illustrates one kind of message that recruitment communications conveys to the outside world—that youth, if combined with talent and initiative, is not a barrier to early success."

What people at all levels of working life most want to know about a potential job is what the job is like, the nature of the working conditions in the organization, and the advantages of the job in relation to their own lives and careers. One of the reasons for the success of the Bendix college ad was its recognition that people want these points not simply asserted, but documented.

The message Merrill Lynch gets over in seeking brokers to join the company is both the capability to handle change in a business notorious for change, and the ability to supply investors with what they need. "Who knows better than Merrill Lynch how to meet the challenges of the eighties in the securities business?" one of the firm's ads asks. The ad copy reports that in the new business climate investors are demanding full financial services, and that the firm has the "broadest product line in the business," more than thirty-five different investment instruments. The ad then goes on to detail four specific ways in which Merrill Lynch helps its representatives succeed. Whether or not you are considering a Merrill Lynch position, you get a definite feeling about the company vis-à-vis coping with change, and the support it gives its representatives.

The best technical recruiting ads deal with the specifics of company projects, summarize corporate achievements, and relate these to the advantages they create for the engineer or scientist who joins the company.

Work advantages and job content appear not only in the ads directed to professionals and executive types, but all down the line. To use another Merrill Lynch example, at the time the company was running the ad just quoted for stockbrokers, it was searching for secretaries with a classified ad with the headline: "Secretaries, Sales Assistants . . . learn the brokerage business as you expand your skills." The copy noted, "You can acquire valuable, first-hand knowledge of the brokerage business. . . . You're needed to function as a true assistant—providing support for our busy dynamic Account Executives. Your diverse duties will range from typing reports and correspondence to handling client calls."

The ads quoted above are characteristic in that they answer not one but two questions applicants consider vital: "What's in this job for me that I won't find elsewhere?" and "What kind of a company is this as a place to work?" This aspect of the recruiting message is often handled directly with a kind of "testimonial" from individuals who work at the organization.

Argonne National Laboratory, a Chicago area research organization, for example, featured its assistant to the laboratory director in an ad directed to technical people. The assistant, who is also responsible for program planning, talked about the organization's work in fast breeder reactors, biomedical and environmental research, and other technical fields. "What is particularly rewarding about the opportunities provided by these programs is the academic atmosphere in which we work," the copy went on. "A recent comment by our director, Dr. Robert G. Sachs, sums it up well. The Laboratory, he said, is an institution whose only product is knowledge. And the quality of that product is determined by the people in the Laboratory." In a few words, this suggests the kind of working atmosphere in the organization and the attitude it holds toward the people who work there. There was more to come, however, in this ad:

"The opportunity to be individually recognized for accomplishment is another rewarding factor—particularly for women and minority professionals. I think this would be the case at Argonne—that ability would come first—even without our strong equal rights policy. With that policy, and with everyone here behind it, I think we have an even stronger base helping solve some of the most important problems facing our world." The ad then listed the current kinds of openings and provided a picture and brief biographical sketch of the assistant to the director—Dr. Patricia M. Failla.

The Argonne Laboratory ad typifies a good recruitment ad, and how recruitment advertising can not only attract needed people but can successfully reveal to important audiences the company's human resources policies and practices.

Other instances could be cited and recruitment brochures and other recruiting literature dissected, but these examples show that the recruitment message, while performing its function of attracting applicants, is doing a great deal more. It is developing an employer image for the company to make recruiting easier and more cost effective in the future. It is acting as a form of employee communications. It showcases achievements, products, growth, diversity, advanced thinking and other favorable aspects of the organization. And recruitment messages—in what they carry and what they don't—tend to position a company in relation to the human resources revolution.

Not all recruitment messages do all of this all of the time. Some never manage because, even after three decades of experience, there are companies placing hundreds of thousands of dollars worth of recruitment advertising without seeing beyond the immediate function of acquiring people. Many ads are too brief to do more than present the basic idea.

Too many are still written strictly from the company viewpoint and give the reader the feeling of being patronized: "We're a great company; are you qualified to work with us?" Such communications are not attuned to the realities of the 1980s, when there is at least an equal relationship between the company and the applicant and, more often than not, it is the applicant who is in the driver's seat. Listen to the language of a job-seeking engineer about to graduate. "I interviewed Du Pont" is the way the recruiting session is likely to be described, and this aptly expresses the new attitude people are bringing to employment.

Perhaps the basic problem is that recruitment is not seen for what it really is—one of the key elements in a corporation's human resources, an element that, as this chapter has attempted to demonstrate, involves a highly diversified, extensive, and sophisticated communications effort.

CHAPTER EIGHT

The Changing Face of Employee Communications

The Caterpillar Tractor Company wanted to deliver a message to its people at its East Peoria, Illinois, plant. The objective was to reinforce the concept of quality workmanship and to improve communications between management and the hourly employees. A few years ago the accepted method for doing this would have been a special issue of the plant newspaper. But Caterpillar's approach was a fifty-minute audiovisual presentation shown around the clock to reach all the 16,000 people working shifts at the plant. The message was, "You make the difference." Carol Todd Puckett, a company spokesperson, explained in *Industrial Marketing*, a journal of business advertising, "We wanted to stress how each person in the plant directly contributes to the manufacture of a quality product and the importance of paying attention to detail in such a job. We created a strong and favorable impression on our people, and the production worked for us." The presentation featured some of Caterpillar's top executives. "By humanizing management," Ed Breese, the plant manager, recalls, "we were able to set the proper tone for a presentation on quality."

In many ways this Caterpillar presentation exemplifies the changing face of corporate employee communications. First there was the use of a new audiovisual medium rather than the traditional print media; second, the message focused on the worker as an important, contributing individual; third was the relationship to the work that the company does; and fourth it involved "humanizing," as the plant manager termed it, the company's top executives.

Shirley A., a production worker at the SmithKline Corporation, pharmaceutical manufacturers, provides another insight into the changing internal communications scene. During her lunch hour at the company's Philadelphia plant, Shirley spends part of her time watching the television screen. What she sees is far from the midday soap operas of commercial television, however. The program she is watching is one of the daily newscasts prepared by SmithKline communications staff, using in-house TV equipment and presented through an extensive closed circuit television network. Television sets throughout the plants enable employees to learn what's happening in the company and see fellow workers on the screen.

Such programs are a dramatic demonstration of the extent to which corporations today are prepared to make substantial investments in new technology to maintain a dialogue with their employees and keep them informed. It also suggests that these communications have become, as one communications director puts it, "employee media," more informal but created with something of the same quality and objectivity as the regular working press.

Just as we still read a daily paper even though we watch TV, employee newspapers have by no means vanished. But in most organizations today house organs have taken up the trend toward frankness. They focus on genuine company issues and avoid the company propaganda that stultified so much of past employee communications. Where such an approach doesn't exist, a new phenomenon is being reported— "underground" employee publications issued surreptitiously as a counter to the "company line."

THE NEW VIEW

Spurred by the changes identified here as the human resources revolution, the new era of employee communications is one in which the company meets the work force directly, talks face-to-face with union leaders, lets everyone in on political or legislative issues that directly concern the company and hence its workers, and presents management executives as people. As Lawrence Parkus of Westinghouse Learning Corporation observes, this is one of the best solutions to the growing problem of employee alienation. "Corporations know their communications have to work and they believe it can be done," he says. "But they often fear doing it. 'We don't want to waste time' is a common reaction." As an example of a company that lets its employees in on issues, Parkus cites one of the major computer manufacturers. "The company, which faced an anti-trust action," he notes, "informed every member of the organization, in groups, about the issues involved and what they might mean to the company and the individual."

Supporting the growing realization that today's employees have special information needs in keeping with the growing participatory trend in the work place is a survey by Syracuse University. This study of some 2,000 corporations confirms that employee publications, as one aspect of the employee-directed spectrum of corporate communications, have indeed changed.

Personal items, the former staple of house organs, are no longer of ranking importance according to the Syracuse findings. Gone, too, are the trite "messages from the president" on upholding the free enterprise system. The new and growing trend, the survey finds, is the independence and professionalism of the company newspaper staff. They are being removed from the circle of personnel or public relations, where they usually ranked low in the hierarchy, and given independent status. Often they report directly to a high-level executive.

This, too, is indicative of the changes now in process with regard to human resources communications as a whole. It is also significant that according to the survey even personal talks and meetings are today considered, along with print, as aspects of employee communications. One result of this recognition has been an extensive proliferation of messages and media directed to company people.

TURNING UP THE VOLUME

One indication of the extent of corporate communications is an estimate that the circulation of printed matter to employees is about 215 million copies at any given time or about four times the total of daily newspaper circulation. Company newspapers in large corporations are reported to exceed 50,000 copies per issue, for example, to which can be added company magazines, notices, newsletters, memos, and many other kinds of print materials.

Part of the reason is that there are many new kinds of information companies want to or must communicate to their people. Some involve compliance with federal law, as for example the requirement that all employees covered by pension plans be given a plain language description of these as mandated by ERISA. In the recent past companies told their people only what, as they saw it, employees "needed to know". This attitude has been largely abandoned. It has been replaced by a desire to communicate about attitudes, as in the Caterpillar presentation; to present news on current developments relating to the company, as SmithKline does; to discuss company achievements, marketing problems, productivity, equal employment, and an almost encyclopedic list of other topics, on a two-way basis if possible.

Training today, and the communications programs it requires, is also more extensive and more continuous than in the past. As the human resources revolution and social change continue to affect corporations in diverse ways, these generate still other company communications. This contributes to the trend away from a single kind of internal medium and toward enlisting many kinds of communications techniques.

Mobil Oil Company provides a good working example. Public attacks against oil companies have caused Mobil to look to its human resources as a major line of defense in terms of public attitudes. To check on its strength, the company had an attitude survey of its people made by an outside organization. This survey disclosed, as expected, that the Mobil employees are tremendously loyal and supportive. "But we also learned that our people didn't have enough information to speak out with authority," says Mobil's vice president for employee relations, Peter Krist. "We also found real communications bottlenecks at the supervisory level, the management group from whom employees preferred to get the facts they wanted."

As a result the company, with management involvement, promptly developed an intensive program for employee communications. It reoriented publications to reflect the diversity of interests, needs, and education of its work force. It expanded bulletin boards, used posters and videotapes, and named communications coordinators in working units. Mobil also began question-and-answer sessions between workers and senior executives, sometimes including company directors, which were taped and shown at company facilities around the world, even on offshore drilling rigs.

THE MULTIFACETED EMPLOYEE

This multimedia approach by Mobil characterizes the sophistication that forward-looking corporations are building into their employee communications, and demonstrates their increased recognition of employees as people who play multiple roles both in and outside the work place.

Al H., for example, is a shop floor steward for his union, a skilled machinist, an advocate of safety and productivity within his work group, a company emissary and recruiter in the community. An ardent outdoorsman, he is a member of local and national environmental organizations, a vice president of the school's PTA, and he is encouraging his oldest daughter to consider a career in engineering.

Bob W. is an MBA, the company's new assistant controller, and a candidate for the zoning board of his suburban town. He commutes to work with friends from a half-dozen major corporations, is the neighbor of a high-level figure in a Wall Street financial house, and plays tennis with the financial writer for a leading business magazine.

Jane C. is an employment executive, a working mother, a volunteer for the local Urban League, an officer in the League of Women Voters, and as the right-hand person to a company vice president of personnel she is privy to many of the policies and practices of her company's management.

These people are targets for human resources communications, not only from their companies but also from external organizations. They are audiences for concerns as diverse as union plans for shorter working hours, corporate desires to establish new facilities and political candidates with programs that may affect their company's taxes or manufacturing processes.

WHAT'S THE MESSAGE?

What are the messages companies are trying to get to their employees today?

"I would say," says a vice president of a large New York bank, "that quality of working life is the most major and the most general communications problem." A corporate manager believes, "It is vital to get over to employees that productivity is the name of the game. If we can't compete, whether with foreign imports or other United States companies, then we go under and their jobs go with us. It's as simple as that." "No, it's not a matter of a particular message," muses an executive in charge of her company's internal communications. "The basic problem is one of developing believability. Company communications are still seen as biased and self-serving. So long as that attitude exists, the company isn't communicating, because nobody out there is receiving the message."

A look at the nature of the information that corporations are providing their employees suggests that all three are right. More spontaneity is showing up, reflecting a more relaxed attitude among editors who are allowed to present contrary viewpoints, survey reader opinions, and respond to employee complaints and questions. In some instances this may extend to reporting on improper behavior by company people, including managers. News such as the foreign bribery scandals is likely to show up in national and local periodicals anyway. But there may be specific reports of troubles with government agencies, or stories about defects that have shown up in company products. Such frankness on once taboo subjects helps build more confidence in other company messages. It also coincides with what people really do want to know.

A survey by Professor David Bateman of Southern Illinois University at Carbondale turned up some data as to what the employees of one large Midwestern manufacturer wanted to hear about. The messages that interested them weren't cartoons, recipes, executive promotion, or the status of the United Fund drive.

What these employees wanted first was information about new or improved company products. They were interested in fringe benefits programs, how sales were going, what other departments and divisions were doing, how company products were being used, business trends, the competition, and the company's stand on union issues—subjects that would not be out of place in the *Wall Street Journal.*

Some of these responses reflect one of the basic problems in the modern work place: the isolation of individual workers from the end products of their work. As this concern with work and the company is becoming recognized, companies are responding in various ways. One of the most original and effective responses was that of a company making mine safety equipment. A relatively small firm, it bundled most of its work force into a fleet of buses and transported them to a coal mine 200 miles away. There company people talked to miners whose lives depended on the equipment they produced, and visited the mine to see it in use. The effect upon morale, pride of workmanship, and quality control is said to have been enormous.

Since images are easier to move than people, motion pictures and videotapes are showing employees how the products and services in which they are involved are actually used by customers, many of whom are pictured commenting on the products. One company helps its work force to be abreast of new products by showing them previews of company commercials on the organization's closed circuit television system. A major auto maker provides two kinds of previews for its dealerships, linked by a video cassette network. Dealers and salespeople get TV tapes that demonstrate the new models before information on them is released to the public. At the same time the dealers' mechanics get cassettes instructing them in the maintenance and repair work the new models will require. No doubt these latter tapes are helpful, since information about the job, ways of working, and career data are among the messages that companies find have great appeal to employees and lead to improved performance.

When the First National Bank of Nevada, for example, learned that communications with both customers and employees were not doing well because both lacked the human touch, it instituted a new in-house program called "Communications and Selling Skills." At a "Top Performers Workshop," tellers and other customer-contact people with outstanding records offered their ideas and opinions. Then upper management took part in a "Personal Effectiveness Workshop," at which the opinions of the first workshop were reviewed through videotapes made at the time and management views were added. In typical current multimedia fashion, learning materials were developed including a handbook, visual aids, and audio cassette tapes. Branch managers attended learning sessions and engaged in role-playing, alternating as customers and employees. Reported results from the program ranged from positive to enthusiastic.

As noted earlier internal recruiting is very much a part of the corporate scene today, a further reaction to the human resources revolution. One unusual example of the use of the employee newspaper as a recruiting vehicle occurred at Lockheed Aircraft Service. There a special edition of the company paper was devoted to openings in the company's operations in Iran. This not only described in detail the kinds of openings but stressed that the nature of the assignments were such that only some people should consider them. Among other points the paper stressed that working in a 2500-year-old culture was not for those who felt uncomfortable without the products of the local supermarket, nor was it the place for a fresh start after a broken marriage.

Career information of a less exotic nature is a regular element in corporate communications today. Professor Fred K. Foulkes, of the Harvard Business School, mentioned some elements of these communications programs in discussing "The Expanding Role of the Personnel Function" in the *Harvard Business Review*. "The organization can help employees develop by making various growth aids available," he observes. "For a number of years, Polaroid and other companies have engaged in career counseling and have recently begun career development workshops. At these voluntary workshops, individuals are given tools to help them better evaluate their own abilities and interests as well as information about various jobs and career possibilities within the company."

At its Greenwich headquarters, American Can has recently established a "Job Information Center" so that employees there can drop in at convenient times, study the information on current openings and their requirements, and discuss with the counselor who operates the center the jobs they find of interest, how to apply for them, or how to prepare to qualify for them.

Dealing with Change

From what has been discussed here, it is obvious that one kind of information companies are making available to their people these days has to do with handling change. This may be a change on the personnel level, as in the orientation, training, and retirement counseling programs we will look at later. It is also likely to include material on the social and economic changes occurring in our society and the issues these raise.

Mobil Corporation's program for dealing with attacks on the oil industry exemplifies this type of message. Northeast Utilities, as another example, puts out a newsletter entitled "Where NU Stands," to keep its employees informed on the company's positions in the complex economics and politics of the highly regulated utilities industry. American Can Company makes use of speeches by corporate officers, neatly packaged in booklet size for ready mailing to employees and other audiences.

Companies have found that motivated employees can do an effective lobbying job. It was largely an employee campaign, for instance, that countered a threat to the development of nuclear energy in California and a loss of jobs in that state. They have also found that employee audiences want to know about issues closer to home. Traditionally such sensitive company developments as the closing of a plant have been officially ignored in internal communications, although the company grapevine and outside news media seldom failed to fill the gap. Now the trend is toward openness on such problems. Sherwin Williams, for example, not only reported on the closing of one of its operations but explained why and described what happened to the workers who were affected. Northwestern Bell Telephone, going into contract negotiations with its union, conducted an intensive survey among its employees to find out what bargaining issues they wished to have raised. The results, fed back from the negotiating table to both management and union representatives, helped ease tension and resulted in a rapid resolution of the talks.

In sum, the corporate message is becoming diverse, responsive, flexible, and heterogeneous. Companies have recognized the spirit if not the scope of the human resources revolution, and have pitched their messages to employees accordingly. They no longer for the most part strive officiously to thrust a company viewpoint upon their employees; the trend instead is to present the facts of business life realistically, with the recognition that American workers have long since come of age, and have done so, moreover, in a culture which has deluged them with information from a variety of the amazing new tools of this Communications Age.

A LOOK AT THE COMMUNICATIONS TOOLS

Tubes and Tapes

After decades in which internal communications were limited to personal meetings, management speeches, and a house organ of often staggering banality, the past few years have seen communications fireworks erupt in the business sector. Companies have borrowed for their own use some of the most sophisticated new information technologies and generated whole new classes of internal communications.

Of these tools, closed circuit television is perhaps the most impressive. Literally scores of companies today have such systems and are using them in different ways, even including in-company news shows. Bethlehem Steel does two a day, "Nine Minutes" and "Nine Minutes Plus." New England Mutual Life Insurance has a video program that substitutes for the company magazine. Pratt & Whitney, a division of United Technologies Corporation, has recently launched its own video news system and invites employee critiques.

Employees see not only the daily news that affects them and the company through these systems but the program shows how company products have been developed, how customers use company products, and they sometimes see themselves in taped panel shows in which employees discuss company affairs. Bank of America has a video system installed in its branches throughout California. "It is more useful and appealing to employees away from the home office," says one executive, "because it helps eliminate their feeling of being cut off from the main center of company life."

In even broader use is the new technology of the video cassette. Programs are put on tape via company television facilities, then the tapes are duplicated and sent out to any number of locations. Videotape machines, which have just begun to be retailed to consumers, play back the tapes through a standard television set at each facility.

One company using this method of employee communications is Standard Oil Company of California. Each month it sends a thirty-minute color video cassette to its many operations. These feature management people discussing significant issues and topics relating to the company. Standard says that after this program began it found that many of its employees, armed with the information provided, began to defend company and industry practices to people both inside and outside the company. Each of these taped programs costs about $500 to produce and the cassettes (reusable, by the way) go to twenty-eight domestic and foreign locations. The only obstacles are the limited number of playback units available and management's concern that the program doesn't reach enough employees.

The Xerox Corporation's "Private Network" is one of the oldest tape networks now in existence, having been started by that technologically minded organization in 1973. Then its primary audience was about 15,000 sales and service people. The company estimates that in the first year of this program, the use of videotape saved 20 percent of what conventional materials would have cost to do the same job. Now the network, operating out of Rochester, has 300 Sony U-matic systems installed in 200 widely scattered locations throughout the United States. Its primary audience is now 22,000, with a potential audience of the corporation's entire work force of some 65,000 people. The company also uses the system to prepare sales tapes seen by visitors who come to the company's sales locations.

Equitable Life Assurance Society of the United States, another communications-conscious corporation, has been using video for employee communications for about ten years. It, too, established a tape network in 1973. A large percentage of the network's forty yearly programs consists of motivational and informational training, including a highly effective "How I Do It" series in which key people demonstrate exactly how they work in the field. General Motors Corporation puts career information on video cassettes for employee viewing and includes a self-assessment exercise with the tape.

Video is obviously an employee communications tool whose time has come. Other audiovisual innovations, such as the new Super-8 sound films and projectors, are also contributing to the broader use of sophisticated but low-cost company films. These methods tend to be highly effective when well done because they reach employee audiences who are products of the television age and relate more readily to images than to print.

Playing It by Ear

To a lesser degree audio tape is finding a niche in employee communications. Typical of its usage is the AT&T Long Lines Division's "Dial U" program. Employees can dial internal phone numbers to get information on personal, medical, consumer, and business subjects. Each tape is from two to five minutes long, and other internal media notify employees about the material available.

Companies are also tending to bring in outside speakers to address large groups of their employees. Often this is on a community basis, with congressional representatives or officeholders invited. Bendix Corporation took a different tack, according to Al Moorhead, former vice president for personnel. "We invited Gloria Steinem, the feminist leader and writer," he recalls. "She was asked to speak by Mike Blumenthal, then Bendix's chief executive. She had a good audience and talked to them about industry's responsibility to women and women's responsibility to industry."

Talking to company people in small groups as a means of involving them personally in company problems or projects is also being more widely used as a communications technique. This stems from recognition of the employee's desire to be on the inside, to be informed and to be consulted, and the pay-offs in response that this can bring.

An unusual variation of this kind of personal involvement has been developed by Boeing Company of Wichita, which calls it a "strategy center." This is a readily accessible room in the company's plant where descriptions of company problems are posted. The problems are set up on the walls in specific and definite categories, such as "shop arrangement" or "equipment use." All of them are real company problems which employees themselves have submitted. Employees visit the center as they wish. The idea of the strategy center is to convey the problems to others in the company who might have a solution, either from past experience or as the result of a bright new idea. When solutions are implemented, the progress is also charted in the center.

Innovations in Print

Two old friends meet on a downtown street in their Connecticut city.

"Well, Stan, how're you doing?" asks one.

"Fine, George, "You keeping busy?"

"Boy, are we," says Stan. "Did you know that last year was the biggest sales year in the company's history?"

"Well, I heard you were doing pretty well."

"Well" exclaims Stan, "Our sales volume was up 23 percent from last year."

"Really?" says George, "How come?"

"Two things. We've started to market a new model that involves solid state circuitry—cuts the operating costs to about a third of the older model. And we've opened up a new marketing area in the Pacific, from Japan to Australia. Pushed up our net income by about 12 percent."

"Well, gotta run along," says George, bemused by his friend's grasp of business matters. "Hang in there."

"Right," says Stan, "Take it easy."

He walks off, thinking to himself, "Reading the old annual report is worthwhile. There aren't many shipping clerks who know that much about their company."

This dialogue is fictional, of course, and, you may add, highly unlikely. For as we know, employees don't read annual reports. Or at least they didn't. Now a new trend is emerging in employee print communications: the employee annual report. It may not inspire employees to lard casual conversations with company statistics, but it appears to be an effective means of providing a picture of what's happening to the company in financial terms—and much else. There are a variety of approaches now in use.

Phillips Petroleum, for instance, simply uses its regular annual report, printing a special letter from its chairman inside the front cover. Addressed to "Fellow Employees of Phillips and its Subsidiaries," the letter points out the specific sections of the report that are meaningful for workers in the company. Ralston Purina prepared a separate employee annual report with financial explanations and illustrations plus an interview with the chief executive. This report also gives major attention to employees, with some biographical short features. In addition a government economist reviews government regulations that affect the company and its work force.

"An Armchair Safari Through the Annual Report" is the tack that

Pfizer Incorporated takes, commenting in print that its report isn't for CPAs but for the employees "who made it all happen."

Typical material in this new form of employee communications (which is also called "jobholder reports," as an analog to shareholder reports), includes company employment and trends, material on the company as a socially responsible organization, company goals and accomplishments, new facilities and products, an analysis of the company's income and expenditures, and often commentary on some of the problems the company faces in its operations.

Pitney-Bowes takes the jobholder report concept a step further. This company not only provides its employees with annual jobholder reports, but follows up with annual jobholder meetings comparable to the company's annual meetings with shareholders. Rather than being centralized, however, they are held at various company facilities. "The workers' questions are much more knowledgeable and comprehensive than questions at stockholder meetings," says Fred T. Allen, the chief executive officer, who has given more than half the company's 18,000 employees the chance to talk with top management at one or another of these sessions. Questions by employees range from complaints about a disliked cafeteria clock to productivity, pensions, and competition from foreign technology, reports *The New York Times* in writing about this new form of human resources communication.

Pitney-Bowes ranks its effort highly. "There is no substitute for talking face-to-face," Allen told the company's jobholders. "These meetings are one of the most important activities of the year. They tell us how you feel about how the company is being run."

INTERFACING

The Pitney-Bowes jobholder meetings are not only innovative but typify another major direction in internal human resources communications—the drive to achieve dialogues within the company between workers and management, to achieve an interface between the people who do and the people who direct.

"One reason for this," says Sanford Browde, vice president of administration and personnel for Litton's Monroe Company, "is the sheer dispersal of company facilities among today's corporations. Our own company, for example, has some 350 locations. We rely heavily on our branch superintendents to provide feedback on what's happening at each plant, and this in turn involves the company employees in the branches. Such communication is essential."

Don Lester of General Electric's Aircraft Engine Group emphasizes the "two-way" aspects of internal communications. "Because of the nature of our product, aircraft engines, high quality is absolutely vital to the product because human life can be directly affected. Simply on technical grounds, therefore, we need continuous feedback from our employees and our technical people. There is a high level of sensitivity here to these exchanges. We're unique, I think, in having what we call a 'red alert' system built into our communications whereby the whole process of information exchange can be speeded up if urgent communication is required either way." He notes, too, the importance of maintaining personal contact, which his organization does through a Boss Talk program in which each manager gives periodic status reports to all employees. This General Electric group has also introduced a new and relatively rare element to the interface between employees and management, which will be discussed shortly.

As with other aspects of communication today, the effort to establish working two-way communications with employees often requires a multimedia approach. General American Life Insurance Company has a program in which employees are free to comment on their first-level management. They also are given walking tours of the company facilities conducted by management people, and suggestion awards, among other devices.

The old standby of communications, the suggestion system, is not only alive and well at General American but is so widespread that it has its own trade association, the National Association of Suggestion Systems. This organization reports that use of the suggestion system continues to increase, although special forms have long replaced the old "idea box" on the wall and some companies have full-time staffs to handle the system. This involves additional employee communications, incidentally, since the workings of the system require posters and other media to prompt participation, publicity for the winners, and cash awards for accepted ideas.

The employee referral systems reported in the previous chapter constitute another ongoing kind of interface, this time with the employees representing the company to outside job prospects as well as being involved with their manager and other executives. Training programs are another area of interface, as are the various job safety, productivity, and other drives that bring managers and employees together in situations that can involve two-way information exchanges.

New Systems for Interfacing

Beyond these familiar and widely used methods, however, new systems are coming into use that aim at maintaining continuous two-way communications channels.

The Xerox Corporation, for example, has instituted a very direct and simple system of expediting the flow from bottom to top. Any Xerox employee, at any time, can direct a written question to the company's chairman, Peter McColough. "Direct" is the operative word, since employees can submit whatever they want to say on the forms provided without clearing it with anyone, including their own boss in the chain of command. Further, the employee needn't sign the questions or comments. Response to the questions come in the form of an answer in the Xerox monthly employee paper.

Corporate newspapers, picking up a technique from their newsstand counterparts, have been creating "action line" columns to which employees can write with problems that bother them. Answers appear from appropriate executives in the company, discussing the subject raised and what the firm may be doing about the employee's concern. The "hot line" telephone which reaches a high-level executive instead of an informative tape recording has been introduced in some organizations, Bendix, for example. There the hot line goes directly to the president's office and workers may give their names or not on these calls, as they choose. Allen Moorhead notes, "I think the workers at Bendix are responsive to these efforts to give them a practical voice in the company's operations. Two-way communications are vital, and ideally, should take the form of continuing discussions at all levels."

Putting two-way discussions into practice is another idea gaining ground in industry's attempt to humanize its operations and its executives. One organization active in this area is General American Life Insurance. Each month twelve employees selected at random are invited to meet with the company's president, Armand C. Stainaker, to participate in question-and-answer sessions. Each of these people—a monthly "advisory panel," the company calls them—submits one or two questions on company activities, policies, or problem areas that they feel should be brought to top management's attention. General American believes this approach is working well as a key "listening post," monitoring attitudes, feelings, and values among its employees.

Worker councils, rap sessions with employees and their immediate and second-level managers, and the jobholders' meetings mentioned earlier are all techniques that respond to the concern of the new work force for information. They stem from a new kind of management that does not govern on an authoritarian, "theirs not to reason why" basis.

One innovation in extending two-way communications is in action at General Electric's Aircraft Engine Group in the form of an "ombudsman". This idea, imported from Europe, is in turn an apparent adaptation of the military "Inspector General" function. The ombudsman—in General Electric's case an ombudswoman, Peggy McAllister—must have two characteristics: one is that he or she be open to the entire work force. Anyone must be able to resort to the ombudsperson with a problem that cannot be handled through the traditional lines of communication, that is, through one's immediate superiors. The other is having leverage within the organization to get action clearing up inequities, resolving conflicts, and otherwise arriving at a satisfactory conclusion.

A typical problem involving the ombudsperson would be a conflict existing between a subordinate and boss, a situation from which the subordinate finds it difficult to appeal. Ms. McAllister notes that the appeals that have come to her have included such subjects as job search, pay, performance appraisal, displacements, lack of work, management practices, benefits, working conditions, and health. She feels that the ombudsman function reaches people on levels that tend to be deeper than other forms of corporate communications. "There is often pain, anxiety, frustration, discontent, bitterness, and unhappiness behind the appeals," she says. "Such feelings are dysfunctional. They invariably have a negative effect on performance. Often a person's associates are contaminated in the process. Resolving the issues, therefore, can and most often does have a salutary effect on performance."

EMPLOYEE COMMUNICATIONS TODAY: BROADER, DEEPER, MULTIMEDIA

The impact of the human resources revolution can readily be seen in this abbreviated review of the function once identified as employee communications, symbolized by the house organ and suggestion box. Today the trend appears to be toward a broader spectrum of communications to accommodate the many roles that the workers themselves have now assumed within the corporate context. This variety reflects the extent to which workers outside the work place are exposed to a multimedia, information society, part of the post-industrial economy into which we are moving.

Our society is moving also toward a humanization of the work place to more closely resemble the normal living environment, rather than the giant machine which has for generations been the implicit ideal in structuring the working environment.

The new directions in employee communications appear to stem from a greater recognition of the findings of behavioral scientists who emphasize that participatory decision making greatly increases the acceptance of decisions. The effective use of these new methods, involving employees and establishing effective two-way interchange of ideas, may also be a long-term answer to the litigious employee. Communication in the work place, in other words, seems to be emerging as a valid alternative to litigation.

CHAPTER NINE

Reaching Special Company Audiences

The broadscale efforts that companies make to acquaint their work forces with information relevant to them and, in turn, to get feedback from their employees, could be compared roughly with the function of such national newsmagazines as *Newsweek* in the world outside the company. Both are concerned with providing a broad coverage of relevant news to a diversified and extensive general audience.

In most large corporations there is a second layer of general communications, directed to a given division or facility. When the divisions themselves are large and divided into further units, there may be a third layer of general communications as well to serve these smaller units. Such second- and third-level communications can be compared to the daily newspapers reaching specific cities, and to the smaller weekly papers that serve the suburbs and neighborhoods of these cities.

Another and different stratum of company communications also exists. This aspect of human resources communications is somewhat like the professional journals, trade papers, and special interest magazines and newsletters which flourish in the outside world. These reach company audiences on a selective rather than a general basis and carry information relevant only to special audiences. Although these metaphoric examples relate only to print media, the internal communications programs themselves may comprise a variety of communications techniques.

THE SPECIAL AUDIENCES

Specialized media reach specific audiences within the company which vary broadly in size and makeup. One corporation found it of value to prepare a videotaped report for the use of just four people in the organization. At the other end of the range, the special audiences may be thousands of production workers, hundreds of engineers, or an entire sales staff.

A person may be a member of a special audience in relation to level of experience within the company, from a new entry-level trainee to an employee facing retirement. Many of these audiences are ad hoc, created by common situations within the company—a group of people being fired, for example. Others may share common personal denominators relating to their work. They have similar problems, perhaps, or common ethnic backgrounds. The audience also may be a product of the hierarchical organization of the company, for example, first-line supervision, or related by a common job function such as secretaries or engineers.

These special audiences will change from company to company and within the company in a free-flowing way, as the organization adapts its communications to meet specific needs. Any single employee is likely to be part of one or more of these special audiences and to get from the company not only the general kinds of information implied by the term "employee communication," but more specific information relative to any of the multiple roles he or she may have.

All of us who work are aware of being targets for such specialized communications, whether they are posters on the production floor exhorting us to support a zero defects program or a memo on saving energy from the front office. We take such communication for granted in our own areas of work. They provide data or information or directions that we need in relation to our jobs. A staff meeting or a seminar may alert us to changes and prepare us to cope with them. We're not likely to identify these things consciously as human resources communications, but that's what they are, since they relate to us in our various employee roles.

Further, this kind of specialized communication appears to be an element of growing importance. In part this is because companies have begun to respond to the perceived demand by their people for more and better information about their working world, and in part because the human resources revolution has added new subjects and new audiences.

EXPERIENCE LEVELS AND
COMMUNICATIONS

"The recruiting effort created a pretty favorable image of the company," the newly minted chemical engineer comments. "I was wined and dined and had several interviews with their managers, and I got the idea that they were really concerned with their engineering staff. Once I was hired though, it was a pretty unpleasant surprise. I was just tossed onto a board job with very little briefing. The engineers I was working with seemed to have no clear idea about what was happening in the company. There wasn't any written material I could use to get a real handle on how the company operates. My only real information source was my boss—and he was too busy most of the time. Frankly, he couldn't answer what I thought were fairly basic questions. Nobody seemed to care whether I was with the company or not. So, after a few weeks, I just moved on—sadder and wiser, as they say."

The company should also have been sadder and wiser. It had invested several thousand dollars in competing for the engineer, and that investment was wasted. The engineer's story will be on the professional grapevine, which won't help the company's image among other technical people and so will push up the cost of recruiting. The slot he left has to be refilled from a highly competitive job market. It would have been wiser to give more attention to orienting new people as a means of decreasing turnover and making them productive sooner.

Welcome Aboard: Orientation and
Communication

Most corporations have some kind of orientation communications for new employees. Most familiar of these is the "welcome to" booklet that outlines basic data about how the company operates in relationship to its employees. These are brass tacks brochures, vetted by the legal department, describing in bland and sometimes opaque details the company medical program, benefits, working times, and other basic facts. Tours of facilities are another common kind of orientation procedure, usually conducted formally in groups or informally for individuals, depending on company size and the entrant's function in it.

In response to the demands for more information surfacing among workers, organizations are adding materials and media to this orientation process. The executive of an electronics company says,

> "When people take a job with us, we think they come to the job with certain expectations. It's a kind of honeymoon period and a good time to

resell them on the company. So we try, right from the beginning, to put them into the picture. We've got a film that shows a lot of the company's products in use. It was made originally for the sales department, but we've adapted it as an orientation on the technical side of the work here. Then we've got some blowups of charts and maps that show the various locations of the company and what they do. One of the company executives gives a talk to each group of new people and tells them about the company philosophy and why we do things the way we do. I've had a lot of favorable comments on the program. Most people just didn't know how many kinds of products we produce, or realize how the company contributes to community projects."

Part of the function of orientation is simply helping new graduates adapt to the vastly different environment of work. Says the personnel director of a Midwest manufacturing company,

"We get a lot of people fresh out of high school, and everything is new to them. So we spend several hours on the first day just showing them how the plant is organized, and where the facilities are, like the lunchroom, and answering their questions about pay, sick leave, and insurance. Then we have a buddy system, so that each new person has someone with more experience to go to with questions. And the people in my department try to follow up personally with each individual during the first six weeks, just to check with them and see how they're doing. It really pays off. Our turnover has dropped since we started this program, and we have people coming in to apply for jobs because of what new people tell them about working here."

Every operation has its own ways of doing things to which new people, however experienced, need to be introduced. At Dow Chemical Corporation a special committee was formed in the company's research laboratory to develop the means for orienting newly hired engineers and scientists to company procedures. It produced "The Inside Track," a loose-leaf book providing guidelines on how to get things done, from using the company library to getting a capital authorization.

For recent technical graduates joining its engineering staff, General Electric's Aircraft Engine Group created a "Dirty Fingernails Engineering" manual which Don Lester, manager of group organization and manpower, describes as "a rather elaborate real world orientation." This is aimed at helping graduates make the transition from academic work to the real world of engineering. Within it are materials of a highly practical nature covering such areas as engine test exposure, product teardown and buildup, and handling on-the-line field assignments from commercial and military customers.

The same General Electric operation has developed another kind of orientation program, according to Lester.

> "In addition to basic orientation, we have developed a process for a more extensive assimilation of a new manager or a new member into the work force. Surprisingly enough, we call it 'the new manager or member assimilation process'. It's basically aimed at facilitating membership rather than just providing knowledge of what the outfit is about. The process is planned and facilitated generally by one of our organization and manpower professionals, and involves identifying what the existing group knows about the new member, what they think they know, what they would like to know—and reciprocally, what the new members know, think they know, and would like to know about the group they are joining. Since it's a fairly elaborate process, we are resource-limited in its application, but slowly we are developing and operating a manager resource that's equipped to conduct assimilations without organization and manpower involvement."

Orientation programs have also proved useful as a means of acquainting new employees with human resources factors. In the employee's working cycle with the company, this is the time to emphasize company commitment to such policies as affirmative action, to demonstrate aids to upward mobility such as job posting, and to set forth the company's program relating to education, training, and development.

Training and Development: Pragmatic Communications

In most organizations training and development is a single distinct function, often associated with the personnel department. While it is not labeled as such and is not often thought of in that way, a corporation's training and development programs, which reach all levels of the company's work force, are often the most intensive human resources communications program within the organization. The training and development staff by the nature of their work are essentially communicators. They usually command the most sophisticated communications equipment within the company. The end product, essential to the organization, is a person prepared to do a particular job or to do it better—that is, a company human resource.

The role of training and development needs little recapitulation here. It is essential to organizations as a means of coping with changes, technical and social. It is also a means to meet human resources goals, such as upward mobility. Training often begins for a worker immediately after entering the company, and may proceed in the form of development programs throughout the employee's working life. Much of the communications materials for this purpose are created within the company itself. Company people may also be trained by outside organizations. The manufacturers of complex business machines, for example, usually also provide the necessary training to operate them. The company which buys computing or word processing equipment sends its people to the manufacturer's training courses as part of the purchase agreement.

Universities, organizations such as the American Management Associations, community colleges, and even consortiums of local employers provide out-of-company training and development. Alternatively the company may pay for the services of outside experts who come in to run special types of training programs.

An entire industry, in fact, now exists to provide training equipment and services. Such major corporations as Xerox and Westinghouse Electric Corporation have established divisions devoted to creating and selling training systems and materials for use by other organizations. IBM is one of the leaders in computer-aided education which permits direct contact between student and computer, the computer enacting the role of the patient and tireless tutor to scores of students simultaneously through its separate terminals.

A number of universities are now cooperating with individual companies to offer university courses for employees by means of closed circuit television from the campus. Companies also use their own internal video capabilities for training—taping salespeople making a presentation, for example, and then criticizing them during a playback. People as different as assemblers and corporate presidents make use of videotape to improve their performances on the job. Management Resources, Inc., is a New York-based organization employing audio cassettes as part of a teaching package which companies can buy and distribute to their managers to learn about important new areas, such as managing in a world in which conventional lines of authority don't count.

Training and development programs are also noted not only for introducing advanced hardware into corporate communications but for bringing new psychological ideas into the business field. Role playing, transactional analysis, and similar tools have become familiar to the newer generation of business people as a means of improving on-the-job performance. Concepts such as management by objectives, and zero base budgeting, introduced as new ideas, are rapidly translated into classroom programs within business and applied to working situations with a speed that more conventional educational techniques cannot match.

Training in business and industry is also responsible to a significant degree for the changing occupational demographics of the work force. The tendency in industry, when craft workers of various kinds are in short supply, is to create new ones—new welders, machinists, or whatever might be needed through extensive in-plant training programs. Curtiss-Wright, for example, needed welders to work to the exacting standards of the nuclear field. Unable to locate them in sufficient numbers, it established a training program at its northern New Jersey location and converted people with general welding experience into nuclear welding specialists by means of a several-week training course. The role of the business machine companies in turning out programmers and other specialists has been noted. They have also created large numbers of experienced technical maintenance people trained to keep the complex machines operating. It is also through the training function, as has been noted in an earlier chapter, that business attempts to remedy the shortcomings of the American educational system by remedial courses—to bring employees up to the standards required in the basics of reading, writing, and arithmetic.

Outplacement: Out But Not Down

If the constant induction of new workers into a company's work force, and the constant need to train, are facts of life in the business world, so is the need to let people go—sometimes a few individuals, sometimes hundreds or even thousands of workers. At one time fired employees were very much on their own. It did not matter that their jobs were terminated because the company was retrenching or restructuring rather than through their own fault. The company door closed behind them and that was that. The human resources revolution, however, has begun to change this situation.

"AVAILABLE: THREE HUNDRED WELL-TRAINED PEOPLE WITH VARIETY OF PRODUCTION SKILLS," the ad in the business section of the newspaper reads. It has been placed not by an employment agency but by a corporation—the company that has fired the 300 people whose skills it is advertising. This large, attention-getting advertisement details the kinds of skills they have, the reasons the company is releasing them, and how to reach the company's personnel department in order to set up in-plant interviews. Such "decruiting" ads turn up from time to time in the *Los Angeles Times,* the *Chicago Tribune,* and other newspapers throughout the country. Recruiters who follow them up often find that the company also has worked with the individuals being fired to help them develop resumes, which are provided on request to interested potential employers. Employment agencies have been alerted to the availability of the people who have been let go. The company's personnel department has called major employers in the area who may have an interest in them.

This new procedure is called "outplacement". It stems from an increased corporate sensitivity toward its work force, and the public and community response to mass layoffs. One recent example is provided by Rockwell International's Los Angeles Division. There, Employment Manager Gilberto H. Espinosa developed a massive outplacement effort when the 1977 cancellation of the B-1 bomber program resulted in the elimination of more than 8,000 jobs. As we will see, this kind of assistance is also provided when companies close down their facilities, resulting in local unemployment. The communications methods involved in the process are similar to those in recruiting, but with a reverse twist. Ads, personal contacts with other companies, internal communications, cooperation with available placement services of government and other organizations—all these are used to *place* workers rather than *hire* them.

Nor is outplacement limited to situations in which the company is firing people en masse. More often than is generally recognized, when a company today makes a decision to terminate a $35,000-a-year manager, for whatever reason, it will hire an outplacement consultant to assist the executive in locating a new job. John Erdlen, secretary of the Employment Management Association and himself an experienced outplacement specialist, says, "Often the work is on a one-to-one basis. The idea is not simply to locate possible openings for the person, but to provide the necessary preparation that will enable the executive to function effectively in the job search. He has to understand what it involves, be counseled on how to put his best foot forward in interviews and on paper, and maintain confidence in himself while the search goes on. In addition, of course, the consultant helps him research the current market for his talent, and advises him on such matters as compensation patterns."

Outplacement, Erdlen believes, is coming into wider use because its advantages to the company as well as to the individual are being recognized. "There is a distinct morale factor in realizing that you're with a company that won't simply throw you to the wolves if something goes wrong. Having an outplacement policy is also of considerable assistance in recruiting, particularly at higher managerial levels. A good candidate is more likely to opt for a company that will help find a different job if things don't work out. I've even heard that provision for outplacement assistance is being written into employment contracts for some kinds of jobs—purchasing executives, for example."

As human resources communications, outplacement ads and other efforts are not only functional in placing discharged company people in new jobs, they also convey a favorable image of the company to its own work force and to outside audiences such as the business community.

Preretirement Counseling: The Long Goodbye

Increased attention is being given to workers who are approaching retirement age, although what constitutes retirement age is in some doubt these days. Outplacement is a kind of reverse image of recruiting. Preretirement counseling is a communications area that parallels orientation, but in this case the orientation is toward a new life-style outside the work place. The current emphasis on this kind of human resources communications stems from the changing conditions that employees face in retiring today, and also the practical concern of the company in keeping its people productive through the years immediately preceding retirement.

Several kinds of communications are involved, and the pattern is similar among most of the organizations that have preretirement programs. It includes group counseling sessions held at intervals in the years immediately before retirement, usually conducted by members of the personnel staff. These sessions tend to focus on the practical aspects of retirement: income, maintaining insurance programs, and similar financial considerations. Often they introduce the preretiree to government agencies that can be of assistance; frequently psychological counseling on making the adjustment to retirement life is part of the program. Some companies provide booklets and newsletters designed to reinforce the information provided during group sessions. Typically, counseling sessions and literature are designed for both the person retiring from the company and the spouse.

"The main communications problem, other than keeping current on all the changes occurring in government programs, is getting people to come to these sessions for the first time," one executive responsible for preretirement counseling comments. "People often find it difficult to face the fact that they are coming to the end of their working lives. Once we've got them involved, however, and they have the chance to talk with other people in the same boat and begin to plan for retirement their attitudes often change. I've had some of our people tell me that this kind of help was one of the best things the company has done for them."

COMMUNICATIONS BY JOB FUNCTION

At a chemical company in New Jersey, an information program was developed for the organization's secretaries. The intent was to give this group a sense of their own role in corporate activities. The written material produced, according to *Industrial Relations News*, was so interesting that it led to the development of a newsletter for company secretaries, now issued as a bimonthly. Sample articles include commentaries on being a secretary, an analysis of a two-day development program for secretaries, and interviews with former secretaries who have moved into management positions. Since most secretaries are women, the article notes that the newsletter has become a significant contribution to development of that human resources area.

The secretaries' newsletter is an example of an internal, specialized communications program directed to employees on the basis of their job functions.

Middle Management: The Print Barrage

Of all the functions within the corporate world, it seems likely that the amorphous group labeled "middle management" is the single audience most often pinpointed by internal communications. Even the baldly factual communications they get on operations and changes are human resources communications in the sense that they link company and manager. Other communications programs to this group aim at specific human resources goals that relate to their management function. Still others, recognizing the potential of middle-management people as representatives of the company to outside audiences, deal with public issues and company views on them.

American Can, a corporation with a reputation for being public affairs conscious, provides a good example of the latter. It has developed a publication for its middle-management people which it calls

"Public Affairs Update." This was started in 1976 as a communications vehicle to tell its management people about the societal and government pressures on its business. Its philosophy was summarized by Senior Vice President Judd H. Alexander. "In my opinion, most of the criticism directed at corporations today is due to misinformation and a lack of understanding of the role of the profit motive in our socioeconomic system," he says. "We in business must share in this blame because of our instinct to be left alone—as the saying goes—to mind our own business. This desire to keep a low profile is a luxury we can no longer afford. Every one of us must be alert to what is going on around us—and prepared to speak up when our interests are threatened."

E. I. du Pont de Nemours & Co. publishes a highly respected periodical for its 32,000 managers. This bimonthly is called *Management Bulletin,* and its function is to report on and interpret Du Pont's position on issues of importance to the company. "If the objectives of *Management Bulletin* could be summed up in one word," the company says, "that word would be 'educational.' The central purpose of the publication is to help improve the business sophistication of Du Pont lower and middle management, particularly those who have been and will be upwardly mobile in the company." Some of the topics that have been covered in *Management Bulletin* include, "Du Pont R&D Today," "Some Basic Questions on Energy," and "Keeping Social Security Strong." One interesting report was on a study conducted by Du Pont of its own employee communications. "Most employees," the story says, "said they usually or always believe Du Pont's communications."

Companies are finding that issues-related human resources communications pay unexpected dividends. Supplying their managers with the company's side of the story has led to numerous instances of company people, equipped with solid background information, strenuously supporting their companies against outside criticism. "He may be President, but he's wrong," one oil company manager was heard to declare on a New York commuter train. "What Mr. Carter has failed to take into consideration about oil company profits . . ." the executive continued, citing chapter and verse on industry earnings to a small but impressed audience of other commuting executives.

The New York Times underlined the political value of such communications in a business page report headlined, "Lobbying by Employees for Companies Increasing." The story presented several examples of this practice as applied to oil companies, airlines, armaments programs, and nuclear energy programs. "In each case," *Times* reporter Robert Lindsey pointed out, "the lobbying was done by employees of corporations that would have been affected adversely by new laws. The incidents are evidence that American businesses are increasingly discovering—and using—a latent political force: their own employees."

Most organizations today have special publications directed to middle management. Often the manager may be the recipient of a half-dozen or more periodicals, newsletters, divisional or department publications, and a stream of manuals, memos, top management speeches, and reprints from business journals. Most middle managers may have the impression that they are the targets not so much of an information explosion as a veritable barrage of data directed at their desks.

Middle Management: Meetings and More

Print materials, numerous and varied as they are, are only part of the picture. Recognizing the value of personal interaction, many organizations are using meetings as a means of two-way communication. In Philadelphia the SmithKline Corporation has a program which includes a series of "president's luncheons" at which some fifteen middle managers at different levels and from different departments lunch with the president and senior vice presidents of the company. "The information and opinion exchanges are usually quite candid and very much two way," says Mary van Roden, manager of corporate communications.

As with print communications, the number and variety of meetings directed to middle management are almost countless and incorporate techniques of communication that range from theatre-sized closed circuit television presentations, by which the company president addresses, nationwide, the company's entire managerial corps, to a new wrinkle recently reported of management spouses attending semiannual all-day meetings on company developments.

It is also middle management that is the principal target of the management development programs noted earlier in this chapter. These programs in recent years have been giving considerable attention to human resources. "We put heavy emphasis on training our managers to be sensitive to the needs of people and to changing values," says Don Lester of General Electric's Aircraft Engine Group. "We have a variety of programs addressed to this need, but they are exemplified by one called 'Managing People in a Changing World.'"

That title, in fact, exemplifies much of the thrust of today's communications programs for middle-management people. In particular, the whole area of affirmative action and equal employment is getting substantial attention. One reason for this is that middle management has been generally regarded as something of a roadblock to change, including those changes necessary to achieve employment equality in the work force. "It isn't top management where we bog down," one frustrated human resources executive sputtered talking about the company's indifferent record in affirmative action, "and it isn't the people on the line who are the problem. It's middle management that messes us up every time." The situation first came to light in the late sixties as companies were pushing ahead on plans to add minority workers as a result of recently passed EEO legislation. Now the rush of women into the work force and into management roles is raising further problems and creating the need for new communications efforts.

For example, since many managers interview job applicants passed along to them by the personnel department, it had become important that these managers understand the new ground rules covering such interviews.

Beyond this lies a whole area in which seminars, meetings, and lectures are developed both by the company and by outside consultants to help middle managers become more sensitive to the psychological aspects of management, and more aware of their own reactions to dealing with women in the work situation. As a corollary, women middle managers are counseled on "surviving in a man's world" and attend seminars intended to help them understand the fears and prejudices that may affect the men with whom they will be working.

Supporting these sessions in many organizations are further print materials concerned with EEO. Some are produced internally, such as the Bendix Corporation's *Monitor*. "Essentially, this describes briefly some of the more effective people programs developed at our various operating units," says corporate EEO Manager E. M. Byrd, "and serves as an added measure to strengthen divisional and/or subsidiary affirmative action programs." Others are purchased from outside sources, such as the *Fair Employment Practices* newsletter issued by Management Resources, Inc., in New York. There are, too, numerous audiovisual presentations, films, and tapes to provide still further support to middle management in dealing with the changing work force the human resources revolution is producing.

Still another human resources subject that has become the focus of middle-management sessions today, both as a group and individually with counselors, is the knotty question of their own futures. "Career pathing," as this kind of personal career planning is now being called, can be described as deciding, in terms of one's own company and background, "where can I go from here?". Bendix, Polaroid, and many other corporations have programs of this kind for middle-management people (and others, notably minorities and women). One current development is the career pathing workshop, another is the "life planning" course, usually designed for the mature manager. Such programs involve personal communications, tie-ins with company information systems, and other methods of transmitting career-related information. Typically, for the middle manager, there is no end to the stream of communications—so copious that sometimes it must seem that the main problem is simply staying afloat.

The Technicals: A Critical Audience

In a Deutsch, Shea & Evans national study of engineer attitudes toward employment, the thousand responding technical people rated the importance of each item on a list of sixty-two job factors. The top ranking factor was "opportunity to express opinions and feelings freely to superiors," listed by 98.5 percent of the sample. Significantly these engineers rated the opportunity for upward communication more important than any other of the listed factors, including "using their skills and abilities," "merit salary increases," or "opportunity for advancement."

Technical people, notably engineers, since there are so many of them employed in American industry, are something of an enigma to the remainder of the work force. Their language, their functions, their status as professionals, their interests and the nature of their work, all tend to set them apart. To call technical people a critical audience for business is accurate in two ways. They are an absolutely vital element in the whole industrial process. The technical professional is an innovator in developing new products and processes, in adapting new scientific findings to practical use. They are the troubleshooters in handling many of the crises that occur in industrial operations, from dealing with breakdowns of all kinds to meeting environmental standards. Technical people frequently work directly with company customers, handle the installation of company equipment, serve as consultants to management, and make contributions to maintaining and improving our entire technologically based society.

In another sense, they are critical because they are fact-oriented, disinclined to accept information on face value, and they are often dissatisfied with their jobs, their working conditions, and the management decisions that come down to them.

One reason for this is their ambiguous status. As both employees and professionals they are accountable, in a sense, to two different masters—their own profession and the organization for which they work. The past history of engineering employment has tended to alienate many of them toward business to some degree, particularly in the wake of the massive hiring and firing waves of the past decade. They face career problems peculiar to their field, notably that of rapid professional obsolescence, plus the same kind of salary compression problems that plague middle managers. One engineer noted that he sees as a major professional problem "the whole attitude of management toward technical personnel. Largely through our own lack of opposition, we are 'graphed' and 'formulated' as to position, authority, and salary. We are treated more like hourly employees than professionals. This applies to almost all companies."

Paralleling the considerable degree of dissatisfaction with the corporate environment is the satisfaction technical people find in their work, perhaps the most important motivating factor. "I am totally satisfied with my present job. It is purely technical, involving analytical and theoretical work. On more than any other job I've had, I can apply directly the things I've learned in college. I also have a great deal of responsibility. I can come and go as I please. No time clocks. In a way, we have an academic atmosphere here and the pressures of routine are minimal." Thus another engineer describes *his* professional work.

Now the social pressures engendered by the human resources revolution are adding other ingredients to the business-professional mix. "The aggressive efforts of organized labor and its success in getting high wages and increased benefits has been a shock to engineers," says Lars G. Soderholm, editorial director of *Design News,* a technical journal, "particularly when they find shop workers making more money. As a result, engineers, frustrated in getting professional recognition from their employers, are looking for attention through collective action. Some organize into engineering unions, some join trade unions, most just grumble about the problem, and a few put pressure on their professional societies to become more militant in protecting their interests."

Technical people, over a substantial period of time, have tended to reject unionization. A study of 1,304 electronic engineers by *Electronics,* a professional journal, indicates that "Not quite 20 percent favored a union in the present survey. Among the reasons given for rejecting an engineers' union were: unions are not professional, they serve no useful function, and they restrict individual initiative or freedom." In a similar survey by the journal conducted in 1971, 22 percent of the respondents had favored a union for engineers.

The technical societies themselves have begun to reflect the various impacts of the human resources revolution. In an earlier chapter we saw how the American Chemical Society analyzed and printed in its journal the background on the firing of chemists and chemical engineers. Thomas Sheffer, director of communications of another technical society, the Society of Automotive Engineers (SAE), describes another direction in which these organizations are moving. Of the SAE Sheffer says, "The new thrust for our Society is making our members aware that their role transcends technical areas. The more we work in transportation, and most all do, the more we feel we are up against broader societal issues of the environment, of human values, and in choosing our material possessions. As we cross these boundaries, our profession requires us to address societal issues as well as technical ones."

The technical professional, consequently, is an important target for company communications, and a difficult one. It is, ultimately, the engineers who are the key to multimillion dollar investments in new technologies, who design the consumer products that sell by the millions, who are able to create the processes of manufacturing and keep them going. These professionals are already involved in an enormous communications web within their profession, including dozens of journals, papers, talks from outside the company, and the need to study (or create) endless computer printouts, proposals, and specification sheets, both to do the job and to keep up with rapidly changing technologies.

Technically Speaking: Person to Person

How can these people be reached? Ideally, person to person, according to Arthur R. Thomson, director of manufacturing engineering, corporate staff, TRW Incorporated. "We are not just dealing with information, but the person. It goes beyond the subject matter," Thomson says. "At TRW, communications is a special concern with us, in a decentralized company like ours. I use the analogy of a convoy, a group of ships. The captain of a ship is like the general manager of a division, but the convoy has common resources and meets common hazards, and it is much stronger when there are good communications. Our idea about communications is that we want something to happen for two reasons. One is for information, and the other is to get people in touch with each other, to get back-and-forth flow by identifying their common interests. It is much the way the professional societies operate in networks— small committees of experts who work and report on problems. The question we ask is: Why should we communicate and who should get involved."

Dr. Richard Kopelman of the City College of New York has published considerable material on the psychological aspects of engineering employment. In reaching engineers, one of the points he makes is that communications must be understood in a total context. "All activities and interactions that transmit meaning are forms of communication," he says. "Any symbolic event that transmits meaning or that is meaningful is communication. The work environment, the office assigned, pay increases—all of these factors communicate things to the engineer. If a person goes to lunch at the company and is served in a dirty dining room, this will be understood as a communication that he or she is not well thought of, even if the company newspaper says that engineers are valued people."

Meetings and seminars, a characteristic mode of communications within the professional societies, have been widely adopted within many technology-intensive corporations. RCA has created a wide-ranging series of meetings for its laboratory staff titled "Colloquium," scheduled on Tuesdays during the winter months. About 300 or 400 of the company's technical people attend each session to hear speakers discuss a variety of subjects. Speakers have ranged from an astronaut to a baseball player, and subjects from medical topics to the application of electronics to automobiles. These meetings are taped for use in other areas of the company. In addition, RCA also holds in-house technical seminars on a regular basis, often on specialized topics, and with an average audience of from 50 to 70.

Dow Chemical Company's personnel director for research and development, George Klumb, says, "Communications here go on in a thousand ways. Some of our research organizations publish a flier of their activities once a month, others rely on monthly meetings of their people. For technical and scientific people, we have formal seminars quarterly or semiannually whose purpose is to present new information on technology, both to other technical people in the company and to management. Our management uses these meetings as a way to maintain two-way communications. Our technical directors, who are both technical people and managers, meet twice a year to exchange ideas, and often to transfer technical people from one group to another, so that people are assigned to projects in areas in which they have a strong interest." He also makes an interesting human resources point: "We had a few programs for technical women, but got out of it quick. They did not want to be treated differently."

Hughes Aircraft makes extensive use of meetings, but in a generally unstructured way, a spokesperson says. "We have a policy of allowing people to participate. There's a fairly free-flowing atmosphere here and we don't feel the need for much in the way of written communications. We practice a high level of interpersonal communications. Groups within the company meet regularly or irregularly, as often as they feel necessary, to resolve issues and exchange information."

These patterns of general meetings, seminars, and ad hoc informal sessions seem to be characteristic of the way major technical organizations deal with the complexities of communicating with their technical audience. The idea of person-to-person interchange is becoming strongly established. "We prefer face-to-face communication." George Klumb of Dow notes. "Some parts of a new employee orientation were on videotape, but we've dropped it for other things; it gets too impersonal." He also comments on the reasons for this trend. "The main cause is something of a change in the general attitudes and thinking of technical people hired in the past seven years. They are much more open. They want to know, and they come and ask you. We try our best to be just as honest as we can."

Technical Publications for Internal Use

Print media are not entirely neglected, however, and in fact some of the most impressive corporate publications are created by and for the technical professionals. These can best be described as internal technical journals. A typical example is Western Electric's *The Engineer*. A recent eighty-page issue focused on a single technical subject, microprocessor applications. The twelve articles in the issue could have been taken from any of the major professional journals. They are written well, replete with photographs, charts, and diagrams, and include a picture and thumbnail biography of each author, all of whom are members of the Western Electric staff. The quarterly also runs sections in each issue listing recent patents, disclosures, articles, and presentations by Western Electric technical people.

Similar journals prepared primarily for internal distribution, but also usually with some external distribution, have been developed by most major technical corporations. They include the *RCA Engineer,* IBM's *Journal of Research and Development* and the *Bell System Technical Journal.* As communications media for the technical staff, these transcend the informational content. For one thing, professional people, like academics, value highly the opportunity to publish their work, in part because of the recognition this brings from their professional colleagues. These journals provide such an opportunity. They also constitute a recognition of the value the corporation places on technology and technical people.

At another level, companies utilize reports and newsletters to some degree. Don Lester of General Electric's Aircraft Engine Group notes, "On the subject of orientation, we believe strongly that it's not just an entry issue but a continuing process. One of the things we do—and I think well—is to engage in a continuing dialogue with various populations in the human resource. For example, we develop reports for our professionals on specific issues that affect them in the work environment. These reports are also teaching tools. In our company publication at Lynn, we also run a 'dialogue' section, which is a kind of continuing open forum that raises questions and answers about business."

Engineering Trend is issued by RCA on a monthly basis. It is a nontechnical publication for engineers that focuses on the business side of the company. *Hughes News,* the only internal company publication which Hughes Aircraft publishes, covers new developments in various technical programs and thus has high readership among employee engineers. These examples represent a common pattern in technical communications.

Technical Training by Wire

Less common are some of the techniques that companies employ to help their technical people combat one of their major career problems: obsolescence. Northrop, for example, enabled its engineers to attend a major aerospace technical meeting by telephone. The California company obtained slides and other audiovisual materials in advance and set up phone connections with the Dallas meeting that relayed the proceedings. The visual material was shown at the company, the presentations were heard as a kind of conference call, and Northrop Corporation's engineers could take part in the Texas meeting through a two-way phone connection through which they could ask questions of participants.

Other companies are enabling their technical people to keep up their education within the company walls. "Many observers attribute some of the drive and leadership shown by electronics companies between Palo Alto and San Jose, California, to a business-supported educational program at Stanford University," a New York *Times* story reports. "This provides live or taped television instruction, for credit, in more than 100 graduate engineering courses, to registrants who attend class in television-equipped rooms at their work places. The taped instruction of small off-campus groups led by a qualified tutor, able to stop the tape at any time to explore a question, produces better scores on examinations than live instruction, according to Dr. James F. Gibbons of Stanford, pioneer of the tape system." The television tie-in between universities and corporations is spreading.

Some companies, RCA for one, are using their own in-house tape programs. The company calls it a "Continuing Engineering Education Program," which includes videotapes prepared both by the company and some outside authorities on a given subject, and used in conjunction with in-plant instructors. Similar programs at Du Pont include a series of economic lectures for technical professionals as an important element. Continuing education, as a pragmatic approach to the speed of technical change, is another element of technical communication that has become standard within industry.

Another highly interesting form of training has also been developed by General Electric's Aircraft Engine Group, again on a pragmatic basis—the imminent loss of some of its key people through retirement. "A high technology operation like ours," Don Lester says of this program, "develops a substantial amount of lore which is invested in the human resource. In the near future, we face fairly heavy retirement attrition and needed to devise a *'lore transference'* process to assure that the organization's new membership was equipped to carry on. In effect, what we have done is to take our manufacturing technology experts and teach them to be teachers, to be training experts as well as technology content experts."

Dr. Richard Kopelman of the City College of New York, commenting on communications with technical professionals, stresses the need for open systems. "There are two kinds of organizational systems, open and closed," he says. "Open systems give people high autonomy, higher interaction, and give professionals influence within the organization—the ability to influence their bosses. The more effective organizations are found in more open systems. To the extent that engineers get complete information, there is a feeling of trust and predictability, and they will be more likely to take risks and be open to new ideas and ways to solve problems."

This open kind of organization, with its associated highly personalized communications, appears to be the trend in this aspect of human resources communications.

OTHER INTERNAL AUDIENCES

"Companies take better care of their computers than their programmers," ran the headline in a journal covering the EDP field. The story outlined the feelings of some programmers of being both isolated from and not understood by company management, a theme that has surfaced in various studies and reports on programmers and systems analysts. As with engineers, theirs is an esoteric profession, although considerably newer, and they are undergoing some of the problems of adjustment that other technical people have encountered in the business world. Consequently they form still another distinct audience, very important to the company's operations, to whom communication must be directed.

There are in fact almost any number of audiences within a corporation beyond those discussed in this chapter. One is the sales group, who recent studies report to be less than enthralled by the traditional rah-rah approach to stimulating their efforts. Another embraces various levels of production people, who with the onset of automation control successively larger investments in capital equipment. Then there are an increasing number of specialists at all levels within the company, important to its operations, yet by their specialization often isolated from the mainstream.

What these constituencies are within a given company often is a question even the company itself cannot yet answer. The development of communications programs to specialized audiences within the company, briefly reviewed here, has been essentially a catch-as-catch-can response to urgent problems. There appears to be little overall analysis within corporations, however, to determine what gaps in the communications pattern may be present now, or may come to pass in the future in the wake of new developments. The success of white-collar unionization drives, for example, and particularly the increasing unionization of professionals outside of business and industry, as reported recently by the Conference Board, suggest the need for a more organized, coherent and forward-looking consideration of the human resources communications effort inside the organization.

CHAPTER TEN

Communicating Affirmative Action

L eonard G., a division manager of a medium-sized food processing company, was humming as he walked along the corridor to the president's office. For one thing, he had found the new man he needed to fill an executive position in his division. Leonard had narrowed it down to two men, both in their early thirties. He had interviewed them again this morning, along with a 29-year-old woman, "just for the record" as he quipped to his secretary when she brought him his morning coffee. The affable man he had liked had accepted the position on the spot, so that was one worry out of the way. His division had done extremely well for the year, ranking third in the company in sales, and it was approaching time for the annual bonus talk with the president. All in all, a happy prospect.

The president noted Leonard's mood. "You're looking cheerful this morning," he said, as the manager took a seat in his office.

"Finally filled that marketing spot," Leonard grinned. "Got a helluva nice guy. Good background."

"Oh," the president observed coolly, "what about the woman you were interviewing for that job?"

"Out of the running," Leonard explained. "Didn't have the right kind of background when we got right down to cases. Just as well. She struck me as a troublemaker, probably a Libber."

"Interesting that you should raise that point, Leonard." The president tossed a piece of paper over his desk to the manager. "Take a look at that."

Leonard studied the paper for a minute. "A class-action suit?"

"That's right. That's what they're considering. A group of our own women employees, Leonard, most of them from your division. They are claiming systematic discrimination in hiring and promoting within the company. I spoke with their representatives this morning, including a very able woman lawyer. It could be very expensive."

"Oh, it'll blow over. They're just sounding off. There's no case. You know I've interviewed a lot of minority people and women over the past couple of years."

"I also know that we've had an audit or whatever they call it from the EEOC, as a result of complaints against discriminatory hiring here. Interviews don't count, you know, not with that outfit. They want to know how many women and minority people we've got on board. Your division didn't come out well. And do you remember a chap named Williams you interviewed a couple of weeks ago for the marketing job?"

"Williams—oh yeah. He's that old guy I talked with. I wrote him off right away. He's over the hill."

"Maybe, but he's also entering a complaint against us on age discrimination."

For the first time, Leonard lost his cheery air. "Seems like a lot of these things hitting us at the same time," he said ruefully.

"Right," the president agreed. "Any one of these would be too many. A class-action suit alone could set us back several million in awards and costs. Not only that, but in our business, women are our major customers. We'd look great on the six o'clock news—especially with our new commercials about helping the working woman. Fortunately, I think, I was able to head that off at the meeting I had with the women this morning. I promised them that we'd make some personnel changes immediately, as a start in correcting the situation."

Leonard smiled, relieved. "You really know how to handle people," he said admiringly. "I hope that means my bonus won't be affected by all this affirmative action bother."

"Not exactly, Leonard," the president said patiently. "You see, the first personnel change I'm going to make is finding a new manager for your division."

In the past few years business has learned, often the hard way, that taking equal employment opportunity (EEO) guidelines lightly can be an expensive business. A number of major corporations have made meeting affirmative action goals one of the conditions on which top-level managers are judged and on which bonuses are computed. There is a report, too, of a meeting at a large corporation at which the chief executive officer (CEO) had gathered all of the organization's top brass. The corporation's chief counsel briefed the assembled managers on the current EEO laws and the penalties that could accrue by ignoring them. After that, the controller made a presentation on the expenditures the company had made in the past eighteen months in legal fees, time, and awards to successful litigants who had sued the company for discrimination. Then the CEO spoke. "You have heard the counsel and the controller," he said. "We can't afford any further litigation. You'll meet the affirmative action goals for your operation or you'll be fired. That's all. Thank you for your attention."

This attitude applies down the line. "Everyone has lawsuits on affirmative action," commented the personnel director of one large Midwestern-based manufacturing company when the talk came around to affirmative action. "We do, too. The question is not whether we have complaints but whether we have had any successful complaints. The answer so far is no. We take EEO seriously; it's the law. We tell our managers they must comply. If they don't get the message, we can always get another $30,000 manager."

Major suits or no, simply meeting the costs of recruiting, settling minor claims, and communicating both in-house and to the government has been estimated by one major division of a Fortune 500 company to be $2.5 million in a single recent year. Given these "operating costs" for affirmative action, and the considerably more expensive alternatives of major class-action suits and other litigation, it is no wonder that communications related to equal employment range from the recruitment brochure to the CEO's office—and beyond.

RECRUITING AND AFFIRMATIVE ACTION

The term "affirmative action" is sometimes used as a synonym for "equal opportunity employment." But while the latter means opening jobs to minorities and women and not discriminating against these or other protected groups in hiring, pay, or advancement, affirmative action is really the process of actively seeking, training, and advancing, minority, female, and other categories of people—Vietnam veterans and the handicapped for example—to fill company openings. Recruiting, then, is one of the principal instruments of affirmative action, and it utilizes many of the communications techniques discussed earlier, but with a difference.

Merrill Lynch's experience exemplifies a part of this difference. The securities firm, though conducting an affirmative action campaign, was cited by the government as having insufficient numbers of women and blacks among its account executives. The company agreed to make further efforts to increase their proportions in the firm.

An affirmative action program was developed which included the creation of a special advertising campaign. Research suggested that the most effective approach would be to zero in on some of the problems that women and minorities were likely to be encountering in their careers, and to demonstrate, in a low-keyed way, how joining Merrill Lynch would be a solution to them. Three sets of ads were developed on this basis: those directed specifically to women, to minorities, and to a general audience. Typical headlines were:

> "If you're running hard and not getting ahead, consider Merrill Lynch."
>
> "If you're a woman who is running fast but not getting ahead, consider Merrill Lynch."
>
> "If you think minorities don't have a chance at high income careers, consider Merrill Lynch."

Each ad, of course, indicated that Merrill Lynch was an equal opportunity employer. They were to run on an alternating basis in newspapers and journals.

Shortly after the campaign started, however, the judge who had presided over the original agreement between government and company called a halt. He ruled that even though the ads indicated the firm was an equal opportunity employer with positions open to all, and that by agreement Merrill Lynch was to take affirmative action to recruit minorities and women for these openings, company advertising could nevertheless not be addressed directly to either women or minorities since this would be discriminatory.

Similar interpretations ("You must take special action to recruit women and minorities but you cannot address women and minorities in your recruitment ads") has led to recruiting ads that rely principally on visual content to affirm equal employment. In college recruitment, in fact, so many ads carried photographs showing a mix of black and white male and female students that one company, Stromberg Carlson, capitalized on the situation. They ran a college ad with a blank space and the query, "What? No photograph of women and minorities in a recruiting ad?" "No," the copy answered. "We think today's college graduates have got the message that industry wants to add women and minorities. Smiling multiracial faces are decorative, but they don't get to the heart of the story, which is—we think—what happens *after* you're hired."

Sophisticated affirmative action recruiting addresses itself to Stromberg-Carlson's point, that is, the organization is hiring on an equal opportunity basis but the important thing is what happens to people on the job. Equal employment opportunity has become an accepted thing. But upward mobility and role models of people who have achieved a measure of success are the more current concern. These themes are also being handled subtly and effectively, as demonstrated by the Argonne ad previously quoted.

Such advertising has quietly become an important part of corporate communications, carrying a human resources message to women and minorities as well as to the large, mixed readership exposed to these ads. But companies have also found a way to carry this message more directly to affirmative action audiences by using the little-known but extensive network of national, regional, and local media directed to women and various minority audiences.

The Affirmative Action Media

"Interior Causes Chaos Over Tribal Water Regs" is not a headline that would fascinate the average suburban reader. To the reader of *Wassaja* it packs a special punch, since that monthly newspaper reaches American Indian audiences throughout the country. *Wassaja* is only one of a group of national minority publications that corporations are using today as recruitment media. Such black publications as *Ebony, Encore, Black Enterprise,* and *Essence* provide their readers with career-related editorial material as part of their overall coverage, and also carry career-oriented ads. The nation's Hispanic population has fewer national media of this type, such as *La Luz* and *Nuestro.* The publisher of *La Luz,* Tom Pino, has established an annual career issue of the magazine both as a handbook to job seeking and to present role models of successful Hispanic people. He feels that business needs to give more attention to getting its affirmative action message to the national Hispanic community, whose numbers he says are now some 16 million and whose buying power, up 23 percent since 1970, is topping $31 billion.

It might be argued that there is, if anything, a surplus of media directed to women. From *Viva* and *Cosmopolitan* to *Ladies Home Journal* and *Woman's Day*, most of the newsstand clutter is devoted primarily to women as consumers. The glamour magazines exist to sell her fashions and life-styles, the service periodicals to sell her on the amenities of homemaking. Most have circulations and page rates that would bankrupt recruiting budgets in short order. For recruiting, corporations have turned to other kinds of magazines.

Ms., launched on the tide of the feminist movement in the early seventies, is one national women's magazine that regularly includes career advertising. From early in its publishing history *Ms.* has carried a human development section focusing on career information and ads. Pat Carbine, the magazine's publisher, says, "We believe that one of the functions of *Ms.* is to focus on the realities of work as an element in a woman's life, on what's happening in society in terms of women as a key element in the work force, and to provide a medium where companies that are serious about affirmative action can reach a national, well-educated, and socially-aware audience."

The women's movement has resulted in the birth of several other feminist publications that are used by corporations to spread an affirmative action message: *Spokeswoman, New Directions for Women, Do It Now, Working Woman.* Specialized periodicals such as *The Society of Women Engineers Newsletter* and *The Woman CPA* also are used as recruitment media.

A similar phenomenon has occurred in the college field, resulting in such affirmative action publications as *Equal Opportunity, Black Collegian,* and *Collegiate Women's Career Magazine, Business World for Women,* and others. Media like these allow organizations to talk directly to potential job candidates among the minority and female populations. By placing such ads, they are also talking in human resources terms to activists, students, and others with strong views on the role of organizations as employers.

The Affirmative Action Message

The human resources messages that are directed to women and minorities in these various media have changed over the few years in which affirmative action has been a fact of life. In the late 1960s when the impact of the Civil Rights Act on employment was just beginning to be felt, the major thrust was simply assuring minority people that the company was interested in hiring them. In a black community that had seen employment doors slammed in its face for the better part of a century, this wasn't a message received with a high level of belief. There was, in fact, a substantial amount of resistance. The consensus was that corporations which had turned black applicants away in previous years were "Mickey Mousing," meaning that they were fooling around, not being serious in making their offers of opportunity. "Companies are placing those ads because they have to," was a frequently expressed thought "but they aren't really going to hire me. If I apply, it will be the same runaround we always get."

In response, the tenor of the affirmative action communications followed that of a classic General Electric recruiting ad. This, later reprinted in the *Encyclopaedia Britannica* as typical of the new genre, was headlined: "There Are no Whites Working at General Electric." A subhead added, "No Blacks Either; Just People." The copy emphasized that the Aircraft Engine Group of General Electric was interested in people who could do a job and not in the color of their skins.

During this early period considerable use was made of minority radio to attract people to production and clerical jobs. Disk jockeys on stations directed to black audiences had a high level of believability within the community. Some companies took groups of these announcers around their facilities so they could see the nature of the jobs that were open, and thus be assured that blacks would be given opportunities. They were invited to use their own words to describe the opportunities, to add to the credibility of the company job offer.

A related technique was to enlist opinion leaders in the black communities—religious leaders, heads of social groups, others with standing and acceptance—to help counteract negative images of business. Another technique which proved to be especially effective was "the walking recruiter." These recruiters were people from the minority community who worked for the company. They assisted affirmative action by talking to neighbors and acquaintances about the company as a place to work, emphasizing its willingness to hire minority people. Such people, concerned with helping both the company and the community, were given time off to spread the word that valid opportunities existed.

Time and the legal requirement that corporations be equal opportunity employers have made the initial message of willingness to hire obsolete. The more usual message today displays evidence that the organization hires minority people and women for all kinds of jobs and provides upward mobility. For example, using the argument that minorities and women could not sell effectively to nonminority, non-female audiences, some organizations resisted affirmative action when it related to sales positions. Companies like Xerox, however, empha-sized their willingness to open sales jobs to everyone in ads that proclaimed, "Xerox has co-ed sales opportunities." A new Merrill Lynch campaign shows a mix of people, one per ad, with the title, "I belong on Wall Street with Merrill Lynch." Other organizations' ads feature pictures and quotes from minority people and women about the company as an employer.

Obviously the basic recruiting situation has changed. It is no longer a question of attempting to lure wary and reluctant people into the unknown business world. Now the name of the game is competing effectively for the still relatively limited numbers of qualified minority people and women. Those with engineering degrees, for example, number less than 20,000. The messages that are used today in recruiting these much sought after groups are essentially those used in other recruiting communications: job interest, opportunities, the nature of the company and its work, advantages, benefits—in brief, what's in it for the individual. The major difference is that the story is supported, in affirmative action advertising, by illustrations, quotes, and examples of women and minority people who are experiencing these advantages, who hold glamorous or prestigious jobs, if possible, and who indicate explicitly or implicitly that in their companies, you, too, can make it. Some firms, particularly in their college ads, indicate the support the company may be giving to relevant programs like supporting minority businesses—another way of documenting that they are "into" affirma-tive action and go beyond the basics.

The affirmative action message that reaches the minority communi-ties and the women to whom they are directed, then, portrays the company—or should—as an involved, responsive organization moving with the times. Most importantly, where an institutional ad might *claim* such desirable qualities, the recruiting ad proves them, not only by demonstrating the equality within the company work force, but by the functional method of inviting the reader to become a part of it. The fact that recruiting ads are functional communications adds significantly to their believability among readers.

Affirmative action communications play an important role in the recruiting effort. They tend to convey, when properly handled, a favor-able picture of the company as a corporate citizen, an image reaching extensive audiences besides the potential employees. Their primary role is to attract qualified women and minorities and other protected groups into the company. Thereafter new affirmative action communications programs come into play.

ORIENTATION, TRAINING, AND DEVELOPMENT

When entry-level people have been hired at American Telephone and Telegraph, one of the first things placed in their hands is a booklet describing all the jobs in the organization open to them. "We want new people to realize, right away, that there are no jobs here that are labeled for men only or for women only and this booklet makes it very clear," says an AT&T employment executive.

Orientation literature at a majority of corporations conforms with their affirmative action stance. The "welcome to" brochures have been carefully edited so that neither language nor illustrations imply racial or sexual homogeneity in any areas of company activity. Visual aids to new employee orientation such as slide and motion picture films are careful to depict women and men in nontraditional roles and include a mix of races. Introductory meetings and plant tours for new employees make a point of stressing the company's policies on equal opportunity during this initial period as a means of impressing *all* newcomers with the seriousness of the effort being made. As one personnel executive puts it, "I find that if you get people started with the idea that the company isn't going to discriminate against anyone, or allow anyone to be discriminatory, it saves a lot of grief later. People know where they stand, they know the company isn't going to allow things such as hazing women on our work crews, they know how they can get action from the company if anything of the kind happens to them." This comment comes from a personnel executive in charge of orientation and training for a utility. It sums up the practical side of such communications.

When the drive to add minority people to the work force first began, some of the manufacturing corporations found new challenges for their training programs to meet. One was helping people from ghetto areas who had never had steady jobs or seen manufacturing plants before to handle such basics as simply getting to work. "We made a special effort to recruit what were called the 'hard core unemployables.' These were people with minimum education and no work histories, who had never had a chance before," a veteran of the auto industries' affirmative action effort recalls. "We found people who never got in on time or never got there at all. At first we thought, well, these people just don't want jobs, don't want to work. But come to find out, a lot of them didn't know how to use an alarm clock. Some got confused trying to get here on city buses because they'd never used them, and didn't know how to transfer. We had a real training job to do."

In some parts of the country the problem was education. One company established a new plant in the South with the intention of adding many local black people to the work force. It was a manufacturing plant and the educational level required was at least completion of the sixth grade. But schooling had been nonexistent for most of the black people in the area. The company called in a consulting organization that specialized in educational training. The consultants established an in-plant program for the minority group that needed it and, using intensive and highly practical training in reading, arithmetic, and other skills, were able to raise most of the people to a sixth-grade level within a matter of a dozen weeks.

In New York City some of the world's largest advertising agencies such as Young & Rubicam and Doyle Dane Bernback established volunteer programs for minority people that taught office skills like typing. The agencies hired some of the people whom they trained; others were snapped up by various New York businesses. Young & Rubicam has maintained its program for more than ten years.

Skills training of this type goes on in many areas of industry. It is doubly practical in that there are a number of manufacturing and office skills in short supply most of the time and the training programs to fill such jobs enable the companies to meet their goals in affirmative action hiring. One of the major trends at the moment is the training of women for blue-collar jobs, both because many women are eager to acquire the security and good pay that such skills can offer and because it gives companies the opportunity to integrate their work forces better.

Nontraditional Work Roles

In the December 6, 1976, issue of *Newsweek* the headline story was "Women at Work." The article gave several examples of women who hold jobs that were traditionally for men only. "Marilyn Butsey slings around more than 8 tons of steel every day—and she's glad to have the chance. Eight months ago, the 20-year old Butsey became the first woman to operate a 'hot press' at Ford Motor Co.'s Vulcan Forge Plant in Dearborn. . . . A high-school dropout at 16, Marilyn Butsey had never earned more than $2.50 an hour before her current job. . . . 'It took me a long while to get used to it,' she admits. . . . 'Now I just lift that steel like it was nothing.' Another example is Madelon Talley who "was bred to be the perfect Manhattan society wife. . . . But now, instead of juggling seating arrangements, (she) is managing $40 million in assets for the Dreyfus Corporation. . . . It was not an easy transition. . . . 'I don't think men understand that women are as ambitious as they are,' she says. 'We really want the top jobs.'"

A considerable amount of human resources communications is devoted to both encouraging and training women for nontraditional positions and supporting them in those work roles. Women working in craft teams, for example, have come in for harassment that sometimes goes beyond the traditional hazing of new people on the job. The result has often been the loss of a worker who was hard to find and was expensively trained. One response has been meetings with supervisors, foremen, and union representatives to develop stringent means of dealing with the problem. Sometimes the communications have to extend beyond the work place, including families and even the community. When a utility company's national advertising featured one of its women workers doing a "man's" craft job, local pressures on the young woman resulted in her quitting the job within a few weeks after the ad appeared.

Though nontraditional work roles have become more accepted, companies find that it often requires a considerable communications effort to convince women to take the step. There is a fear of the unknown, of failing in a new task, of working with potentially hostile people, and many other psychological barriers. Cultural backgrounds tend to create problems, as in the case of women with Hispanic backgrounds mentioned earlier. Tours of work areas where the jobs can be demonstrated, films showing how the needed skills can be acquired, and talks by people who have made the transition from one role to another are among the techniques that have been used successfully. One company brought in a leading advocate of Hispanic women's rights to talk with some of the company's semiskilled workers, urging them to train for the skilled jobs the company was offering.

Commenting on this point, Frank J. Toner, vice president of human resources for Boise Cascade Corporation, says:

> "Companies that have made solid progress generally stress a business rationale for action supplemented by social, legal, or attitudinal programs. A recent program that Boise Cascade has undertaken is a seminar for

approximately 300 key management people on women in business. It involved the use of an outside consulting firm, Boyle/Kirkman. The focus was at the division level and actual operating EEO statistics were used to surface areas where affirmative action progress could be improved. Through case studies and role playing, management skill needs were identified and goals, timetables, and programs were established for every division to improve their performance in effectively utilizing women's talent in the organization.''

Sharon Kirkman Donegan, vice president and cofounder of the New York-based consulting firm Boyle/Kirkman, says:

"It is imperative for an organization to train its managers and employees in order for affirmative action to be significant and for equal opportunity to become a reality. The needs of every company are so diverse that prepackaged modules have little practical value as no prototype can be consistent with the individual company's styles and values. In the training programs we develop and conduct, we use a variety of communications techniques—case studies, role playing, videotapes, films, cassettes—to teach managers how to deal with women and minority employees as they do other employees, especially where interviewing and counseling are concerned. In awareness workshops for women and minorities, the basics for success within the corporate structure are stressed.''

The Interview Problem

One landmine in the affirmative action process is the employment interview. While personnel people are carefully trained in the equal opportunity interviewing process, follow-up interviews by supervisors and managers have produced a rash of discrimination suits. A casual inquiry about a woman's family after a formal interview had been completed, for example, led to a threat of legal action.

What one can say and ask in an employment interview is extensively circumscribed by EEO legislation. Outside organizations are providing communications for corporations to meet this problem. Executive Enterprises, New York, puts out guidelines for interviewing women which companies can purchase and distribute to their management and supervisory people. They cover avoiding sex discrimination, attitudes to take during the interview, and other relevant material. Corporations themselves also have developed interview seminars for their supervisors, including such techniques as role playing, to sensitize them to the techniques and hazards now implicit in the interviewer's role.

Industrial Relations News reports that a program developed at Motorola Incorporated to teach managers how to avoid illegal bias yielded a game called "EEO—It's Your Job." It has sixty situation cards which players pick in turn. Wrong answers lead to bias charges, investigations, and litigation. A player is fired when poor decisions lead to $1 million in "fines." The game was developed for managers who are concerned with hiring and firing people. It attracted enough outside interest that Motorola is now selling it to other firms and is using the money for social action programs.

Internal Channels

The need for internal programs related to affirmative action has also stimulated a search for communications channels linking the company's minority group members and women with management, a search that has resulted in several instances in connecting top management into the communications loop.

When Secretary of the Treasury W. Michael Blumenthal was chief executive of Bendix Corporation, the company established a Minority Advisory Council of which he was a member. The purpose was to explore methods for furthering the company's employment and advancement opportunities for women and minorities. The council, in addition to Mr. Blumenthal and other members of management, included women and minority group representatives who were there to represent their own groups within the company, and to cite problems and make suggestions to help the company assure the effectiveness of its various affirmative action programs.

When women working for the Columbia Broadcasting System (CBS) organized a protest against that firm's treatment of women as employees, one of the company's reponses was to establish a program in which the chief executive officer met with a group of women periodically. At these sessions women were encouraged to point out the problems and inequities they perceived and recommend approaches to changing the situation.

The impact of these top-level meetings is often enhanced by using other internal communications. Bendix, for example, publicized its Minority Advisory Council widely within the company, both when it was originally formed and later when policies were developed from the council meetings. The CBS meetings got similar exposure, and among the communications materials resulting from them was a printed statement from the CEO emphasizing the absolute commitment of the company to function as an equal opportunity employer in all phases of the employment process.

The idea of hotlines, discussed earlier as a form of general employee communications, has also been adapted to affirmative action use. Several companies have an internal phone number which minorities and women are invited to use to make known any complaints they may have on equal employment, or to get answers to questions on that issue. Organizations today may have an affirmative action executive, often called a human resources director, part of whose function is to be a sort of ombudsperson to receive and act on problems which the company's protected groups may have.

These and similar programs of two-way communication have the intent of providing a special voice for these special groups within the company, in itself a useful safety valve, and of enabling the organizations to take rapid action on human resources problems that surface so that these do not lead to more extensive and expensive actions by individuals or groups who feel aggrieved.

THE EDUCATION CONNECTION

The National Alliance of Businessmen (NAB) is composed of business people who, with the cooperation of their companies, volunteer to work toward national human resources goals. Following the initial Jobs for Veterans program to help cope with the immediate flood of veterans released as the Vietnam war ended, a program developed by Deutsch, Shea & Evans for the government and the Advertising Council, the NAB has assumed follow-up responsibility for this project. These veterans are one of the protected groups to whom companies are now asked to direct affirmative action efforts.

The NAB is also working with local school systems to help minority children think and plan and prepare for working careers. The program it has developed utilizes three methods, all of which involve local businesses in communications programs: the classroom connection, career exploration, and living witness. The classroom connection enlists a person from a local company with a specific skill, such as mathematics. That person works with a teacher to create a lesson plan and a half-day presentation tailored for elementary or junior high school. This includes information on the skill, the relationship it has to working, and the role it plays in the business world. The career exploration program involves an expert in a particular career area at a company— engineering or accounting, for example. This person spends a day at a high school talking about career possibilities, the preparation required, and much other information designed to stimulate interest among students. The living witness program is based upon someone from a local company with the same kind of background as the students who is a real-life role model with whom they can identify. These individuals— a black woman programmer, for example, or a Hispanic bank executive—give a three-hour orientation at the school with the underlying theme "I made it—you can, too," in which they answer questions from the student audience.

The National Urban League, which has branches throughout the country, has had a long-standing program that cooperates with local companies in communicating to black students about work opportunities. In recent years companies, some working on their own and some in conjunction with organizations like the Urban League and the NAB, have been reaching minority community schools with a variety of messages and programs to orient youngsters to the working world. Some have, in effect, "adopted" certain schools within their locality on which they concentrate their communications efforts, supplying speakers and audiovisual materials, conducting facilities tours, and assisting the schools financially to obtain needed equipment. Major corporations have prepared guidelines on how to develop programs with high schools, conduct work forums, and provide tours of the company operations.

These local efforts to reach and influence young minority people are reflected in national programs that many corporations now maintain, directed to minority and women students. They are aimed at the black and the women's colleges in addition to minority and women students enrolled in the general universities. They are part of a whole network of human resources communications programs directed to campuses.

Just as there are recruitment media and ads directed specifically to women and minority students, there are also corresponding campus programs, in which the individual corporations work either directly or through other agencies. For example, many organizations contribute financially to the United Negro College Fund; a number also provide financial grants independently to specific black schools with whom they have developed a close relationship. More than a dozen major firms have been working with the Georgia Institute of Technology in two national programs it conducts which in 1976 won its president the Employment Management Association/Deutsch, Shea & Evans Award for outstanding contributions to the human resources field.

The university conducts what is called a "3/2" program directed to women and minority students at more than ninety of the smaller liberal arts colleges throughout the country. The objective is to attract these students into engineering, where the numbers of female and minority professionals are small. With the support of some major corporations, Georgia Tech encourages students to complete their third year in liberal arts and then spend two years studying engineering at Georgia Tech, acquiring two degrees simultaneously: one in liberal arts and the other in engineering.

Northrop Corporation has established a Business Management Fellowship, working with the Department of Commerce's Office of Business Enterprise. This program sponsors summer jobs for students who come from disadvantaged backgrounds and have strong academic records. The program provides income and work experience for the students and can lead to permanent employment. In 1976 Inland Steel allocated a third of its scholarship aid funds, at schools near the company's Midwestern location for women and minority students to study engineering. A member of the board of directors of General Motors is chairman of Howard University's International Sponsors Council, the school's fund-raising group. The list could be extended indefinitely. These activities suggest, however briefly, the extent to which corporations have established communications programs to meet affirmative action aims.

What has been the internal impact of these efforts? Frank J. Toner of Boise Cascade sees them as beneficial beyond only affirmative action. "The EEO effort has caused industry to re-evaluate its personnel systems and this has been good for *all* employees. Clarity of job specifications, self-nomination systems, career development programs, assessment centers to identify management potential, etc., have helped tremendously to break down systemic discrimination. In-depth analysis of a company's work force structure and the flow dynamics of how people are recruited and move through an organization has led to a better understanding of the dimensions of the problem by all employees. It has also helped companies do a better job of realistic goal setting at reasonable levels to meet most employee and management expectations. It also segments the problems into manageable proportions for special attention like the lack of parity in managerial and professional categories. This enables industry to concentrate on specific bottlenecks so the base of qualified minorities and women can be expanded for future hiring and promotions."

AFFIRMATIVE ACTION AND EXTERNAL
AUDIENCES

A homely but telling piece of evidence about the extent to which business is becoming aware of the relationship between human resources and marketing is a panel from a milk carton distributed by a local dairy in the New York area. It bears this legend: "From Dellwood with Love. An Equal Opportunity Employer."

We have noted the extent to which companies marketing consumer goods have been including minorities and women in their advertising. Viewers see on their television screen any night at least one commercial in which a sponsor's work force is pictured by a representational group that carefully includes women and blacks. Not always would these commercials pass muster with an EEO agency. A recent airline advertisement was careful to provide a mixed group in its pitch about the airline's concern for its customers, but presented its people in stereotyped roles—the white male captain, white female cabin attendant, black female counter clerk, and Hispanic baggage handler.

Television in general is not faring so well. *New Directions for Women*, a quarterly newspaper, based in Westwood, New Jersey, cited a recent study by the United States Commission on Civil Rights, "Window Dressing on the Set: Women and Minorities in Television." This shows, the feminist quarterly reports, that "despite advances made in portrayal as well as in employment opportunity, minorities and women continue to be underrepresented in dramatic programs and on the news, and their portrayals continue to be stereotyped." The publication advises its readers to watch television with a critical eye and a positive, not a passive attitude. "If you see something good, send letters in support of the program and spread the word around. But be just as quick to protest programs and commercials that offend you, demean women and encourage violence towards women."

That almost all aspects of a company's communications are subjected to a critical scrutiny from a human resources viewpoint is also demonstrated in *New York* magazine, where Jane Trahey reported on an examination she made of the annual reports of "the top fifty" American corporations. Specifically she examined the illustrations in these to determine how such corporations portray women. So few women are shown in these reports, she says, that she was able to itemize them and did so on a company-by-company basis. "The smell of tokenism is everywhere," she concludes.

What Organizations Are Doing—and Not Doing

As a later chapter will show, there are many corporations whose annual reports today reflect the human activities and assets of the organization as well as its financial condition. Consumer ads and commercials and institutional advertising for many organizations are designed to reflect a multiracial, two-sex work force.

Other ways are being found to build an image of the company as a supporter of equal opportunity to external publics. Some organizations for example, have an EEO speakers bureau. Pfizer has run ads in minority publications illustrating their increasing use of minority businesses as suppliers. Westinghouse places institutional ads in black publications featuring its minority employees and their activities on and off the job, such as teaching weekly science seminars to high school students. Business leaders speak before minority groups, and vice versa. Corporate films push nontraditional jobs for women, and stories about women and minority people at work appear from time to time in national and specialized publications.

Few companies, however, appear to be presenting themselves as affirmative action employers in an organized way. One reason seems to be that some top executives see affirmative action as strictly an internal problem and largely the domain of personnel. Implicit in this thinking is its corollary that affirmative action takes place in isolation from such other company activities as marketing and finance. In other instances it seems that top management is aware of the implications to the company of its affirmative action image, but has failed to translate this sensitivity into action, perhaps from lack of a central human resources communications function charged with getting the word to communicators within the organization.

A national poll taken in 1977 showed a majority support the Equal Rights Amendment. It indicated similar support for the concept of equal pay for equal work. The human resources revolution has apparently succeeded in raising the national consciousness regarding affirmative action. Corporate communications to external audiences need to follow suit.

CHAPTER ELEVEN

Shaping the Future Work Force

Sixteen-year-old Susan E.'s parents talk with her teacher. "We'd thought Susan ought to go into something more practical," her mother says. "Her cousin, now, is a dental hygienist and she has a good job. But, well, this makes a difference." The difference is that Susan has just won an award in a national science competition sponsored by a major corporation. Her project, a painstaking and carefully presented analysis of local geological features, was rated among the top entries and the award carries a scholarship with it. Susan, from a family which has never produced a college graduate, has aimed at a career as a geologist. Now the goal is in sight.

Bill L. is enrolled in a course in computer programming at the local community college near his New Jersey home. "All you have to do is look at a paper to see how much programmers are in demand. My folks always wanted me to be a lawyer, like my uncle, but my grades weren't good enough to swing a scholarship, and tuition at a good law school is out of sight. The family just can't afford that kind of money. But this two-year college is something else. It doesn't cost much, I live at home, and I've got a good instructor. He's a programming manager, in fact, at a big company, so he's giving us a lot of info on how to get a job after we've finished our courses."

In Michigan an accounting senior near the top of his class picks up his mail at the dorm. It includes a recruiting brochure from one corporation, an annual report from another, an invitation from a top CPA firm to attend an off-campus talk on careers by one of its partners, and a copy of *Black Collegian*, a bimonthly publication which carries advice on career choices on its editorial pages and recruiting ads from a number of major corporations.

In New York the placement director of an upstate school has dinner with a group of colleagues from other schools, courtesy of a New York bank, which is giving them an extensive presentation on the career aspects of banking.

On the campus of a noted Ivy League school, a distinguished professor of engineering strolls the quad with a former student. "One of the areas the company's heavily into now," the alumnus is telling his companion, "is holography, particularly some advanced industrial applications. I was thinking that if you'd like to have us set up a demonstration for some of your classes, we could probably do it sometime in the next semester."

HUMAN RESOURCES COMMUNICATIONS AND THE CAMPUS

The human resources cooperation between school and corporation is of long standing and constitutes a field of its own, as those involved with it are aware. The campus audiences are not like any others. A different time element is involved in communicating with them, reflecting not only the cycle of the school year but the life cycles of the principal campus audience, the students, whose decisions on careers and companies are conditioned and made within a very few years.

There are also different media used in communicating with school audiences, who are not reached effectively with human resources messages through the conventional channels (although what appears in conventional media can affect the students and academic attitudes toward a company as employer).

The corporation today is, or should be, concerned with several levels of schools, ranging from graduate schools to the high school, perhaps even into junior high and grammar schools. The target audiences for human resources communication are similar, whatever the educational level. They are the students themselves, who constitute the future work force; those who teach them; and those who counsel or assist them, directly or indirectly, in their career choices and job seeking.

There are several objectives for this campus communication:

- Influencing students in selecting their career directions, with the intent of providing a pool of qualified people from which the company, the industry, and the economy can meet their needs for human resources.

- Educating and influencing those whose opinions will affect such career choices, including, to some degree, parents.
- Developing a positive awareness of the company as an employer.
- Actually recruiting the newly trained people the company needs.
- Creating a favorable general image of the company, its industry, and the business system as a whole.

To achieve these ends corporations are involved in communications programs of a scope surprising to everyone but the personnel people who organize them and carry them out. Particularly notable is the extent to which companies rely on a communications technique which is in decreasing use in product marketing, that is, face-to-face, person-to-person contact.

COMMUNICATING WITH COLLEGES

College Relations: Person to Person, Plus

"It was a problem of time. We wanted to talk with placement officers of twenty colleges at the beginning of the school year, but we couldn't take the time to visit each campus. Our solution was to arrange a two-day seminar at our headquarters. The placement officers were delighted with the chance to visit New York, and in terms of getting our needs and interests across, the seminar was an outstanding success."

This is Jeannette Gadomski, assistant treasurer, describing part of The Bank of New York's college relations program. It was a seminar to provide placement officers with an on-the-spot look at the bank's training programs and a chance to talk directly with company people about the kind of employee the bank is looking for and careers that beginning jobs can lead to.

The seminar included a dinner and reception for the college representatives and "gave us a chance to tell them about our specific goals," Ms. Gadomski reports. "We're already getting results. We've been invited to speak on a number of campuses before student groups, classes, minority associations, and the like." She explains that the bank's college relations staff will follow up the seminar with campus visits and career fairs at about twenty colleges, mostly in surrounding states. Over the next few months the bank hopes to hire thirty or so new graduates who will build successful careers in banking.

The bank's college relations program goes beyond recruiting. For instance, in the hope of increasing the number of minority graduates on which to draw, the bank participates in career days and small group career counseling on campus as well as in the bank.

There are about as many sides to college relations as there are jobs companies want to fill. While The Bank of New York brought college placement officers to its own headquarters, the more customary method is to send representatives to the college campuses.

A highly personal kind of business, college relations depends heavily on one-to-one meetings between company representatives and college placement officers, professors, and students, both in general and those being considered for positions.

Many companies rely on full-time college recruiters to handle college relations. Stauffer Chemical Company, for example, has regional recruiters, each one responsible for building and keeping good relationships with the colleges and universities in a particular section of the country. Other companies use other employees in college relations. Engineers, for example, may recruit this year's graduates for new engineering positions. Alumni often are sent as company "ambassadors" to their alma maters in the belief that a college's graduates have special familiarity with the teaching staff and the curriculum, as well as with the placement department.

Apart from seeking the best qualified students for job openings, the college relations programs strive to build a solid rapport between the company and the school, a bond that will encourage the college to direct its outstanding graduates to the firm. Knowing the company's projected needs for nuclear engineers over the next several years, for example, the college can use such information in counseling undergraduates as they make their program decisions.

Companies use different ways to build this relationship. One way is to help a school solve some of its problems. It may be done through financial grants or awards, donations or loans of equipment, company data, or even company computer time. Use of company personnel as guest lecturers, instructors, or consultants adds another dimension to a college's programs. Such generosity and indication of concern and interest builds a foundation for successful recruiting.

A main thrust of these efforts is, of course, hiring people. At the same time the company's image as a corporation and as an employer is being built on campus. Faculty members generally are community leaders; today's students will be tomorrow's consumers and leaders in business and government. The attitudes and decisions of both groups strongly influence a company's success.

We have touched on how a company's future needs can help influence a student's career choice. In that way, to some degree, a recruiting program helps shape the work force. A broad recruiting and image building program does this in other ways as well, as a special program of Bell Laboratories illustrates.

To help develop more minority engineers, the research arm of the Bell System Companies each year provides a visiting professor to one of the six black colleges with engineering programs. The professor's full salary and relocation costs are paid by Bell Labs. For the last two years, for example, a Bell engineer who had graduated from Cornell's electrical engineering school taught at Prairie View A & M College in Houston. "The costs to the school of adding an outstanding, experienced teacher to its faculty is virtually nil," Rod Parker, an employment specialist with Bell Telephone Laboratories points out. "And our standing with the school is given a big boost. Furthermore, we've helped a number of young black people to become the engineers we'll need tomorrow."

In addition to this involvement and also financial support to minority schools, Bell Laboratories extends its recruiting to reach women as well. "We've added a number of women to our recruiting staff," Parker notes, "and we make special efforts at traditionally female campuses like Hunter College and Mount St. Vincent College in New York City."

Campus recruitment is the source of most of the company's employees and, like many others, Bell Laboratories relies on its own technical staff rather than full-time recruiters to find candidates for technical positions. The consequence is an extensive person-to-person communications program in which nearly 450 staff people visit campuses, including their own alma maters, as often as three times a year, renewing acquaintances with faculty and other staff.

Stauffer Chemical Company's college relations program on the other hand includes a network of regional recruiters, as earlier noted, to build communications with the nearly sixty schools it looks to for technical employees. It also provides scholarships, particularly in chemical engineering programs; gives grants to college departments; and funds several programs for minority groups and women engineering students. "The number of women we are able to hire for engineering positions is definitely increasing," Joan Gable, one of the company's employment executives reports. "A real problem," she adds with a note of disappointment, "is the low number of black engineering graduates."

Building for Tomorrow

College relations programs have another objective for many leading corporations. They hope to use their communications with campuses to help build a pool of the kinds of people they will be needing in the future. Among the most visible consequences of the human resources revolution in the college area, therefore, are the programs aimed at creating more minority and women technical students with degrees in fields relevant to company needs.

Less visible but more pervasive are the many internal programs that have been established to help students, through guidance and through financial investments. Many organizations utilize the services of faculty, as previously noted, who gain experience they can communicate to their students to help them make career choices. One company with an extensive program incorporating all of these elements is United Technologies Corporation's Pratt & Whitney Aircraft Engine Division. Its personnel manager, Paul E. Willhide, says, "The division is represented on the board of Eastern College Personnel Officers which aids students in career planning and placement. Like many other businesses, the company awards annual scholarships to employees' children—in this case, forty awards of $2,000 each. Because a lack of money can halt an education, Pratt & Whitney also hires college students during the summer to help them defray their costs, as well as get first-hand experience in business and manufacturing. The Connecticut and Florida plants also offer summer jobs for about 200 professors. Pratt & Whitney benefits from their technical expertise, and the professors get first-hand experience in current operations—experience they can pass on to their students."

Using Campus Media

The fact that the chief executive officer of a major corporation appears as a role model in a company ad directed to college students suggests the importance being placed on getting messages about the organization as a potential employer to this audience. There is a virtual web of specialized media reaching campus audiences of which major corporations make extensive use. The Bendix ad, for instance, appeared in *College Placement Annual,* a guide for student job seekers published by the College Placement Council, which contains scores of ads and thumbnail descriptions of hundreds of companies with openings. The council also publishes the *Journal of College Placement,* directed to campus placement and corporate recruitment executives. "A number of companies use the *Journal* regularly as a means of communicating to placement people what's happening in the organization, the range of opportunities it presents graduates, and the company's advantages as an employer," says Warren Kauffman, director of communications for the council. "In addition," he adds, "the editorial pages of the *Journal* are often a forum for discussions by placement people about corporate recruiting practices, and by corporate people about the problems they encounter in attempting to reach the schools' graduates."

Other national campus-directed media have emerged to serve human resources communications needs. University Communications, Inc., a division of Cox Broadcasting, has a group of publications directed to graduating seniors on campuses throughout the country. *Equal Opportunity,* a semiannual publication which as its name suggests is aimed at minority students, carries substantial numbers of recruitment ads directed to this group, as does its sister publication, the *Collegiate Women's Career Magazine.* Students in the Harvard Graduate School of Business issue an annual called *Careers and the MBA. The Graduate* is a career-oriented magazine directed annually at all college seniors.

In addition, a variety of media exist on individual campuses. Student newspapers ranging from monthlies to dailies are widely used to announce corporate recruitment interviews. Campus radio is sometimes utilized for the same purpose, and the growing numbers of schools with campus video facilities are adding television to the available communications media. In addition there are student publications directed to special campus groups, such as engineering students. Some companies—for example Westinghouse—not only utilize campus publications for advertising but direct special public relations packages to them, which may include photographs of company technical projects and shots of school alumni at work in the company.

Many graduate business schools have their own newspapers like the *Harbus News* and the *Wharton Journal,* in which corporations can speak directly to aspiring MBAs. A growing roster of such schools, responding to corporate concern with recruiting, also issue annual books of resumes that present the qualifications of their entire class of graduating students.

Posters in prominent campus locations, direct mail pieces to promising student contacts that may include the company's annual report, the indispensable college recruiting brochure that outlines, often in full color, the organization's fields, history, advantages, locations, and types of openings—all these are part of the human resources communi-cations scene. Some companies are adding audiovisual presentations, including film strips in the placement offices.

The Campus Message: "A Good Place to Grow"

A recent Atlantic Richfield Company ad typifies the high-level, almost "institutional" kind of message that top corporations are directing to key campus audiences in this broad range of media. Under an illustra-tion showing an ethnically mixed group of men and women in Atlantic Richfield hard hats, the copy says: "Our most important resources are the ones we can't drill for, mine or refine. Because they're not natural resources, they're human resources. Men and women of many different races and backgrounds. At Atlantic Richfield, the only common denom-inator we seek is talent—the ability to take on difficult energy problems and solve them. The skill to help manage a corporation doing business in the billions. The creativity to find better ways of preserving and protecting an environment that's given us so much. And the pioneering spirit to discover new energy sources."

The ad also points out that the company has created a minority business program, attempts to stem high school dropout rates by using employees as speakers at high schools, sponsors a film on nontradi-tional work roles for women, and is involved in community councils and related activities. Finally it indicates the kinds of openings availa-ble and how students can find out more about them. Both illustration and ad copy stress that Atlantic Richfield is an equal opportunity employer.

The themes in the Atlantic Richfield ad—the importance of people to the company, the interest and importance of the company's work, its role as a responsible corporate citizen, the diversity of its openings, and its adherence to equal opportunity—are recurrent in most of the exten-sive communications efforts companies direct to college audiences. Each organization stresses some of its special advantages. General Dynamics emphasizes broad involvement in high technology; Xerox, its social role in communications; others their wide choice of locations, their leadership in an industry, patterns of growth, or future prospects.

The message that comes through in print and in audiovisual material, by and large, is that of the corporations as "good guys"—concerned, responsive, involved, and offering graduating students both interesting work and a chance to remake the world as they advance along with the company's growth.

But the message that really penetrates, however, is more likely to be the one that develops through the person-to-person communications programs that parallel and reinforce the ads and posters. Image, as noted, tends to spring more from these contacts and from the campus grapevine. The actual working experiences the company provides conveyed by co-op students and alumni; the impression made by its recruiters and speakers; the human resources news reported from the outside world on hiring and firing, discrimination suits, and contract awards—all of these, plus experience with company products and articles in business and technical journals modify the messages that advertisers direct to their sophisticated campus audiences.

Coming through, too, is the message that recruiting attention focuses on the business and engineering schools. "One of our major problems in placement," says one university placement executive, "is the liberal arts student. The companies just don't see much of a role in their organizations for people with degrees in English lit or ancient history. We've been finding some applications for such degrees—sales jobs, for example—but not many. It's a problem that needs more attention from both the schools and business. There are a lot of good minds that may go to waste otherwise."

One response to the recent recession has been a wholesale switch among new students from the "soft" disciplines of the sixties into courses that provide better opportunities for employment. Business is, in this sense, shaping an important segment of the future work force.

THE COMMUNITY COLLEGES

The growing importance of the country's 1,200 two-year schools, often called community colleges, is another evidence both of business's impact in shaping the work force and the human resources revolution's effect on career thinking. There are more than 4 million students enrolled in these schools, most of which were established in the affluent sixties as one answer to the overflow of college enrollments. Today, however, nearly half of these two-year students are enrolled in highly practical courses such as lab technology, computer programming, and business administration.

As a result not all corporate campus relations efforts and scholarship support go to the four-year colleges. "We keep the closest possible relations with two-year colleges and technical institutes," says the college relations director of one of the nation's leading companies. "Those schools provide us with well-trained people, ready to step into many positions that we're having trouble filling."

The success of the two-year schools seems to stem from two advantages. First, they are meeting the growing need within the economy for people to fill complex jobs that require considerable training, but which are not at a professional level. The lower echelons of computer programming are one good example; the need for technicians is another, and that is desperate in many fields with the increase in automation, which requires high-level maintenance and repair skills.

The second advantage is that while the costs of a four-year degree program are skyrocketing—the current average cost for a year's tuition and fees at a private university is now an estimated $3139 per year—publically operated two-year schooling remains within the financial range of most families. The average tuition at such schools is about $300 a year and usually doesn't require a student to live away from home.

Indicative of the importance companies are giving these schools is the support they get from such organizations as Bell Labs. "We recruit regularly from a number of New Jersey two-year schools," says Rod Parker of that organization. "As a research laboratory, we have a substantial need for people trained as technicians. One of the programs we have adopted to meet that need is to provide grants which will encourage people to acquire engineering technology certificates that community colleges confer. And at the same time, we provide equal amounts to the school as a way to encourage them to maintain such programs. This, incidentally, has been a boon to encouraging minority and women students to enter such occupations."

The kind of communications efforts directed on a national basis to four-year colleges have yet to emerge in relationship to the two-year schools. In part this is due to a lack of available media for corporate recruiting to use. Only a comparative handful of these small schools have their own newspapers, for example. Outside publishers have made only limited attempts to tap the community college market, in contrast to the many publications directed toward four-year college students. Also, as in the Bell Labs program, most corporate involvement with community colleges is on the local or regional level.

Yet the community colleges may be sleepers as far as their human resources potential is concerned. More flexible and responsive than their four-year counterparts, more accessible in financial terms both to students and to smaller companies needing trained people, these schools are ideally suited to deal with the new second-career trends that are emerging. In a period when students are increasingly vocation-conscious, they may also be the successors to the high schools in producing people trained for the new kinds of entry-level jobs emerging in the post-industrial economy.

HIGH SCHOOLS: POINT OF DECISION

When Jimmy B., a high school freshman in Greenville, opens his next copy of *Senior Scholastic*, the national news publication for high school students used in thousands of classrooms across the nation, he will probably encounter an exciting message from a potential employer.

"Careers are important," the ad will tell him, "and if you want to get ahead in life, you should be thinking now what you'd like to do." The ad will then go on to list and show, in full color, some of the training the organization can offer: electronics equipment maintenance and repair, cooking, medical technician work, skydiving, scuba diving, boat handling, off-the-road driving (in a strictly nonrecreational vehicle), and piloting small aircraft.

The organization, of course, is the Army. The Department of Defense, for its various divisions—Army, Navy, Air Force, Marines, Coast Guard—is doing some of the best and most extensive human resources communications directed to high school audiences, supplemented on occasion by such show-and-tell projects as an air show by the Blue Angels.

The military services are doing two valuable jobs for business and industry. They are training young people by the millions in skills that often have an application outside military service—operating computers and servicing jet engines, for example. More important in human resources terms is that the military, year after year, has been pounding home the idea of thinking and preparing for the world of work to millions of high school youngsters. They have been doing it in a skilled, professional, and extensive way, which business, by and large, has not equaled.

Shaping Career Decisions

Helping and hiring young people who have studied beyond high school can be compared with remodeling a house. A wall or a window may be added or removed, but the basic house remains intact. By contrast, the carpenter who sets out to build a home determines its size, shape, and features. It seems apparent today that business in its human resources communications directed to schools puts the major emphasis on reaching students after they have made and implemented a career decision. Only a relatively few companies are attempting to influence student attitudes at the high school level on a national scale.

One of the notable individual efforts at human resources communication on the high school level is conducted by Westinghouse. The company's annual Science Fair for students, offering substantial scholarship aid to winning entrants, attracts major interest throughout the country and has stimulated a generation or more of students to consider careers in science and engineering.

Another is the New York Life Insurance Company's careers program entitled "Careers for a Changing World." A key element of this is a film developed for and distributed to reach high school students. "What Will I Do with My Time" portrays a group situation in which students express their hopes and doubts, and experienced people at work in different fields comment on their own career choices. The company reinforces this effort with related booklets that describe various career fields such as health care, the arts, business, and office jobs.

Mirroring the human resources thrust of the last decade, special programs are aimed at minority high school students. Under the Minority Introduction To Engineering (MITE) program, minority high school juniors attend two-week summer sessions at the University of California at Irvine and other schools to learn about opportunities in engineering and their educational requirements. A special program at the University of Kansas, which is sponsored by twenty-nine companies and the National Science Foundation, also encourages minority high school students to pursue engineering careers.

But only half our high school graduates now go to college, and it is frequently acknowledged today that fewer students should commit themselves to college studies, at least not until some time after high school graduation when their interests have crystallized.

Furthermore, business and industry are looking askance at a college degree, stating it is "way oversold" and that people who in years past would have become skilled workers after high school now go to college and emerge with "no salable skills."

Given the costs of most college educations, more high school students are looking at jobs in industries and more companies are making efforts to encourage them, with good reason. A survey by *Industry Week* reported in that business magazine's August 29, 1977 issue shows that more than half of United States manufacturers are victims of the skilled labor shortage. Most of them report that the shortage is hurting their businesses in terms of efficient operation, quality, and profits. Philip G. Marquis, plant engineering manager for Litton Industries, Inc., in San Carlos, California, says that part of the shortage is due to the attitudes of teachers who malign the blue-collar worker from grade school on up. "Teachers make a big mistake," he says, "in not impressing on students that a good skilled worker can make better than $20,000 a year once apprenticeship is completed."

General Electric has taken another approach to help high school students who will be working in its factories. Faced with a high turnover and problems in filling jobs with people who have basic skills, one plant has developed a program focusing on teachers and guidance counselors in local high schools. The goal is to show what factory work really is like and what skills it requires, in the hope that teachers and counselors will pass the knowledge on to their students.

Except for the first and final sessions at local colleges, the classes meet weekly at the plant, where managers volunteer their time for discussing everything from apprentice problems to union-management relations, environmental problems, and quality control—even the atmosphere of the plant cafeteria. Then each teacher "shadows" an employee for a day, watching him or her doing the job, and explaining what it is and why it is done.

More than sixty teachers and counselors have completed the program to date. The results? One counselor noted that for any job in the plant, whether it is working in the stockroom or drawing on a knowledge of fractions to use blueprints and scaled-down drawings, the employee without mathematics is "just out of it." Previously, the counselor said, advice to the student not going to college might have been to avoid difficult math. Now, "I would tell him to make the effort."

Many authorities think there can be a better matching of youth with available jobs, and many believe that, with help like that provided by the General Electric plant, high school teachers and counselors can do more for those who aren't bound for college.

CORPORATIONS AS EDUCATORS

"Guidance and counseling on the high school level is the weakest link in the bridge between education and work," according to Willard Wirtz, who as former Secretary of Labor and now head of the National

Manpower Institute knows whereof he speaks. He might well have added that even those students with specific goals, at both high school and advanced levels, are also coming into the work force woefully deficient not only in understanding of the opportunities open to them but in the basics of writing, reading, and arithmetic, as we observed earlier.

The result is another area in which companies are deeply involved in human resources communications—the education and training of their own personnel. Confronted with ill-prepared employees, or those who want to move up in the job or want to enter another field, companies are spending an estimated $220 million every year just in underwriting employee study.

Shirley Y. is one of these students. "I graduated from high school two years ago with good grades," she says, "but I really didn't know what to do with myself. I was lucky to get a job in the office here. After about a year, I decided if I was going to go places, I should get a degree as an accountant. I'm taking two evening courses now and my company is paying all my tuition. My supervisor says I should be ready for promotion next year, based on the courses I'm taking, and the company will back me all the way to a degree under their tuition program."

The number of employees utilizing this employee benefit is apparently increasing. Merrill Lynch, Pierce, Fenner & Smith, which is the nation's largest security firm, for example, reports that 6,000 of its employees studied under the company's tuition refund plan in the 1975–1976 school year, up 50 percent from five years earlier.

Is it profitable for companies to teach Johnny to read or help Shirley to be an accountant? Most personnel directors think so. The skills the company's tuition buys are as valuable to the employer as to the person who acquires them. "And with the number of young people entering the labor force about to take a sharp drop in the eighties," says one employment executive, "competition for skilled entry-level workers is going to climb. This kind of program enables us both to get people and hold them. There's a certain loyalty engendered when your company helps you get a marketable skill or a degree."

In the belief that well-informed employees are an asset to a company, Kimberly-Clark Corporation also has expanded its educational assistance program from only job-related courses to inclusion of cultural opportunities. In the 1976–1977 school year, when the company paid out $833,000 under the program, more than 30 percent of its employees were enrolled in courses, a sharp contrast to the three percent under the more restricted plan a few years earlier.

Richard C. Hupp, who administers Kimberly-Clark's Educational Opportunities Plan, says that in addition to the educational value to present employees, the program is a drawing card for new employees. It has had another effect, too. Colleges and universities in areas where the company has its plants are increasing the number of their night and weekend courses, a sign that the program benefits those institutions as well as the employees and Kimberly-Clark.

Every semester 1,100 employees take advantage of Pratt & Whitney's educational assistance program, and the firm's annual tuition bill is $750,000. The need for more skilled craftspeople prompted the company to expand its program of paying tuition for graduate studies in engineering and the sciences to include study on the undergraduate level and in high schools, trade, and correspondence schools where the programs also include business, trade, and technical studies.

Co-ops—Combining Work and Study

In the search for skilled and educated employees, more and more companies are taking another approach, the co-op program in which a person goes to school part of the day or year and works the remainder of the time in a job closely related to the school work. In the typical college co-op program, the student spends the first year on campus, then alternates semesters in the classroom and on the job.

Edward N. Cole, president of General Motors and himself a product of co-op education, believes that cooperative education is a realistic one and is especially suited to the needs of students and employers in this age of industrialization and urbanization.

The Burroughs Corporation's president, Paul S. Mirabit, sees co-op education as a means of creating good communications between industry and the universities, making it possible for the schools to do a better job of preparing students for careers.

Another aspect of communications is the employer image factor. Co-op students, as people with actual working experience at a company, can be important in building or downgrading the corporate image as employer, depending upon the experiences students have on the job.

The main company objective, that of being able to recruit trained people, is apparently achieved through the co-op programs they operate. Most companies with co-op experience, of which there are now literally hundreds, report that many of the students who work at the organization on a co-op basis come back to it as full-time employees after graduation.

Colleges and Corporate Training

Obviously colleges and local schools at every level are becoming more important to businesses and industries as extensions of their own training departments. The Manassas campus of Northern Virginia Community College, for example, developed a certified program in electronics technology to meet the need of employees at IBM's Manassas plant. The program now enrolls 100 other residents of the suburban Washington, D.C., area. In line with that success, a committee representing community colleges and training and development managers is considering the kinds of programs that community colleges might offer in conjunction with corporate training goals.

CORPORATIONS AND IN-HOUSE TRAINING

One of the most extensive elements of human resources communications by organizations occurs within the companies themselves in their in-house training programs.

At the 3M Company where the primary purpose of on-the-job training is immediate job results and the secondary purpose is to help people develop for future jobs, President L. W. Lehr asserts that intelligent and careful use of the training dollar pays big dividends. With in-house training programs for sales representatives, for example, the company has been able to "save valuable management time and still maintain increased productivity, to an extent we wouldn't have thought possible fifteen years ago."

Company training programs have other merits. For Wigwam Mills, Inc., in Sheboygan, Wisconsin, it has meant a stable work force. Previously, skilled knitting mechanics recruited from out of state vanished at the sign of the first snowflake. Thanks to an in-house four-year program for mechanics begun in 1971, the company hires locally and its turnover problem is solved.

The nation's largest manufacturing company, General Motors Corporation, believes that in-house training is the key to developing a solid, skilled worker force, according to Donald F. Pheifer, assistant director of the company's labor relations. Some 15,000 workers are being trained for skilled jobs in the traditional apprenticeship program and the company's Employees in Training (EIT) system. The latter establishes a pool of trained people who normally work on production lines but who are ready to fill in a skilled position when sudden peak business or a vacancy occurs. The big auto manufacturer relies on the talents of 65,000 skilled employees and, in the opinion of Mr. Pheifer, "You're a lot more certain of getting good skilled workers if you train them properly in-house than if you just advertise for help."

General Motors' program is based on the company's estimated needs four years down the line. Other companies initiate programs to meet needs created by particular situations. A Dallas construction subsidiary of Centex Corporation, Fox & Jacobs, Inc., has begun its own training program for bricklayers and other skilled workers to fill its requirements because of the building boom in the Sun Belt.

In the same labor-short region, a group of companies (Dow, Fluor Corporation, Fish Engineering & Construction, Foster Wheeler Corporation, Kellogg Company, and Lummus Company) are training piping designers and drafters in a course developed by Fluor. Students who have completed two years of college studies in pre-engineering and other topics and who pass an examination continue attending college for eleven forty-hour weeks as salaried employees of one of the sponsors. On graduation they are assigned jobs as beginner designers, and given a raise. The success of the first program prompted the companies to offer an advanced course in piping design. Other companies are expected to join the sponsoring group, and additional courses are being considered for the program.

Fluor, which spends more than $9 million annually on training and recruiting, conducts an extensive in-house technical training program through its subsidiary, People Growth, Inc. It is now training 500 high school graduates for drafting jobs that normally require two years of schooling.

The Business-Education Web: Continuing Challenge, Continuing Change

Most people well remember their first day at school and their first "real" job. Like so many other milestones in life, they were markers in our career development. Looking backward, we can see that in reality there aren't sharp dividing lines between our education and training and what we do today for a living. The first prepared us for the second, and to advance, we have had to update and upgrade our skills and knowledge continuously.

"The shape of the work force has changed," observes William B. Chew of General Motors' personnel department. "It's no longer a pyramid; today it's more like a diamond. The number of entry-level jobs that require no skill is shrinking, and the technical force is increasing."

The situation at General Motors where there are some 700,000 jobs illustrates changes throughout industry. Legislation like pollution control laws force manufacturers to develop new technology. Time brings other changes. Dr. Jules Mirabal, a corporate engineering executive with General Electric, remembers that only twenty-five years ago groups of women painstakingly hand-wrapped three layers of resin-soaked tape around each large metal conductor bar used in turbine generators. Today the task is done by operators controlling machines worth $300,000 each that replace scores of tedious and repetitious jobs. A main motive for the change was to raise product quality, but the change also calls for greater responsibility and skill in using the complex machines.

Technology has brought about sweeping changes in the United States work force since 1950. A United States Census Bureau study shows that the percentage of "professional, technical and kindred" workers has risen 167 percent. This group plus "managers and administrators" now make up nearly 26 percent of all workers. By way of comparison, "craftsmen, foremen, etc." in the work force rose 40 percent, and "operatives and kindred" rose about 20 percent. In other words, our sophisticated computers and complex equipment require a greater number of skilled, educated people in the work force.

Our post-industrial age has brought us new problems we're just beginning to solve. One of them is more competition for jobs, and the competition puts a new premium on education and training, from the basic skills we acquire in grade school to the highly specialized knowledge earned on the graduate level.

Another of these new problems, described at length in Alvin Toffler's *Future Shock,* is accelerating change. Studies show that an engineer's college training is outdated in only ten years as new methods and equipment filter into our manufacturing systems. Lasers were unheard of three decades ago, but in the last few years there has been a steady stream of applications, from cutting cloth in garment manufacturing to mending retinas. Even diligent reading of the general and business newspapers and magazines can't keep us abreast of new information and its meaning in our lives. And that's where more education enters the picture, whether it's on-the-job training, special courses, or even sabbaticals for extended study. Reaching those in education, telling them what business needs, helping them prepare tomorrow's employees, has a new importance in a company's communications.

CHAPTER TWELVE

Communicating with Outside Audiences

The city is Grand Rapids, Michigan. The company is Doehler-Jarvis, which has an 800-person manufacturing operation in the city, one of its several Midwestern locations. The company intends to shut down the plant.

This is a familiar situation. Markets change. Facilities age. The economic climate dictates consolidation or retrenchment, and the decision has to be made. What follows a plant closing is also familiar. People are out of work suddenly; they have problems with mortgages and medical expenses and school costs for their families; there is an adverse economic impact on the community as a large number of wage earners lose their buying power. This chain reaction produces strong negative reactions against the company (and business in general) for allowing disaster to happen. There may even be lawsuits to avert the closing.

With Doehler-Jarvis in Grand Rapids, however, the scenario was different. When the closing became inevitable, the company turned to the University of Michigan's Institute for Social Research (ISR) for suggestions on how best to cope with the human aspects of the plant closing. The resulting company/union planning team, under advisement from ISR, put together a community-wide task force in the Grand Rapids area that acted to coordinate efforts of groups able to help those who would become unemployed. With four subgroups headed by community leaders, a Community Service Council was established to work with a liaison unit of union and management people and the United Way staff. The subgroups were organized around four areas of need: manpower, health, education, and finance. The manpower group included representatives from the Michigan Employment Security Commission, private employment agencies, the Chamber of Commerce, the United Auto Workers, and the Urban League. It talked to employers throughout western Michigan about jobs. Ads were placed by Doehler-Jarvis to publicize this available work force and its skills. Employees were given information on the unemployment laws, available benefits, and training grants.

At the same time the health group, comprised of members of area hospitals, clinics, the local health department, and family service agencies, notified the hospitals and clinics of the problem. These were urged to make special arrangements for paying health care costs, since many workers would be forced to drop their medical coverage. The education group looked for grants and loans that would help pay for education and arranged additional training for almost a hundred of the newly unemployed workers. A financial group helped in the planning for changed family finances and in getting monthly charge payments eased until the workers could find other jobs.

This extensive program substantially reduced the problems created by the plant closing. It gave the community a different view of Doehler-Jarvis, and it provides a good working example of how the human resources revolution is altering the ways in which companies deal with their communities, and the extensive human resources communications this may involve.

A NEW CORPORATE VIEW

There is a classic Bill Mauldin cartoon that pictures two diplomats walking away from the United Nations. "Who do you think you're working for," one chides the other, "us—or the rest of the damned world?" If politics appear to have stood still in this regard, business seems to be moving beyond the "us or them" stage.

Once it was possible to draw the line between the company, that monolith within its unassailable corporate walls, and the outside world. The latter was seen primarily as a medium for achieving the corporate will, whether that meant selling goods or passing laws. "What is good for General Motors," as Charlie Wilson's philosophy had it, "is good for America." The human resources revolution is changing that attitude with discernible speed. Sophisticated management is increasingly sensitive to the total social environment in which the organization operates.

One reflection of this new view is the way human resources communications are being extended to external audiences important to the company, audiences which themselves are increasingly sensitized to the implications of this change.

Among the most important of these audiences are the communities in which organizations have facilities, the unions, which are becoming a part of the changes the human resources revolution is creating; its retirees; and that highly sensitive group, the stockholders.

INTERFACING WITH THE COMMUNITY

Employees as Communicators

Like any organization classified as a public utility, Continental Telephone Corporation has always considered community relations important. Officers and employees took active roles in community affairs, the company provided educational materials and assistance to local schools, and public relations people worked actively with local news media to keep the public informed about company activities and plans in the extensive region in which this phone company operates.

But the company found that rate increases and other developments in recent years had dimmed its image with many of its subscribers, including local business people. One response by Continental was to involve its own employees as a part of its community communications efforts. District Manager David Batchelder set up a series of meetings between employees and the utility's community relations staff to stress the importance to the company of public and community relations, and explore ways to improve its communications with subscribers in each locality.

A community action team consisting of local management and employees was formed for each community in which the company operated, and a committee on public relations was organized among craft and clerical employees. The aim was to encourage a flow of suggestions for improving daily contacts with subscribers. In addition a representative of the craft committee was chosen to participate in community action team meetings.

One result, which management considers highly effective, was face-to-face communication with local opinion leaders by plant supervisors. These leaders were identified, then the managers visited them personally to discuss areas of concern. It was important that the community members had a company person, not just an abstract name or title, to talk to about problems. "By keeping the lines of communication open, by actively making sure they are kept open, we should be able to head off problems before they become serious," Batchelder says.

The company's public relations committee generated a series of suggestions that were adopted by local management. Most of them were easily implemented ideas aimed at encouraging employees to deal with subscribers as people rather than as job assignments. One example was a call-back program to ask if newly installed services met the customer's requirements.

The human resources communications involved in this one program are many. They include internal, two-way communications with various levels of employees; involving employees in company projects; a specialized suggestion system; the contacts by employees with company customers; and the overall idea of handling community relations by means of the company's own work force.

Pulling Out—and Moving In

The Doehler-Jarvis example shows how companies have begun to exhibit a larger concern when business needs dictate closing down or moving a facility, and it indicates some of the human resources communications involved. Westinghouse Electric Company provides another example.

Westinghouse made a $10 million investment in a television tube plant and warehousing facilities in Elmira, New York. Within two years foreign competition in this field produced drastic changes in the whole industry. Westinghouse had to make the decision to end its manufacturing at the Elmira location, which meant cutting 1,100 workers from the local payroll.

The company announced its decision to its employees, to community leaders, and to the news media a month before the first layoffs were scheduled. The announcement was followed by information to the work force (and the community) on the severance benefits that Westinghouse would provide. (These were described by one community leader as "very liberal.") Westinghouse also determined that those who were let go were eligible for special benefits, since the layoffs were precipitated by foreign competition. Employees were informed that they would have doubled unemployment insurance benefits as a result of the government's Trade Adjustment Assistance program. The company worked with a job task force from the community to reach employers on behalf of the laid-off Westinghouse people, and the company compiled and provided information on employee skills to aid in the search for new jobs. These steps, communicated to the community and involving company-community programs, helped Westinghouse maintain good relations in Elmira where it still employs 750 people in other operations.

When a company is looking for a location for a new plant or headquarters facility, where once they were welcomed, they now meet a different reception. Environmental concerns must increasingly be considered. Dow Corporation's attempt to establish a petrochemical complex in a rural area 40 miles northeast of San Francisco, for example, was to be the spearhead of an industrial development program that would have added $1 billion in industrial facilities, involved 1,000 construction jobs, and required a permanent staff of 1,000 more. All this in an area where unemployment was running at twice the national average.

But even support from government officials did not stem a furious tide of opposition to siting industry near one of the nation's largest tidal marshes, already declared a vital wildlife area, and within terrain crisscrossed by hundreds of miles of waterways. Environmentalists saw the plant as precipitating the destruction of a unique area. Other groups feared the pollution that would result from manufacturing operations. "It would be the first of a series of plants that would completely change the character of southeast Solano County," argued one Sierra Club member, voicing local opinion. "Industrial growth should be placed where there has been industrial growth." A lawsuit against both the company and the county brought to a halt Dow's plans, on which it had already spent $10 million.

Because the Dow story is far from unique, companies today tread carefully when approaching new communities. Not all of the mine fields are environmental; others may be in human resources. Du Pont has established operating procedures on communicating with a community about locating a facility. Opinion leaders, the press and local broadcast media, and the community at large are informed about the plans. Considerable information is given about the numbers and kinds of jobs that will be open, the pay scales and benefits programs, and other human resources data concerning hiring and equal employment policies.

"When we go into a community," one Du Pont spokesperson notes, "we adopt the policy of being completely open and factual with the people. The first impression is a lasting one, and we strive to get across that Du Pont will be a responsible employer who will make a positive contribution to the community, in addition to providing jobs."

The traumas of moving out and moving in aside, many other aspects of human resources are involved in communications between organizations and their communities. For example, there could be local labor problems, with the threat of extended strikes; concerns about working conditions at company facilities, augmented today by increasing public awareness of hazards connected with handling various kinds of materials. There are the various problems that can arise in establishing equal opportunity and counteracting backlash effects; problems with service industries which may not have sufficient staff to meet critical local problems; and concerns with the impact of new equipment at company facilities on the local work force. Often these have a direct impact on the company's local customers. One reason the local Bell systems, for example, used nontraditional recruiting ads showing women as telephone installers and men as operators was to accustom local subscribers to the idea that they would be encountering male telephone operators and women installers.

The other important interrelationship between community relations and human resources is the extent to which the company's own human resources—its work force, from management down—are becoming a key element in communicating company ideas and achievements to the community, and in return reflecting community problems and attitudes back to the company.

NEW INTERCHANGES WITH UNIONS

Interviewed about company communications with its unions, one industrial relations executive said, "Our production workers are members of the unions. We communicate with our production workers. That's it." This is a pretty accurate summing up of the situation in most corporations. Union communications involve the traditional channels of grievance procedures, collective bargaining sessions, and other familiar interchanges.

While these remain solidly in place, the human resources revolution is bringing some companies and unions together in creating new kinds of responses to the changes occurring within the work force. One area of shared concern is the effort to make work life more satisfying for the worker through job enrichment programs.

"Job enrichment really does work, but it's 98 percent a communications device," says Richard Neitlich, assistance vice president for personnel for the Metropolitan Life Insurance Company. "It does perk up the job for awhile, but unless constant efforts are made by both sides—management and employees or unions—it will fail. Labeling it a 'program' is bad because it frightens people. They often feel that the program is there simply to get more work for less money. The solution is to communicate continuously and through all media. Both management and supervisors must be taught how to work closer with labor and 'share the glory.'"

Another kind of shared program is helping current workers adapt to changed technologies. The pace of change in the working world necessitates, for both union and company survival, that the past processes of long-term stubborn resistance to change by the unions, and equally determined insistence on instant automation by the company, be moderated.

Common human resources problems are also a factor in new facets of the company-union relationship. OSHA's drive to make the work place safer accords with union goals for its members, and company-union teams are working together on this human resources project in a number of organizations. More efficient use of energy, as a national concern, has engendered instances of unions and companies cooperating on developing new work methods and processes that can conserve energy, with inputs from employees. The problem of providing equal employment opportunity, pushed by some unions and resisted by others, is also providing a common meeting ground. Cooperative company-union programs have been established in skills training, in recruiting for particular jobs, and in making the essential on-the-job human adjustments.

Lifetime Security

Potentially the most radical of all recent developments in terms of its human resources implications and the need for union-company information interchange is the new demand for "lifetime" security by some of the major unions.

From the union viewpoint this is a logical response to the extensive technical, demographic, and economic changes in process. The loss of manufacturing jobs to more sophisticated machinery is one reason for the diminishing percentage of unionized workers. As the centers of population and industry shift from the traditionally unionized Northeast and Midwest, many industries are forced to follow. The can manufacturers, to name one industry, already faced with lifetime security demands, are closely tied to their customers the beverage producers, who in turn are following *their* customers in the demographic shifts now occurring. Such changes are of economic importance to companies, too, since the moves often result in a better tax climate and a lower-cost work force.

As a result it seems likely that unions will be willing to make concessions to companies on automation and on radical alterations in some long-agreed-upon work rules in order to achieve a better level of job security for their members. One implication of this new development appeared in a October 31, 1977 *Business Week* review of lifetime security in the can industry:

> To win the lifetime-security measures it wants, the USW may have to yield to management demands on productivity issues. The companies want to replace inefficient high cost lines that produce three-piece cans with computerized machinery that turns out two-piece containers. To run these lines with greatest efficiency, they must be operated 24 hours a day, and management is asking for more freedom in scheduling hours of work. Overtime is already a matter of bitter contention in some plants.

In the eighties the issues involved in lifetime security alone are likely to create extensive changes in the whole relationship between workers and company, and at all levels. The long-standing pattern has been to pass on union gains for blue-collar people into comparable advantages for the white-collar group, and for these to spread through the economy.

REACHING THE RETIREES

Every Wednesday is Senior Citizens' Day at Korvette's fifty-eight department stores, a chain concentrated on the East Coast and in the Midwest. On that day older people get a 10 percent discount on most of the company's merchandise. Korvette's president, David Brous, says this new program is in recognition of the "emergence of the senior citizen as a major factor in retailing today." The growing economic and political power of this group has been noted earlier. What's happening in the marketplace is being reflected in human resources communications.

Company communications on retirement begin well before people reach their actual retirement date. An American Management Associations survey indicates that about 90 percent of the 300 companies responding have some form of preretirement communications program. In most of these companies, 72 percent of the respondents report counseling on such retirement-related issues as Social Security benefits, Medicare, and legal and health matters.

Once an individual has retired, the chances are increasing that he or she will be hearing more from the company. Bristol-Myers, for example, recently introduced a new bimonthly publication which it calls *AlumNews*. Its aim is to maintain communications between the company and the organization's retirees. The publication is written in a newsmagazine style and carries information on benefits, pertinent company news, and articles on the activities of individual retirees. A "Class Notes" section provides brief data on other retirees, and there is a column of reader response. *AlumNews* is printed in 11-point type for easy readability by older people, and is mailed first class to Bristol-Myers retirees throughout the country.

As part of its extensive communications program, Bethlehem Steel issues a quarterly publication, the *Bethlehem Review*. The company sends it not only to its current employees but to its entire roster of retirees. These reviews carry information about the company's attitudes toward major issues of public policy—energy, for example—in terms of how these affect the company.

Many prepare periodic newsletters on company affairs, providing advice and information of special interest to their retired work forces. Often they are mailed in the same envelope as the pension check. Other organizations use an outside professional service like Retirement Advisors, Inc. (RAI), which provides a monthly newsletter closely tied to current economic and other developments that relate to the interests and needs of a retiree audience. An organization using RAI's service can also include company information in the newsletter.

Retiree response to communications provided by their companies is highly enthusiastic, says Henry Wallfesh, executive vice president of Retirement Advisors, Inc. He cites surveys made by various corporations to determine to what extent such material is read, and the reactions of retired people to receiving it. "You would have to see the surveys' responses to realize what a fantastic impact this form of human resources communications has on a retiree audience," he says. "You can recognize it right from the beginning when the questionnaires rack up response rates of 80 percent and 90 percent, with no incentives offered. The questionnaire data indicates a consistent 90 percent plus favorable reaction to the retiree publication and almost 100 percent readership of it. We receive literally hundreds of comments from these retired people about the value of the information, what particularly interests them, and the appreciation they feel because the company hasn't forgotten them." He cites the responses to a recent study by the Borden Company which included comments such as, "The newsletter gives me a feeling that the company I loyally served for years does care," and, "The letter makes me feel that I am still part of a great company."

Some companies go beyond print communication. A Midwestern steel company, located in a small city where such personal communication is feasible, employs a person in its human resources department to reach regularly as many of the company's retirees as possible, either in person or by phone. This involves chatting with individuals, telling them about what's happening in the company, and determining if there are ways in which the company can help them. As an interesting by-product, the program is helping create an archive of company history, since the retiree relations person also writes down the reminiscences of long-time employees about the company's early days.

An electronics firm maintains a special office for its retirees, available to them at any time, to which they can bring any problems they may have. A machine tool firm organizes clubs for its retirees, patterned after school alumni associations, in various communities where there are concentrations of its "alumni."

Prudential Life Insurance is one of the leaders in this area of retirement communications, starting more than fifteen years ago with what is known as the "We Care" program. Prudential has its own retiree association, makes facilities available for meetings, and through the Prudential Athletic Club sets up trips and special events for retirees. The company also supplies speakers for association meetings. Retirees get the regular employee publication plus their own monthly retirement newsletter. Researchers are available in the company to answer questions from retired people, and the company provides other services as well.

One of the results of the human resources revolution has been a change of attitude that is occurring among the older population, patronized as "senior citizens," and often written off by both their former employers and the community. Having the examples of the minority communities and the women's rights groups, who have succeeded in using their political and economic power to better their lot, older people are moving toward an active militancy. The upcoming generations of retirees can be expected to reinforce this movement. Most of these older citizens are veterans of the work force; many carry psychic scars to prove it. As their numbers grow and solid leadership emerges, retirees seem likely to become a very important audience to the business world, both economically and socially.

The general approach to retiree communications, however, has yet to come to grips with the potential impact of the human resources revolution on this group. The aim seems to be that of providing information helpful to the retired individual and to maintaining a connection with the company. In this, the programs are successful. Yet they appear to be very much in the style of yesterday's "employee communications" programs, with their happy house organs and simplistic view of the world and the worker. This is no longer enough.

For one thing, retirees are no longer enjoying the "peace and leisure" that has been the standard image of retirement life. Inflation has wracked them financially; government programs for older people are often erratic and imcomprehensible; they are targets for street crime and shady manipulators. These experiences are creating a concerned, informed, and sophisticated core of older people with whom business should be maintaining a correspondingly more sophisticated dialogue.

THE SENSITIVE STOCKHOLDERS

A resolution from the floor at a recent Celanese Corporation annual meeting was significant in two ways. One was the nature of the resolution. It asked the company to provide a report to shareholders on its employment practices, including data by race and sex. It further asked the company to explain its problems, progress, and achievements in affirmative action. The other significant point was that this resolution was introduced by a stockholder who was also a company employee.

The resolution reflects the kind of question that is more and more often raised by investors. They are questions that relate to social factors in the company's operations, including the human resources area. The employee stockholder symbolizes the increase in the number of shareholding employees (and retirees) resulting from compensation plans at higher levels and, in the lower echelons, thrift programs involving company stock. It also reflects an increasing awareness in the financial community of the monetary importance of human resources issues. Securities Exchange Commission regulations, for example, now require that organizations disclose to potential investors any suits pending against the company, such as class-action litigation regarding employment discrimination.

There is also the marketing factor. We have seen how marketing communications have been building minorities and women in working roles into ads and commercials. How effective will this effort be when a company is facing a suit by its own people for failing to provide equal employment? The company's human resources practices must match the attitudes expressed in its marketing communications or every TV commercial with minority or female workers is likely to reemphasize the company's discriminatory practices. Financial people have become increasingly sensitive, therefore, to this direct relationship between marketing and human resources.

Companies, in turn, are becoming sensitive to attitudes within the financial community and among their own investors. They have begun to extend their human resources communications to include these two pivotal audiences. A survey of company annual reports by *Industrial Relations News* (May 20, 1978) found that 42 percent of the 132 organizations studied included material related to human resources in this basic corporate document, or that they published separate reports on social or human resources aspects of the company's activities.

Celanese, for example, devoted three pages of a recent annual report to "Public Responsibility." That section included several paragraphs on its activities in equal employment opportunity; reports on its safety record under the title "Employee Safety and Health"; and under "Employee Job Satisfaction," summarized a recent attitude study among the company's people, and reported on eight employees at one Celanese location "who are working toward graduate degrees in engineering administration by watching lectures that were videotaped at the University of Tennessee." A chart, in color, also provided statistical data on the number of women and minority employees in each job category at the company.

A recent American Can annual report featured a woman employee on the cover. She is identified and quoted on the inside cover as an administrator in Information Services at the Greenwich, Connecticut headquarters, who began with the company as a trainee. "This year's annual report," the copy notes, "is focused on young people with significant responsibilities at American Can." Other color photos in the report include younger workers, including women and minority people, in various company operations in a variety of working roles. All are quoted briefly, and a capsule background on each accompanies the photograph.

Many other organizations use the annual report cover as a kind of affirmation of equal employment, displaying many shots of company employees, and depicting a mix of men and women, whites and minorities, in many different roles. These companies, too, provide investors with information on human resources matters.

Texaco takes another tack. Their magazine includes articles on working life and photographs of the company's people at work. It also reports on various corporate social projects in detail. This publication is issued not only to internal audiences but to company stockholders, providing them with an ongoing update on human resources along with other company developments.

More corporate annual meetings are including comments from the chief executive officer about the company as an employer, often supported by visual aids reinforcing the verbal report. Such information also surfaces in corporate publications efforts directed to the financial community.

Much of the effort is defensive, of course, forced on the organization by the demands of its shareholders and of activist groups who use the technique of acquiring shares to give them a voice at annual meetings. Other aspects relate directly to government requirements, such as those of the Securities and Exchange Commission, that mandate disclosure of some human resources matters. Another reason for the increase also relates to the government. Because of the reporting requirements of the equal employment opportunity agencies and other government bodies, more data on this aspect of company activities is available now than ever before.

The key element, however, is the extent to which the average person, shareholder or no, is becoming aware of corporate financial matters and the human factors involved. Major television networks have news people who are financial reporters; this has been a long-time tradition among major newspapers. Business publications have in recent years been providing more coverage of human resources (although they may not recognize it as such) and increasingly deep coverage. It is now quite common, for example, for a lead front-page story in the *Wall Street Journal* to deal with such subjects as women in nontraditional work roles, business executives who have opted out of the working world to find other life-styles, or the performance of the Equal Opportunity Employment Commission. A dozen years ago the only human resources topics likely to surface in any business publication would be changes in the employment level or labor-management negotiations.

Consumer publications such as *Money* provide additional sophistication for average people on financial matters. Syndicated columns like

Sylvia Porter's appear in scores of newspapers. Courses and seminars (some of them, like Merrill Lynch's, conducted by securities firms themselves) have multiplied in recent years to provide education on financial matters and, of course, each year sees a best-seller on some aspect of making money.

To speak of a sensitive investor, then, is no poetic license. Business has never had so broad or so sensitive an audience for its offerings. Nor, perhaps, one so ready to turn from corporate securities to other forms of investment, as the activities of the market have shown, nor more prepared to take action—to litigate, if necessary—to achieve a greater degree of responsiveness from management in the area of human resources.

An Information Science, Inc., study estimates that human resources matters now occupy 20 percent of top management's time, and many executives expect this to increase to 30 percent within the next five years. Daniel Yankelovich, the noted business forecaster, believes human resources will be a primary focus of attention by business during at least the next decade and will be the key to shaping business in the years to follow. People, he observes, have changed more rapidly than management has been able to adapt to that change.

CHAPTER THIRTEEN

Adding the Third Dimension

W e have seen what the human resources revolution is about and how it is affecting the relations between the company, its work force, and the outside world. Further, we have explored in some detail the many kinds of communications programs which companies have developed that relate to human resources factors. Now the question is: How can this kind of corporate communications best be structured into the company?

Though a multitude of communications programs exist, there are only a few companies which have attempted to create a corporate framework for these new messages and the media they utilize. Instead, as Figure 1 shows, the tendency has been to fragmentize rather than to concentrate responsibility for various kinds of communications related to human resources.

This fragmentation is the understandable result of the rapid and unexpected growth of the whole human resources area, which has blossomed in the past five years. It created unforeseen and urgent demands for new ways to transmit messages to a variety of audiences. Under those circumstances, the tendency was to assign each new program to whatever function seemed best able to handle it at the time. Often, as the survey shows, this has been public relations.

Now, however, given the increasing costs for communications of all kinds, the size to which this new field has grown, the critical importance of human resources communications to many key corporate goals, and the need to bring it under direct top management control, it is time to structure this new dimension in corporate communications into a unified, coordinated, and coherent function.

FIGURE 1

Human Resources Communications: Department with Prime Responsibility among Fortune 500 Companies

(All figures in percentages. Base: 106 respondents = 100%.)

Dept. responsible	Type of Human Resources Communications						
	Employees	Affirmative action	Academic & educational community	Student career	Stockholder	Government-related	Community
Personnel	52	91	72	79	8	86	15
Personnel/PR jointly	25	4	8	3	6	5	27
PR	18	2	10	5	66	5	47
Other	6	9	3	4	19	14	8
Don't know	0	0	6	*	2	0	0
Doesn't apply	0	0	4	8	3	0	2
No answer	2	*	0	*	*	0	3
Total	†	†	†	100	†	†	†

*Less than 1%.
†Total exceeds 100%, due to multiple response.

WHAT SOME COMPANIES ARE DOING

Discussions and interviews with executives throughout the country and a search through the limited literature confirm that the concept of a new kind of corporate communications, concerned with human resources, has yet to surface. Yet there are unmistakable signs of ferment, and a few companies are making tentative efforts in this direction. Their various approaches are instructive.

Westinghouse, for example, recently established a Department of Human Resources under the direction of N. V. Petrou, vice president of human resources, who says:

> "One of our most important functions is to reorient the thinking of management in every area, so that manpower, its use and development, will be considered in all aspects of operations. Our department includes a communications unit, with responsibility for publications and other materials focusing on employees and their relationships with the company, from benefits to on-the-job safety. We have established carefully constructed lines of responsibility so that conflicting departmental interests are avoided in the human resources situation. For example, our surveys show that employees are highly interested in company sales and earnings, and we use such material in our employee publications. But announcements of company sales and earnings originate with the public relations office. So the human resources department has established formal communications with both the public relations and the marketing functions."

Westinghouse is one of very few companies that have established its own human resources communications unit within the company, in the human resources department, and staffed by its own communications specialists. The formal working liaison that has been established with the other two principal communications functions is noteworthy, as dealing with one of the practical aspects of developing a new kind of communications function. So far, however, the Westinghouse program is focused almost entirely on internal communications, following the pattern of past "employee communications" functions.

The Continental Group Incorporated, a New York-headquartered manufacturing organization in the packaging field, is an example of companies that are providing a communications arm for their human resources organization but doing it within a totally separate company framework. This was established in May 1977 when the company reorganized its communications functions, dividing them between external and internal matters. The external group is concerned with all the traditional areas of public relations. The internal group, headed by

Stuart A. Segal, director of internal policy and programs, has responsibility for a variety of communications programs relating to human resources.

"We have a Human Resources Department," Mr. Segal says, "but the principle is that the human resources people contact us when they have a communications matter: the ERISA requirements, savings plans, or basic benefits, for example. We act as an in-house consultant on communications programs, problems, techniques, and materials. What is new in this arrangement," he points out, "is the fact of a centralized communications function that *supports* other departments. More typically, as in some corporations, such a unit would generate material on its own; we, however, provide support for other arms of the corporation. We attempt, for example, to centralize communications for employees of all kinds. Over the next five years we will be tailoring these communications not just to employees in general, but to constituencies and subgroups within the employee population."

The Continental Group approach is instructive as indicating a strong corporate awareness of the need for a special organization to handle human resources communications. Mr. Segal notes that his group also does some external communications directed to government audiences. On the whole, however, like Westinghouse, the emphasis is predominantly toward internal communications.

Mobil has long been considered a corporate leader in terms of communications of all types. As noted earlier, it has also expanded its human resources communications efforts recently. Peter Krist, the company's vice president of employee relations, quoted in *Industrial Relations News*, attributes these changes to the number and kinds of attacks on the large oil companies, "that require extensive communication to people outside the company so that it will be able to recruit the kinds of people that it needs and also maintain the morale of those already employed." To an already extensive internal communications program, these activities were added at Mobil, according to Krist:

- More emphasis on the personal role of line management in communications.
- A programmatic approach to employee communications, based on a bottom-up formulation of objectives.
- Clearer organization for generating and distributing employee information, based on agreed-to line management objectives and input from both field and headquarters.
- Increased emphasis on local communications system improvement by adding communications coordinators at each Mobil unit and by

providing more communications support for local publications and first-line supervisors.

- Reorienting and adding to existing employee and retiree publications to reflect the diversity of interests, needs, and education of the work force.
- A greatly expanded bulletin board and poster campaign program.
- An improved videotape production facility tied in with an Employee Information Center for headquarters people.
- Three expanded upward communication efforts: a confidential Q & A program running outside normal channels, Executive Forums (frank talks by senior executives with employee audiences), and more systematic use of attitude surveys.

This is of interest as showing the rapid and extensive response that a corporation, already highly communications-minded, is able to develop under the pressure of social events that impinge upon its well-being. Mobil, however, follows the pattern of many other companies in adding these programs to the communications load of its public relations department. "The public relations department creates the materials and employee relations is responsible for delivery and monitoring their results," Mr. Krist says.

Obviously the need to organize means of implementing the company's human resources communications has begun to be felt. The extensive involvement of corporations in programs that go well beyond traditional employee communications has been recognized, both by companies and by such organizations as the Conference Board, which reports in a study on the personnel function, "Examining position guides and organization charts, as well as discussing job duties with public affairs executives themselves, a number of major new activities emerge that are related to the management of the personnel function: external communications, government programs, environmental forecasting and surveillance, public issue exploration." As the handful of company examples indicates, though organizations intuitively feel a need for a total human resources communications strategy and the structure on which it can be developed, present efforts in these directions are limited. What is the answer?

CREATING A HUMAN RESOURCES COMMUNICATIONS FUNCTION

The obvious first step is corporate recognition that a third dimension in communications does indeed exist, and how this newly developing field relates to the other, long-established elements in the company.

Figure 2 provides a working view of the three major elements in today's corporate communications structure in terms of their individual concerns, objectives, audiences, and the broad kinds of communications techniques that each employs. The similarities and differences of these three kinds of corporate communications can readily be seen.

Figure 2 also can be a guide to the second step: developing a comprehensive audit of the company's entire communications spectrum. The purpose is to identify all of the kinds of programs within the company that involve communications, including not only the formal and familiar programs in print and audiovisual forms but the entire range of meetings, training sessions, counseling, and similar activities. This audit should identify the program by name, purpose, nature of its contents, the audiences to whom it is directed, the unit in the company responsible, and the executive to whom the unit reports.

With the results of the audit in hand, it will be possible to clearly determine the range of the company's total communications programs (which are likely to prove more extensive than most managements are aware). Using Figure 2 (and the descriptions of human resources communications elements presented in earlier chapters) it should be possible to work out a clear-cut, three-dimensional division of the company's marketing, institutional, and human resources areas. It should also become clear which of these are currently improperly assigned in terms of internal responsibility for the particular program, that is, which are essentially human resources programs that are being handled within the institutional and marketing functions, or are floating without roots as independent efforts. In human resources terms, the audit will also provide a useful summary of which audiences are being reached and how. It will indicate areas of possible communications "overkill" and those which are insufficiently covered.

Once the scope of the company's human resources communications effort becomes apparent through the audit, it is likely the need for a three-dimensional approach to corporate communications will be made clear. Figure 3 suggests one way in which these areas can interrelate within the company structure.

Defining the Human Resources Communications Function

Each company has an internal structure peculiar to itself and not readily subject to change. As one observer has commented, once an organizational pattern has been established it tends to become institutionalized,

FIGURE 2
The Three Dimensions of Corporate Communications

MARKETING COMMUNICATIONS

Concerns	Objectives	Audiences	Elements
Product advantages	Sales	Original equipment manufacturers	Advertising: consumer industrial business etc.
New products	Product and brand image	Government	Public relations: product promotion trade shows exhibits etc.
Product applications	Increasing share of market	Distributors	Sales literature/AVs distributor relations retailer relations market research etc.
Etc.	Meeting competition	Retailers	
	Etc.	Consumers, general	
		Consumers, specific demographics, etc.	
		Buying influences	
		Etc.	

INSTITUTIONAL COMMUNICATIONS

Concerns	Objectives	Audiences	Elements
Profitability	Raising capital	Stockholders	Advertising: institutional financial issue-oriented community-oriented etc.
Achievements	Financial image	Investors	
Growth	Corporate image	Financial community	
Diversity	Influencing public attitudes	Business community	
Acquisitions	Influencing community attitudes	"Influentials"	
"Citizenship" issues	Influencing government deci-	Activists	

FIGURE 2 (*Continued*)
The Three Dimensions of Corporate Communications

INSTITUTIONAL COMMUNICATIONS

Concerns	Objectives	Audiences	Elements
Attitudes toward company	sions, legislation, etc.	Government	Public relations:
Attitudes toward industry, business	Countering attacks on company, industry	Company communities	financial
Etc.	Demonstrating corporate social responsibility	Special groups	institutional
	Etc.	General public	image building
		Specific elements of public	issue-oriented
		Media	etc.
		Etc.	Exhibits
			Meetings
			Stockholder relations
			Financial community relations
			Government relations
			Opinion surveys
			Etc.

HUMAN RESOURCES COMMUNICATIONS

Concerns	Objectives	Audiences	Elements
Employment opportunities	Staffing	Employee prospects	Advertising:
Employee information	Employer image	Company employees	recruiting, local
Affirmative action	Morale	Retirees	recruiting, professional
	Staff retention	Minority/female work force	recruiting, affirmative

Development and training Productivity
Company HR* policies
Company HR*
  achievements
Labor relations
Etc.

Meeting government require-
  ments for EEO, etc.
Upgrading staff
Developing sources of
  employees
Handling labor problems
Informing employees, general
Informing employees, specific
  groups
Influencing public attitudes on
  HR* issues
Influencing community attitudes
  on HR* issues

Other employee groups
Activist groups in HR* area
"Influentials"
Minority community
Local community
Educational community
Unions
Professional associations
Government, re HR*
Stockholders, re HR*

action
recruiting, college
employer image
etc.
Public relations:
  recruiting
  affirmative action
  college
  special audiences, re HR*
  etc.
Mailing
HR*/recruiting exhibits
Career seminars
Open House
Recruiting literature
Employee publications
Training materials
A/V materials: HR*
Annual Report: HR*
  section
Reports to government
Etc.

*HR = Human Resources

FIGURE 3
Structuring Corporate Three Dimensional Communications: One Approach

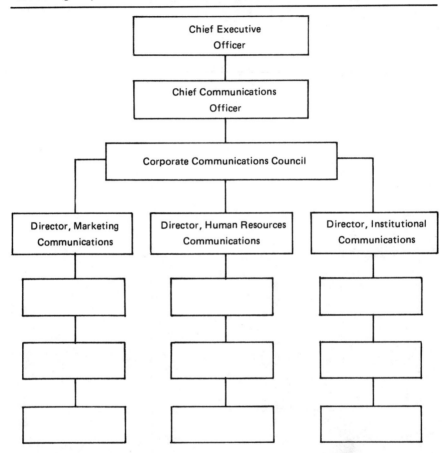

and few significant modifications ever occur. The human resources revolution, however, has, willy-nilly, imposed change upon organizations, even if they do not yet recognize the direction or scope of the structural modification. The emergence of a new form of corporate communications, for example, has been quite successfully disguised by the corporate habit of scattering the new programs among existing functions, as we have noted. But these expedients are nearing the end of their usefulness.

What is ultimately needed is the establishment of a clearly defined human resources communications function preferably within the company's human resources department, incorporating all the internal *and* external communications serving human resources purposes. Figure 4 provides a simplified view of how such a function might be set up. Each company, of course, would have to arrive at its own particular format for this function, based on management philosophies and corporate makeup.

Many organizations see change of this magnitude as resulting from a slow evolution. In the process of arriving at a new framework, it is likely that numerous hybrid combinations will be tried, as in the examples just described, in order to find a compatible means of fitting human resources communications within the individual corporate structure. The concept presented in Figure 4 should be regarded as a basic matrix on which to mold individual working models that will then be modified on the basis of company experience.

Note that this proposed organizational chart covers not only corporate level but unit levels, whether these are separate companies within a conglomerate or manufacturing facilities or divisions. Sanford Browde, vice president of administration and personnel of Litton's Monroe Company, comments on this need for creating capabilities below headquarters level.

"Divisions of major conglomerates have particular problems as far as human resources communications are concerned. The division has all of the problems which are directly raised by employees and customers and vicariously inherits the problems raised by stockholders and the public with respect to the large corporate entity. In my view it is important for the division to build its *own* human resources communications effort to enhance its own identity and image in the eyes of employees, customers, and the public. Employees want to identify with their own business. And to the extent that the image is strengthened or weakened by the large corporate public image, the division must be in a position to react in a planned and organized manner.

"At Monroe, in addition to the overall divisional publications and ongoing written communications to employees, we have sought to bring the human resource effort to the work station by decentralizing the personnel function. In this way, personnel managers are meeting constantly with line managers and their people in order to insure a feedback and quick response to ever-present problems.

"This approach, supplementing written or formal communications efforts, is necessary in today's work force. They want to be heard. They have something to say and the sooner they can be heard, the sooner productive efforts can continue. The human resources effort is no longer an administrative and caretaker function as in the past. It must get down to the line level, listen and react. While decentralizing personnel responsibil-

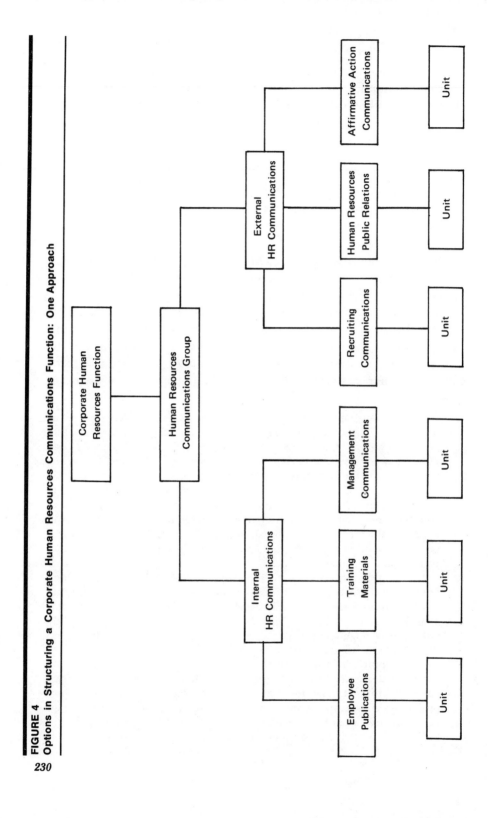

ity and authority, we are, at the same time, moving in the direction of unifying divisional control over written employee communications and public relations. Progress in this regard is slow, in view of years of organization deficiencies which have left these functions fragmented and pigeonholed, but we will progress more rapidly toward this goal in the future."

Directing the Function

Most corporations today have directors of public relations and of marketing communications, though the exact titles may vary. Such positions exist to provide overall direction for functions increasingly extensive, intricate, and sensitive for the company. They require a special combination of talent that includes administrative ability, a feel for nuances of communication, a thorough knowledge of their respective fields, and the ability to manage intangibles. These directors are also involved in a kind of quality control—responsibility for seeing the company communications meet standards of design, content, style, and other characteristics that the corporation requires of its communications.

In establishing a human resources communications function, many companies will feel that similar direction should be provided by creating a corresponding position, to be filled by an executive with special capability and grounding in human resources as well as communications. He or she would be responsible for existing human resources communications programs, for generating new kinds of communications vehicles as needed, for building and motivating a staff of the special kind of hybrid communications specialists the operation will require, and for maintaining levels of communications quality consonant with other corporate programs.

A director of human resources communications could also act as liaison with the company's other communications areas, as Figure 3 suggests. The importance of such liaison has already been cited by some of the companies whose programs have been described here. An arrangement of this type can be considered as a means of coordinating company communications as a whole, so that they will all reflect, both in internal and external programs, the basic corporate style and philosophy. It might be organized in the form of a communications council of the directors of the three areas, whose purpose would be to make decisions involving overlapping areas of interest, to exchange information with the other communications functions, and so on. This could facilitate the exchange of expertise, the maximum use of various materials developed by any one of the three areas, and cost-saving sharing of facilities and equipment.

As Figure 3 indicates, a top-level executive who will act as the company's chief of communications is advisable. Under various titles, a number of leading corporations have already established positions of this type to provide overall, high-level integration and direction to the corporate communications output. Adding the third dimension in the communications mix, as suggested here, makes the case for such a position even more compelling.

Staffing: Needed, a New Breed

"We have turned to the new dynamics of the changing American worker with new emphasis on changing expectations and desires. You do it gracefully and with style or you get dragged into it kicking and screaming, but you are not going to escape it. This kind of communication, done with realization and understanding of change, is a new field, and there is a lot more growth to come; we are dealing with a fluid, moving target." This comment by Laurence S. Sewell, manager of public relations for Alcoa, is a vivid summary of this new field of human resources communications. It is, indeed, as Mr. Sewell defines it, a new field. And, as with all new areas, needs a new breed of specialist to deal with it.

Why a new breed, and not the marketing and public relations people who staff the company's communications activities today? For one reason, experience suggests that there is a critical difference in attitude among people involved in those functions and those concerned with human resources. In many years of hiring people to create human resources communications, it has become apparent that most people with training and experience in areas such as consumer product advertising find it difficult to make the transition. What makes people successful in such fields is a strong orientation toward selling. This sales orientation is based not on providing information, but on working on the prospect's emotions. As a communications technique this may be suitable for influencing the choice of toothpaste or cigarettes, but not for the more important and personal decisions such as choosing a job or achieving a company goal. Public relations people also deal with methods that involve manipulating people's attitudes, often on an emotional rather than an informative basis. But in the human resources context, this manipulative approach is often the least effective; it is perceived, resented, and stimulates resistance and backlash.

A second reason is that human resources, as has been demonstrated, is very much a field of its own, one as complex, professional, and demanding as the marketing and institutional fields, but very different from them in the types of knowledge and background and experience it requires. It is the recognition of this basic difference that has led top managements to turn to the human resources executives within the company to deal with the troubles and traumas of the human resources revolution.

To staff a human resources communications function, therefore, a new breed of communicator is needed: a hybrid, if you will, who combines the communications and information skills of the journalist with training and experience in the human resources field.

Where is business to find such communicators? They are, at present, rare birds. The industrial relations schools, of which there are a handful, have been remarkably backward in understanding that their graduates find themselves deeply involved in communications of many kinds from the day they begin their jobs. Most people with formal schooling in personnel or human resources have not had more than passing academic exposure to communications. The journalism schools, on the other hand, though they provide courses relating to marketing and public relations, remain largely unaware of the burgeoning volume of business communications concerned with various aspects of human resources. There are a handful of personnel magazines, services, and newsletters whose writers have a solid background in the field. Internally the company may find that within its own training and employee communications functions it has some of the talent required. And it can also turn to outside organizations for assistance in meeting communications needs.

External Support Organizations

As do the public relations and marketing functions, the human resources area is able to call on an increasing number of outside organizations to stretch its capabilities and meet unexpected new needs for communications. Some of these have been relied upon by personnel people for years: recruitment advertising specialists, organizations that design booklets and brochures for internal and external use, audiovisual specialists, and so on.

The human resources revolution has stimulated the development of many other types of support organizations. Some, like Boyle/Kirkman, specialize in the affirmative action field and produce in-house seminars and other programs. Others provide the elements for management training and programs. Still others provide written materials, tapes, or audiovisuals for particular human resources purposes and corporate audiences. There are research firms that specialize in employee attitude surveys and outplacement counseling firms to help companies find new positions for the people they are serving.

As this new aspect of corporate communications develops, it can be expected that an extensive range of such external support organizations will be available to a company in supplementing its own in-house programs.

The Advantages to the Company

Human resources communications already exist on an extensive scale within most corporations today. Regulating and systematizing these within a specific, clearly defined function will have the advantages of developing more effective management control of these programs, creating a visible framework in which responsibilities can be assigned, establishing corporate goals and budgets, developing policies, and so on.

This is a most appropriate time for organizations to take the step toward a separate function of this type. We are far enough into the human resources revolution to comprehend its nature and scope and yet recognize that much more change is ahead. Increased militancy among older workers, the handicapped, and others; problems of high unemployment among young blacks; rapid technological change; and new directions in the Equal Employment Opportunity Commission are just a few of the problem areas visible immediately ahead.

If the company has a well-established, adequately staffed communications capability for this purpose, then it is prepared to deal with new developments in human resources in an organized and rational way, rather than generating new programs in the heat of a crisis. One of the responsibilities of this new function should be to anticipate new needs and prepare for them in good time. It should also be aware when programs have outlived their usefulness and discontinue those which circumstances make obsolete.

But the real values are much broader. An effective human resources communication program should have a positive effect upon the entire range of audiences concerned with the company as an employer. If this can be accomplished, then the expensive legal embroilments so frequent today which inspired the title of this book will dwindle as a threat to the company. Communications, properly handled, are also the key to other important corporate goals, including that of increased productivity, perhaps the most vital problem management faces today. A well-informed work force, as Mobil among others has found, is an asset that contributes to the company outside the work place as well as within. And good communications, with the favorable image these create of the company as an employer, are vital in attracting and holding high-calibre people at every level. In the end, they are the difference in the company's ability to compete effectively in the marketplace.

THE METAMORPHOSIS: A VIEW AHEAD

The metamorphosis in Franz Kafka's famous story about a person who turned into an insect described a change away from the human. The metamorphosis in the business world is in the opposite direction: the organization is in the process of changing from a bloodless and impersonal monolith into a strongly human-oriented entity. It may be doing so "kicking and screaming" as some executives have commented in interviews, but the momentum is there and the direction is clear.

The idea of accountable social leadership by business, pioneered by a few leaders such as Joe Wilson of Xerox, was not readily accepted a few years ago. But social changes such as the human resources revolution have cracked the corporate shell and altered the tradition of untouchability and exclusivity from social involvement that formerly characterized the business world. Much of the driving force behind corporate change has come from the top—corporate executive officers (CEOs) such as W. Michael Blumenthal, formerly of Bendix, Reginald H. Jones of General Electric, and many others. They made clear their organizations' commitments to goals like affirmative action and set up policies and incentives to assure that such goals were met.

It is top management, too, that has led the way in recognizing the importance of human resources to the company and the consequent need for more open, intense, and personal levels of communication with the work force. These executives have seen clearly the relationships among an informed and motivated work force, the achievement of vital company goals, and the impact on outside audiences. It seems likely that the impetus to establish a human resources communications function will also come from the top, from CEOs who are themselves already deeply involved with the economics of human resources.

Monolith to House of Glass

The observer walking down Park Avenue in New York might see a certain symbolism in the style of the corporate headquarters buildings concentrated there. The older buildings are structures of massive concrete with small windows peering out of their stony facades. But there are few of these. Instead the avenue is dominated by buildings in the newer style of the Lever House: great sheets of glass open to the view of the outside beholder and broad vistas of the world for the people within.

These new buildings are a visible metaphor for what is happening as the human resources revolution rolls on. Business is no longer protected by monolithic walls of privilege and custom. Today it lives in glass houses, literally and figuratively. It operates with a high degree of openness, in part because it is required to do so and in part because it suits the new view of what business should be. No longer is the company, wherever it may be located, an isolated "corporate community." It is now the corporation *in* the community, a community that ranges from small towns to the international scene.

Operating this way requires new management capabilities. Chief executives, for example, can no longer solely be business specialists skilled in administering large enterprises. They must also be more political, alert not only to the classic realities of markets, money, and materials but to the constituencies that now comprise the company and its environment, constituencies in which the worker, social advocate, voter, and stockholder are often the same individual. It is indicative that *Time* not long ago editorialized on the many capable business leaders who would make good presidential candidates. A recent study by the executive recruiting firm of Heidrick and Struggles—a five-year profile of the chief executive officer—seems to confirm this trend. It notes that today's CEO tends to be more adept at communicating with the outside environment.

In this new corporate environment, communications is integrated into the working structure of the organization and not just superimposed upon it, and the value of the individual is recognized in fact, not by lip service and clichés. Monsanto, for example, is noted for its sensitivity in the employee communications area and for keeping its people conscious of their individual potential. General Electric has been a pioneer in stressing the value of the individual as a decisive factor in company performance. Delta Airlines, which has established an exceptional performance record in the airline field, focuses on its people as the factor that makes the difference. Xerox is noted as a company that encourages its people to think in terms of social responsibility, inside and outside the company. Many others can be added to the list.

These organizations have moved away from the view of people as objects, as interchangeable parts in the business machine, that has characterized business thinking since the dawn of the industrial revolution. Instead, in keeping with the new social views that are emerging, they see the company as a social system in which people are essential, individual, and play many different roles in achieving personal and company goals.

The Communications Catalyst

Despite econometrics, computer modeling, and other sophisticated business forecasting tools, the human resources revolution has been an unpredicted and suddenly swelling tidal wave crashing down upon an unprepared American economy. Social change has spawned new ethics and new attitudes at an unprecedented rate. The very nature of the work force, for long considered a bastion of stability, is undergoing radical alteration. The attitudinal changes of people as employees are even broader, and are supported by a spectrum of constituencies ready to encourage litigation and other actions against corporations on the basis of business human resources practices and policies.

Yet amid the welter of class-action suits, attacks on individual corporations by advocacy groups, a recession-intensified disenchantment with business as an employer, and a revolt against the conventional working life, something new is emerging. While the work ethic continues to erode, we are seeing that people who feel themselves a part of an organization—not mere human machinery—are more productive, more innovative, contribute more in the work place. We are seeing another phenomenon: workers who are ready to go out and be advocates in support of their company and its goals because they understand these goals and how they relate to themselves. Further, business and some of its critics are beginning to establish dialogues with each other and there is a lessening of the confrontation psychology.

Communications has been the catalyst in these developments. Communicate or litigate has been the challenge of the human resources revolution. Slowly the balance is shifting toward communications—the new kind of corporate communications that has been described here. That is why it is important to recognize human resources communications as a new element in corporate operations; it is a keystone, to be put together now to deal with the massive changes ahead.

No chief executive would attempt to operate an organization in today's market conditions and economic climate without a sophisticated capability to communicate with customers and the financial community. In the eighties it will be equally rash for a company to exist without a communications capability fine-tuned to the special needs of human resources, able to effectively reach both internal and external audiences, whether they are entry-level workers, students, or Wall Street analysts.

It is a time to dare, to pioneer, to restructure corporate thinking—and the corporate organization chart—to accommodate this vital new dimension of communications. Those companies that do so will reap the benefits of leadership in this new Era of Human Resources. Theirs will be a more productive relationship among their own people, and a more peaceful coexistence in a litigation-oriented society.

Index

First National Bank of Nevada, 136
Fish Engineering and Construction, 203
Fluor Corporation, 203
Ford administration, 81
Ford Motor Company, 84
Fortune, 220
Foster Wheeler Corporation, 203
Foulkes, Fred K., 109, 136
Four-day week, 47
Fox & Jacobs, Inc., 203
France-Soir, 120
Franchising, 44–45
Fred E. Lee & Associates, 51

Gable, Joan, 191
Gadomski, Jeannette, 189
Galbraith, John Kenneth, 27
General American Life Insurance Company, 143, 144
General Dynamics, 194
  Electric Boat Division of, 115, 118, 124
General Electric, 14, 32, 199, 235, 236
  blue- to white-collar change at, 41
  Aircraft Engine Group of, 143, 145, 150–151, 158, 165, 166, 175
  Space Division of, 41
  technical seminars and, 123
General Motors, 56, 139, 184, 201, 203–204, 206
  in-house training at, 202–203
  retirement age at, 40
Georgia Institute of Technology, 38, 183–184
Gibbons, James F., 166
Ginzberg, Eli, 36
Government:
  communication with, 12, 82
  as customer, 81–82
  as competing employer, 48–49
  (*See also* Federal government)
Graduate, The, 193
Grey Advertising, 85
Grey Matter, 85
Guggenheim, Simon, 59

Harbus News, 193
Hardee's, 115
Harper's, 21
Harvard Business Review, 99, 109, 136
Harvard Business School, 65, 109, 136
Harvard Graduate School of Business, 196
Harvard University, 57
Hauser, Philip, 39–40
Health insurance, 19
Heidrick and Struggles, 236
Heinz, Robert, 54
Hercules, Inc., 54
HEW (*see* Department of Health, Education and Welfare, U.S.)
High schools, 197–199
Hispanics, 19, 38, 120
  equal opportunity for women and, 39, 116–117
  publications of, 173
  (*See also* Minorities)

HMD, 19
Holiday Inn, 45
Homosexuals, 19
Hooks, Benjamin, 69
Howard University, 184
Human resources, definition of, 7–8
Human resources communications, 93–97, 100–108, 219–238
  affirmative action and (*see* Affirmative action)
  as catalyst, 227–238
  consumers and, 12
  definition of, 100–102, 224–231
  direction of function of, 231–232
  educational community and, 12, 82–84, 105, 182–184, 187–202
  elements of, 102–106
  employees and (*see* Employee communications)
  external support for, 233–234
  Fortune 500 companies and, 220
  four functions of, 102
  future employees and, 87–89
  general remarks on, 10–13, 93–97, 106
  government and, 12, 82
  local communities and, 85–87, 106, 207–210
  middle management and, 156–160
  organization of, 107–108, 224–231
  orientation and, 149–151, 177–182
  outplacement and, 153–155
  place of, within corporate communications structure, 225–227
  potential investors and, 12
  preretirement counseling and, 155–156
  professionals and, 76–79, 160–167
  recruiting and (*see* Recruiting)
  retirees and, 74–76, 106, 212–215
  staffing for, 232–233
  stockholders and, 12, 89–92, 106, 215–218
  technical personnel and, 160–167
  training and development and, 104–105, 151–153
  unions and, 210–212
Hupp, Richard C., 201
Hughes Aircraft, 164, 165
Hughes News, 165
Hunter College, 191

IBM, 152, 202
Indians, American, 19, 38, 117, 120
Industrial Marketing, 130
Industrial Relations News, 47, 55, 156, 180–181, 216, 222
Industry Week, 198–199
Informador, El, 120
Information Science, Inc., 218
Inland Steel, 184
Institute for Demographic and Economic Studies, 48
Institute of Electrical and Electronic Engineers, 71, 78, 83
Institute for Social Research (ISR) of University of Michigan, 205–206
Institutional communications, 99–101, 225–226